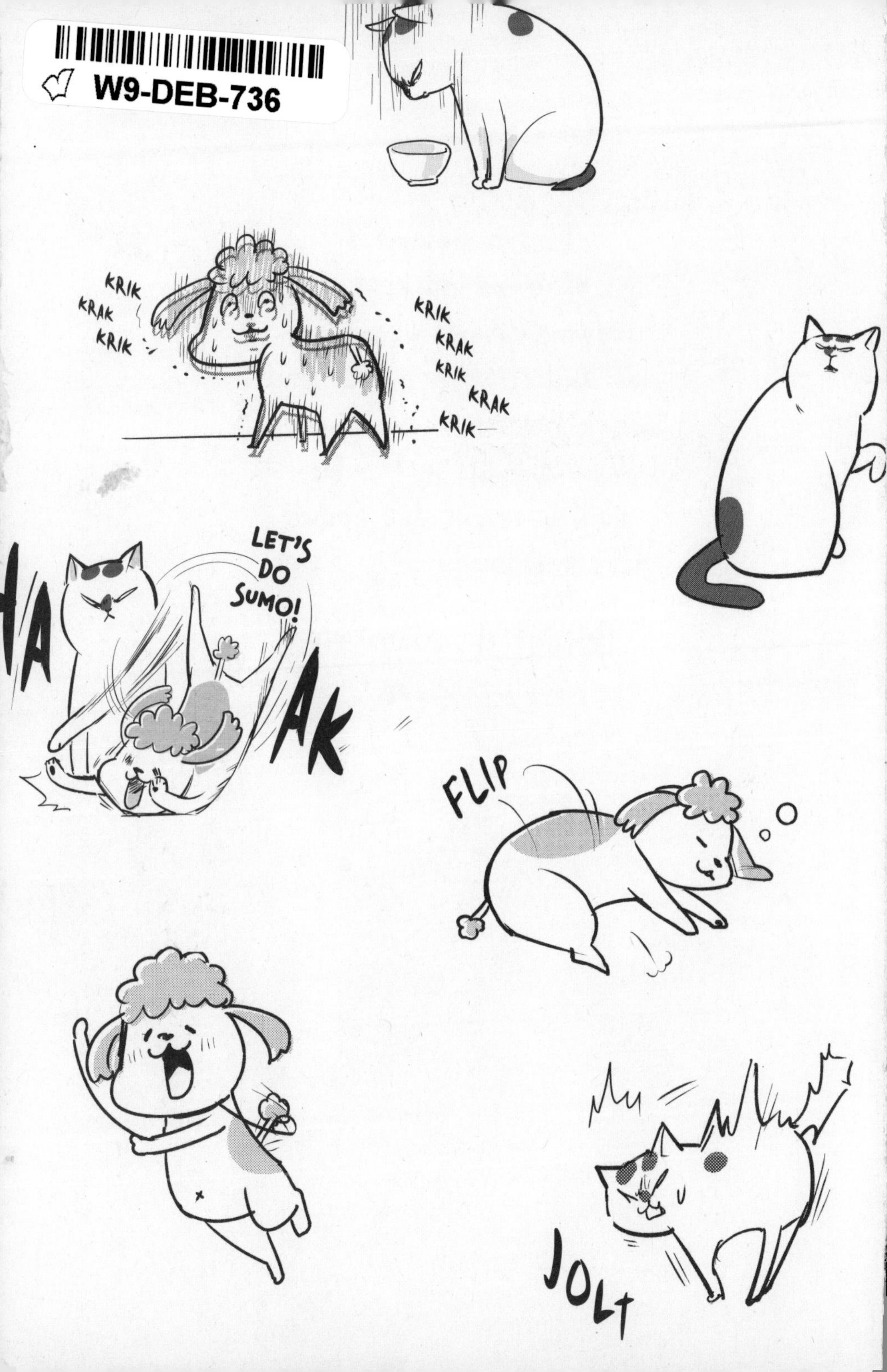
KRIK
KRAK
KRIK
KRAK
KRIK
KRIK
KRAK
KRIK
LET'S DO SUMO!
HA
AK
FLIP
JOLT

This is Volume 3.
I have indeed kept on
drawing comics about how
Inu and Neko are cute and
here we are at Volume 3.
The animals in question
still have no idea about
this and lazily sleep away.

Hidekichi Matsumoto

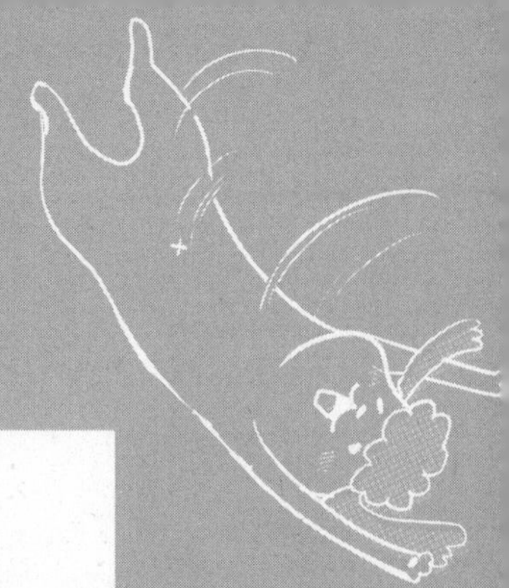

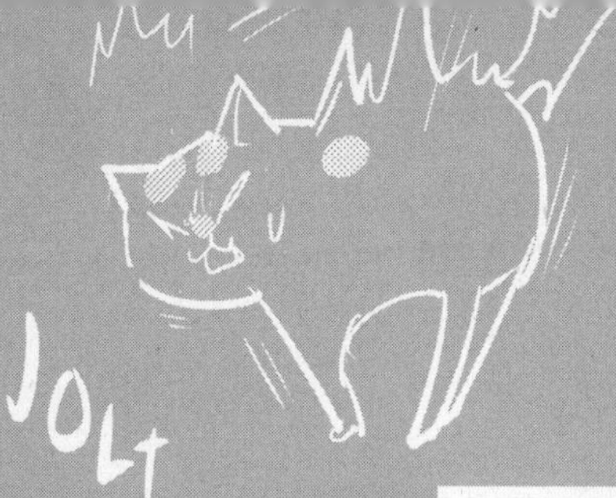
JOLT

With a Dog AND a Cat, Every Day is Fun

③

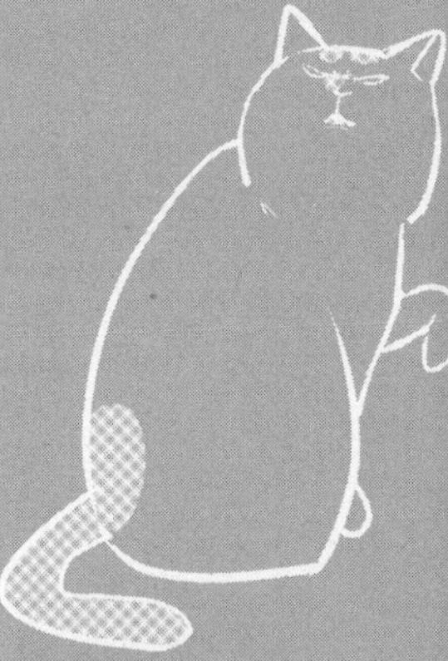

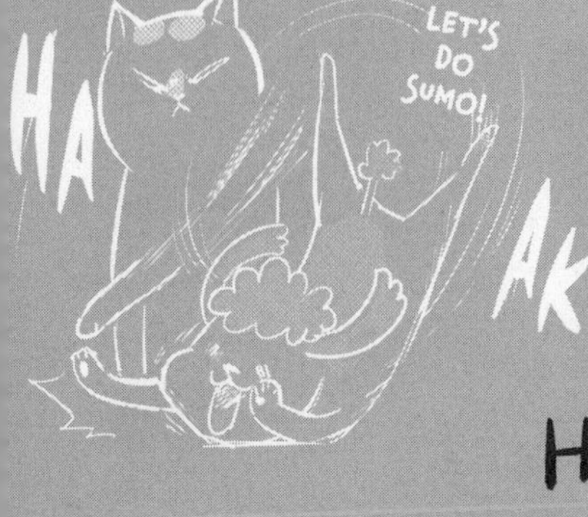
LET'S DO SUMO!
HA
AK

Hidekichi Matsumoto

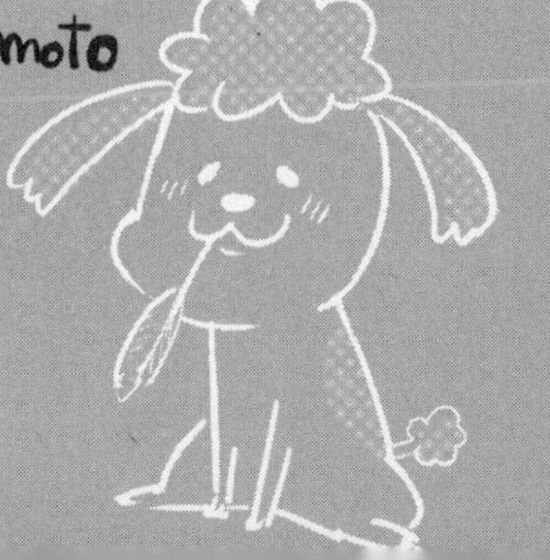

CAST

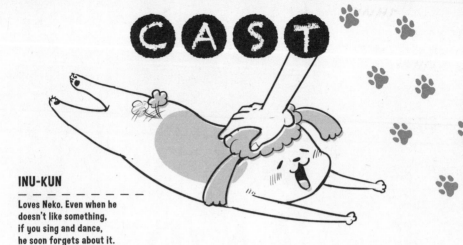

INU-KUN

Loves Neko. Even when he doesn't like something, if you sing and dance, he soon forgets about it.

NEKO-SAMA

A fearsome face. A cool customer. His passion for theft is staggering.

LEOPA

Nickname: Tokage-chan. A constant object of Neko's gaze. Has none of the cool composure you expect from reptiles.

MOM

Hidekichi's mother. Holds the #1 ranking in the Matsumoto household.

HIDEKICHI MATSUMOTO

Manga artist. Loves animals.

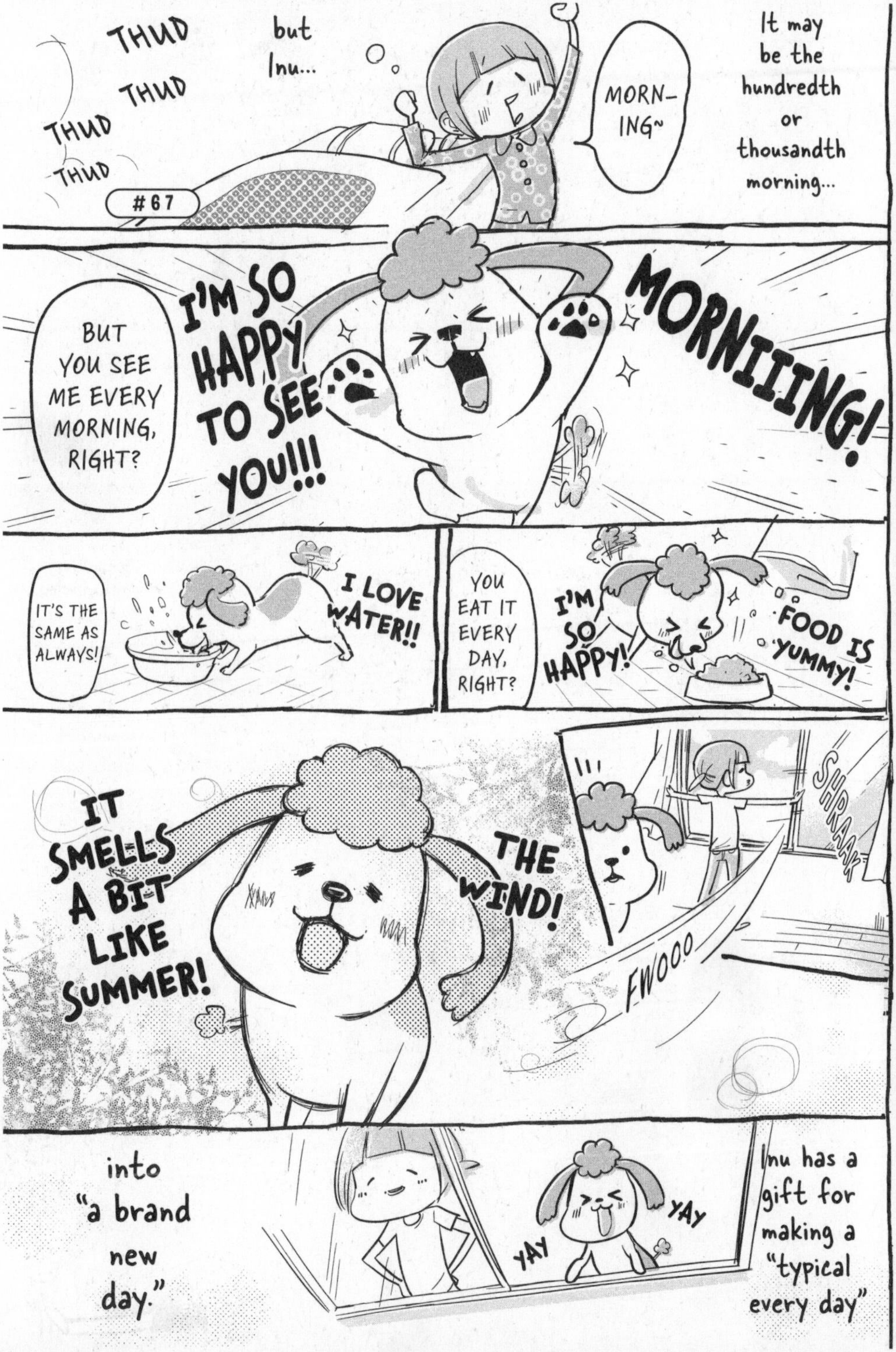
It may be the hundredth or thousandth morning...
MORN-ING~
but Inu...
THUD
THUD
THUD
THUD
#67
MORNIIING!
I'M SO HAPPY TO SEE YOU!!!
BUT YOU SEE ME EVERY MORNING, RIGHT?
FOOD IS YUMMY!
I'M SO HAPPY!
YOU EAT IT EVERY DAY, RIGHT?
I LOVE WATER!!
IT'S THE SAME AS ALWAYS!
SHRAAK
FWOOO
THE WIND!
IT SMELLS A BIT LIKE SUMMER!
Inu has a gift for making a "typical every day"
YAY
YAY
into "a brand new day."

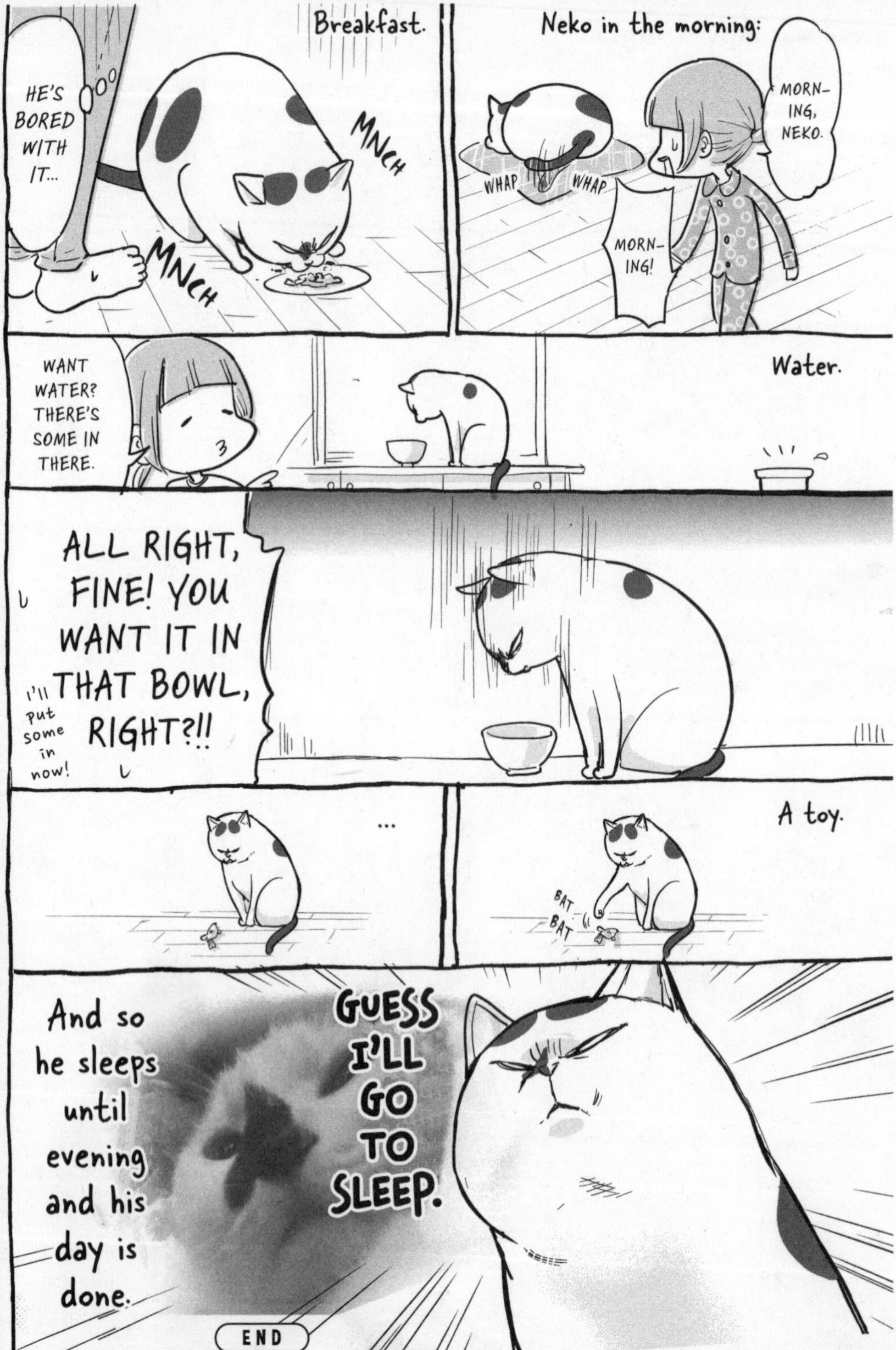

Neko in the morning:
MORNING, NEKO.
WHAP WHAP
MORNING!
Breakfast.
MNCH MNCH
HE'S BORED WITH IT...
Water.
WANT WATER? THERE'S SOME IN THERE.
ALL RIGHT, FINE! YOU WANT IT IN THAT BOWL, RIGHT?!!
I'll put some in now!
A toy.
BAT BAT
...
GUESS I'LL GO TO SLEEP.
And so he sleeps until evening and his day is done.
END

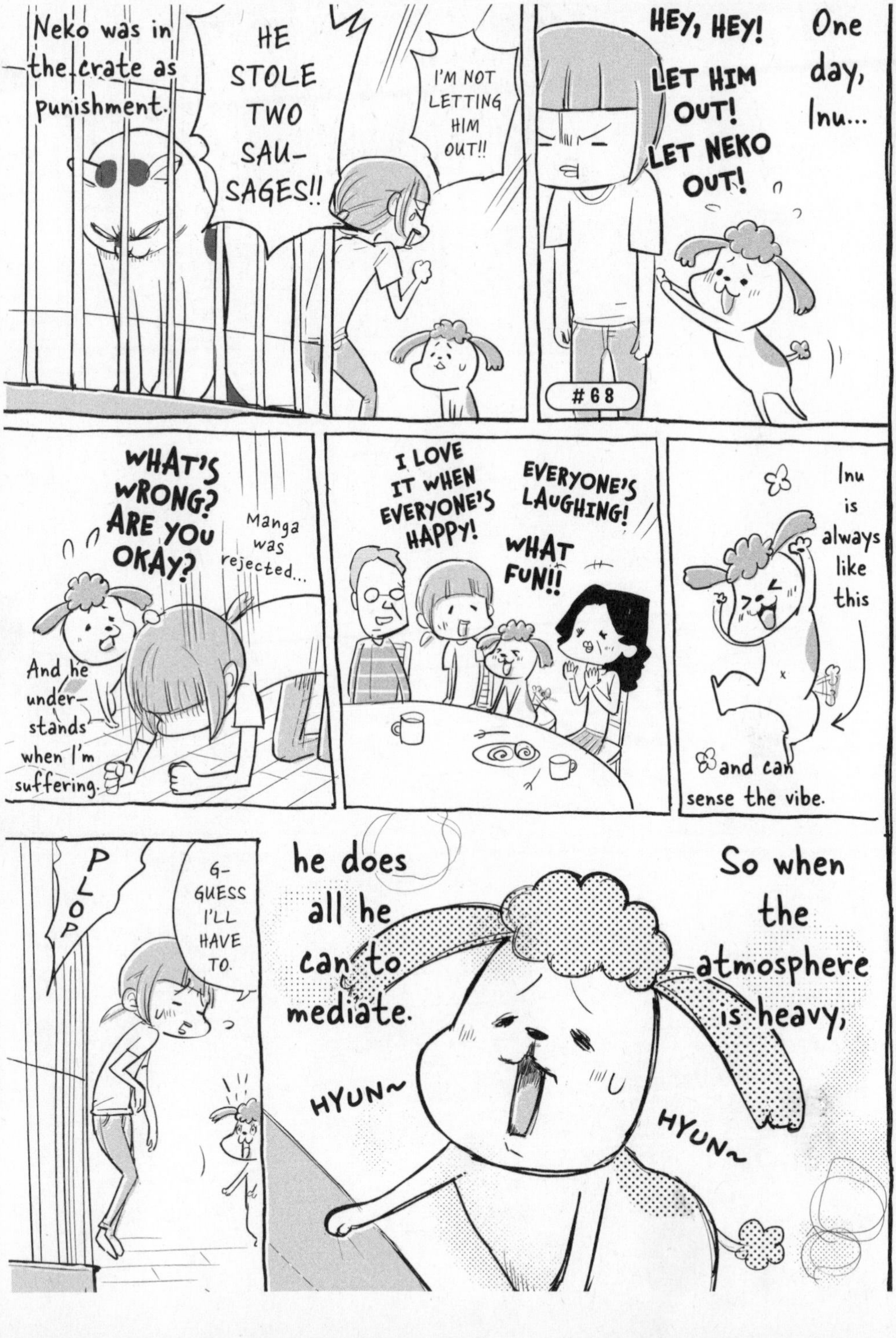
One day, Inu...
HEY, HEY! LET HIM OUT! LET NEKO OUT!
#68
I'M NOT LETTING HIM OUT!!
HE STOLE TWO SAU-SAGES!!
Neko was in the crate as punishment.
Inu is always like this
and can sense the vibe.
EVERYONE'S LAUGHING!
I LOVE IT WHEN EVERYONE'S HAPPY!
WHAT FUN!!
Manga was rejected...
WHAT'S WRONG? ARE YOU OKAY?
And he under-stands when I'm suffering.
So when the atmosphere is heavy,
he does all he can to mediate.
HYUN~
HYUN~
PLOP
G-GUESS I'LL HAVE TO.

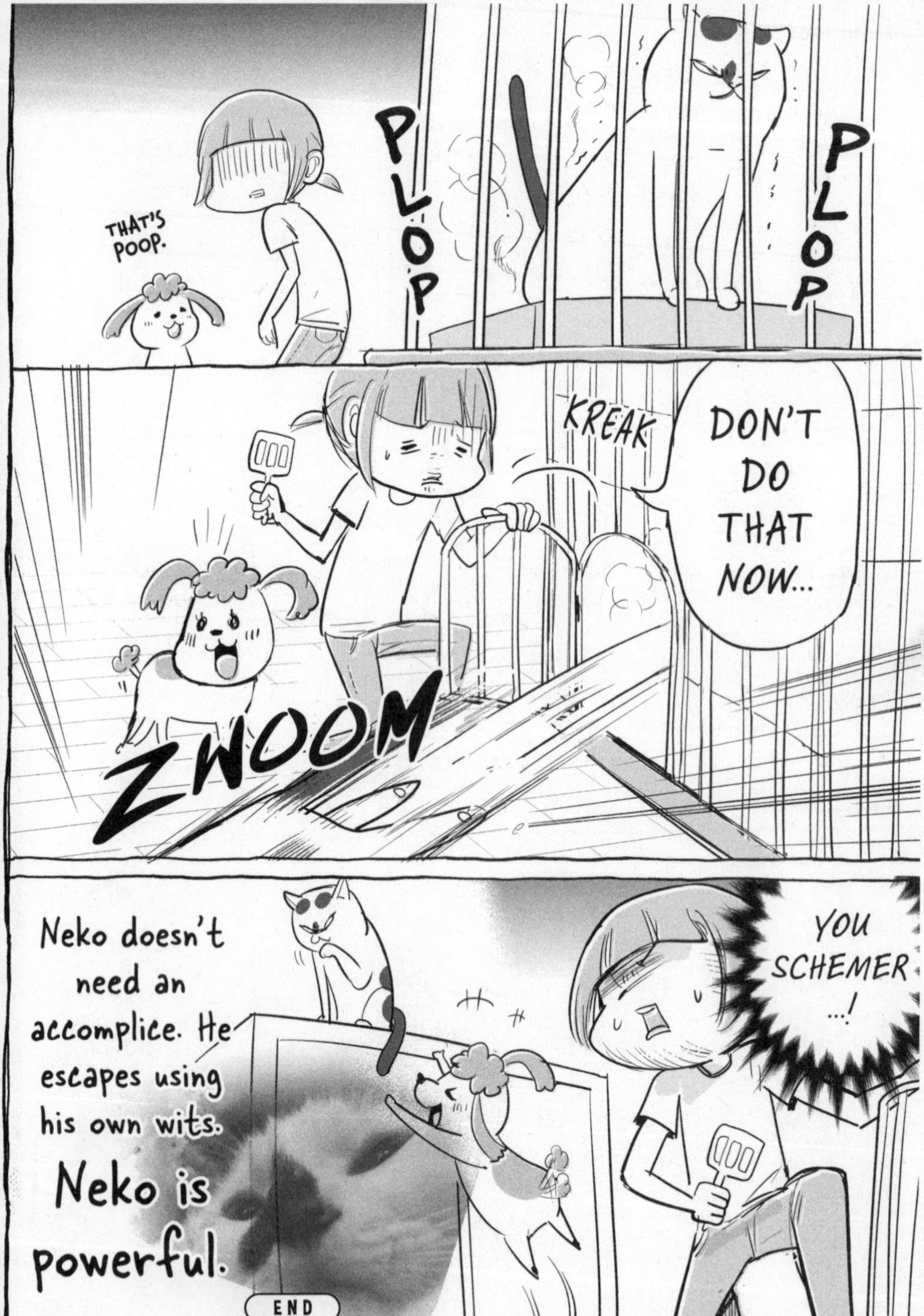
PLOP
PLOP
THAT'S POOP.
DON'T DO THAT NOW...
KREAK
ZWOOM
YOU SCHEMER ...!
Neko doesn't need an accomplice. He escapes using his own wits.
Neko is powerful.
END

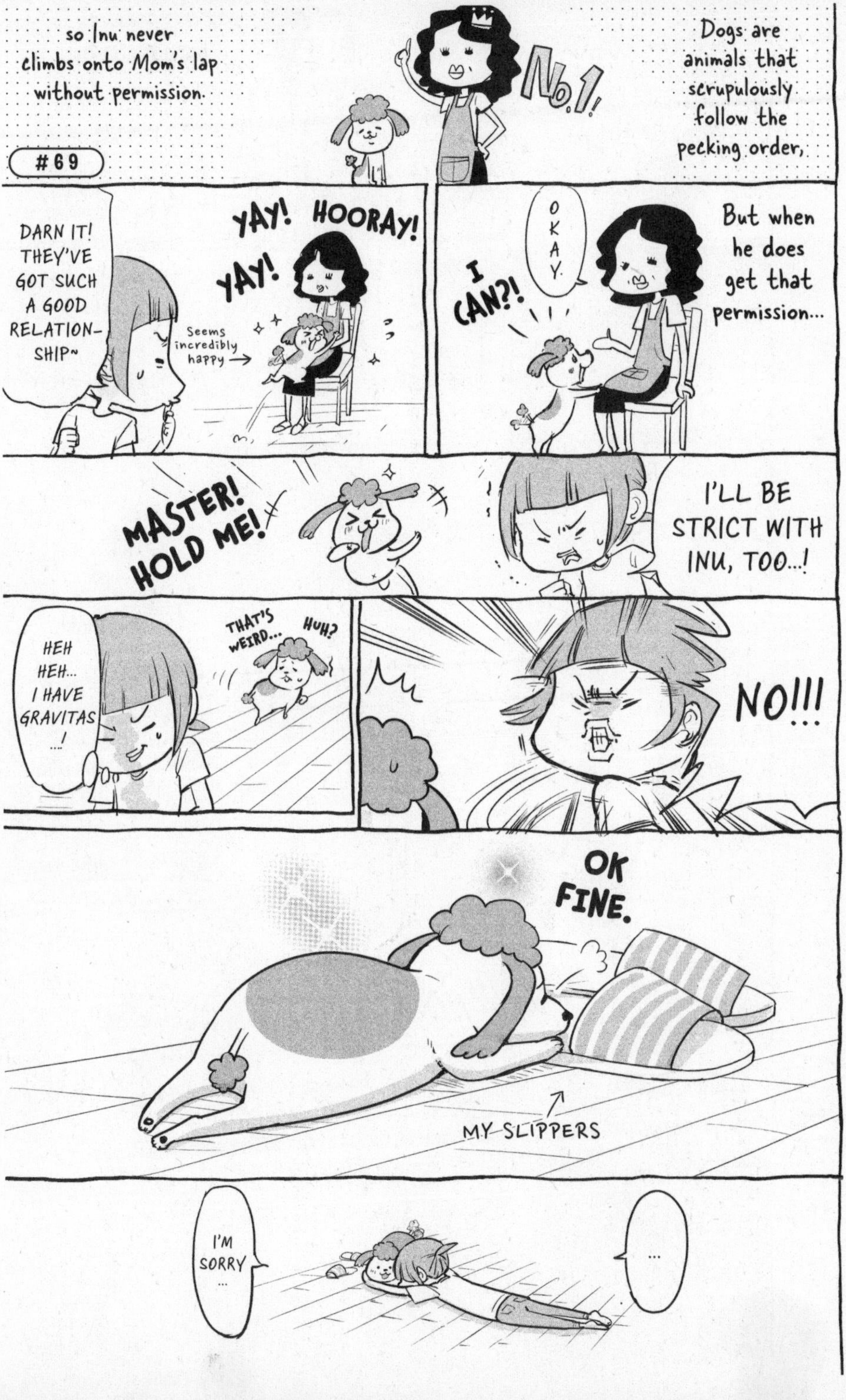
Dogs are animals that scrupulously follow the pecking order,
No.1!
so Inu never climbs onto Mom's lap without permission.
#69
But when he does get that permission...
OKAY.
I CAN?!
YAY! HOORAY!
YAY!
Seems incredibly happy
DARN IT! THEY'VE GOT SUCH A GOOD RELATIONSHIP~
I'LL BE STRICT WITH INU, TOO...!
MASTER! HOLD ME!
NO!!!...
HUH?
THAT'S WEIRD...
HEH HEH... I HAVE GRAVITAS...!
OK FINE.
MY SLIPPERS
...
I'M SORRY...

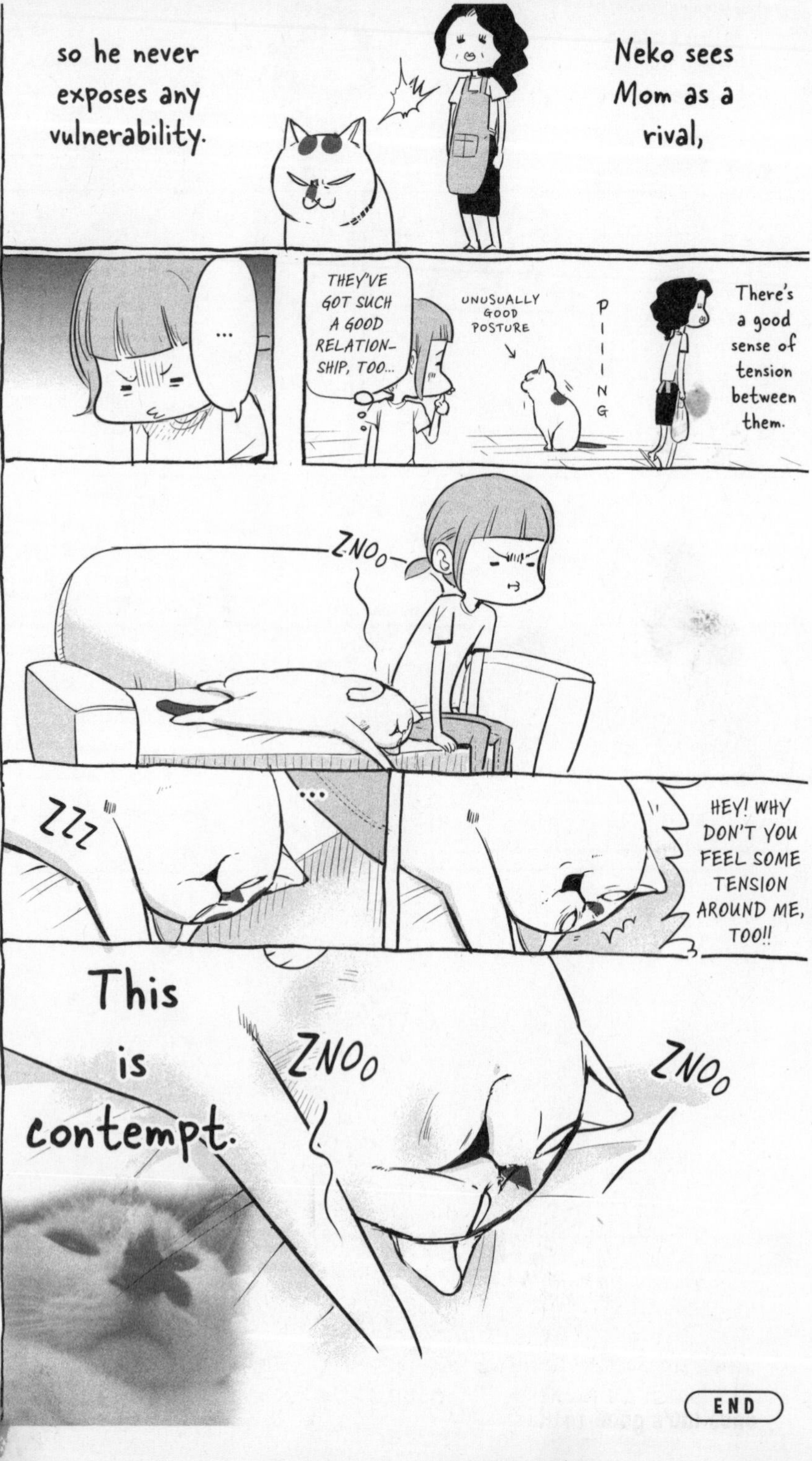

Neko sees Mom as a rival,
so he never exposes any vulnerability.
There's a good sense of tension between them.
PIIING
UNUSUALLY GOOD POSTURE
THEY'VE GOT SUCH A GOOD RELATIONSHIP, TOO...
...
ZNOOO
HEY! WHY DON'T YOU FEEL SOME TENSION AROUND ME, TOO!!
...
ZZZ
This is contempt.
ZNOOO
ZNOOO
END

The two of us sneakily having fun on my phone
once Inu's gone to sleep.

Newly-Drawn 4-Panel Strip

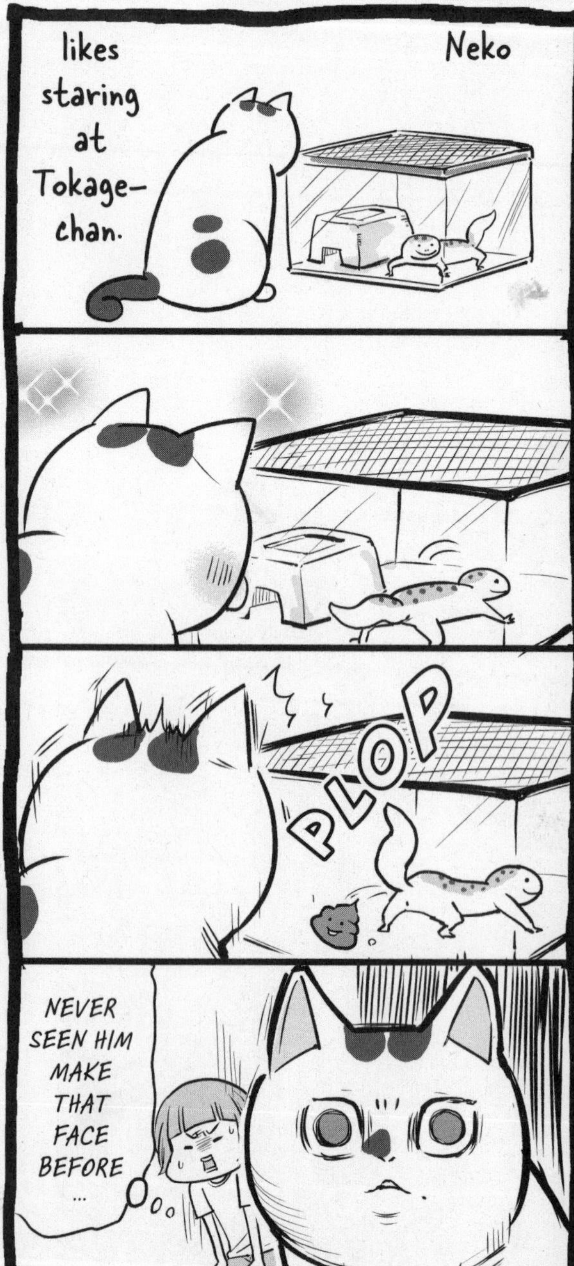

Neko
likes staring at Tokage-chan.
PLOP
NEVER SEEN HIM MAKE THAT FACE BEFORE ...

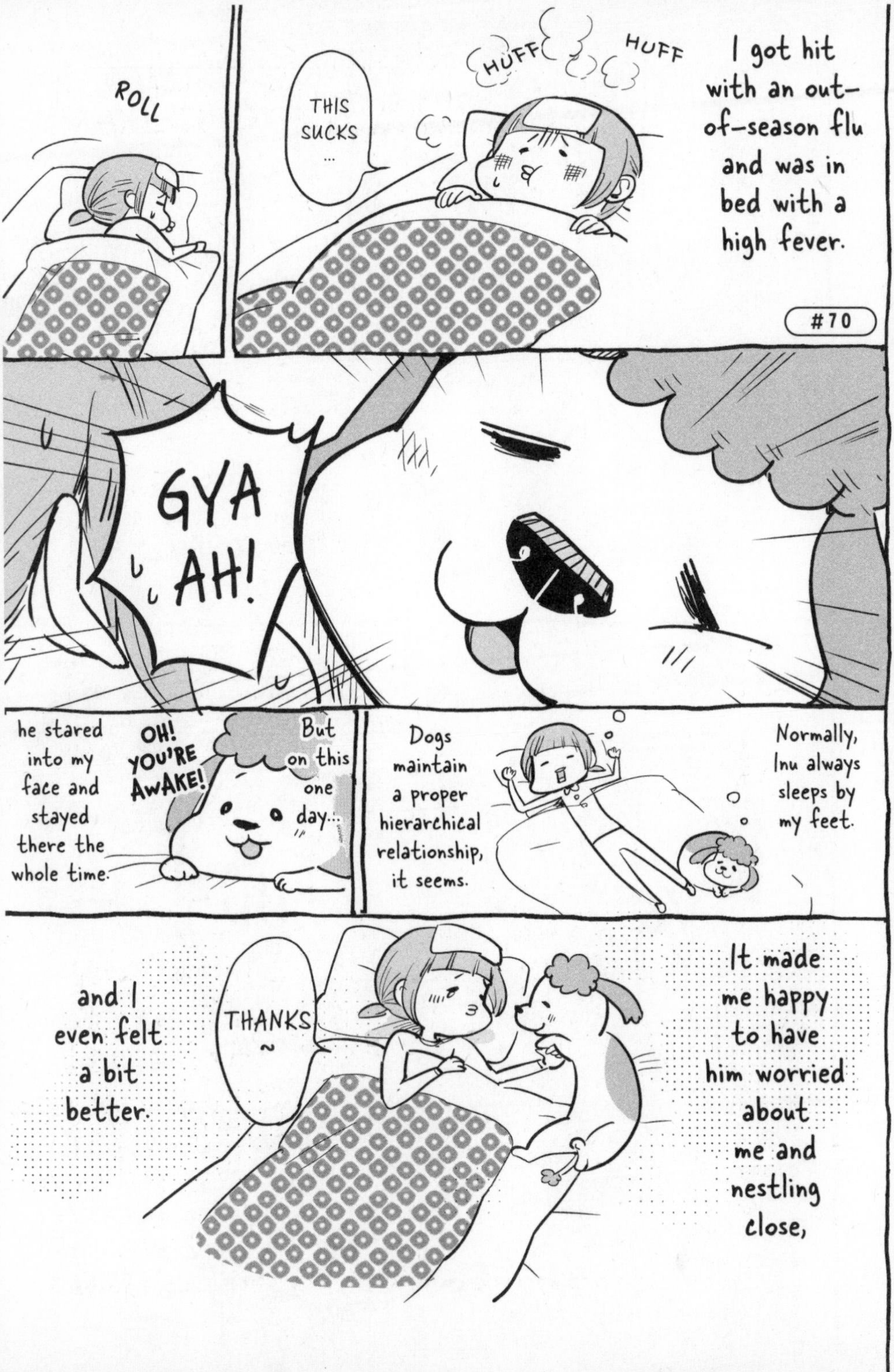

I got hit with an out-of-season flu and was in bed with a high fever.
HUFF HUFF
THIS SUCKS ...
ROLL
#70
GYA AH!
Normally, Inu always sleeps by my feet.
Dogs maintain a proper hierarchical relationship, it seems.
But on this one day...
OH! YOU'RE AWAKE!
he stared into my face and stayed there the whole time.
It made me happy to have him worried about me and nestling close,
THANKS ~
and I even felt a bit better.

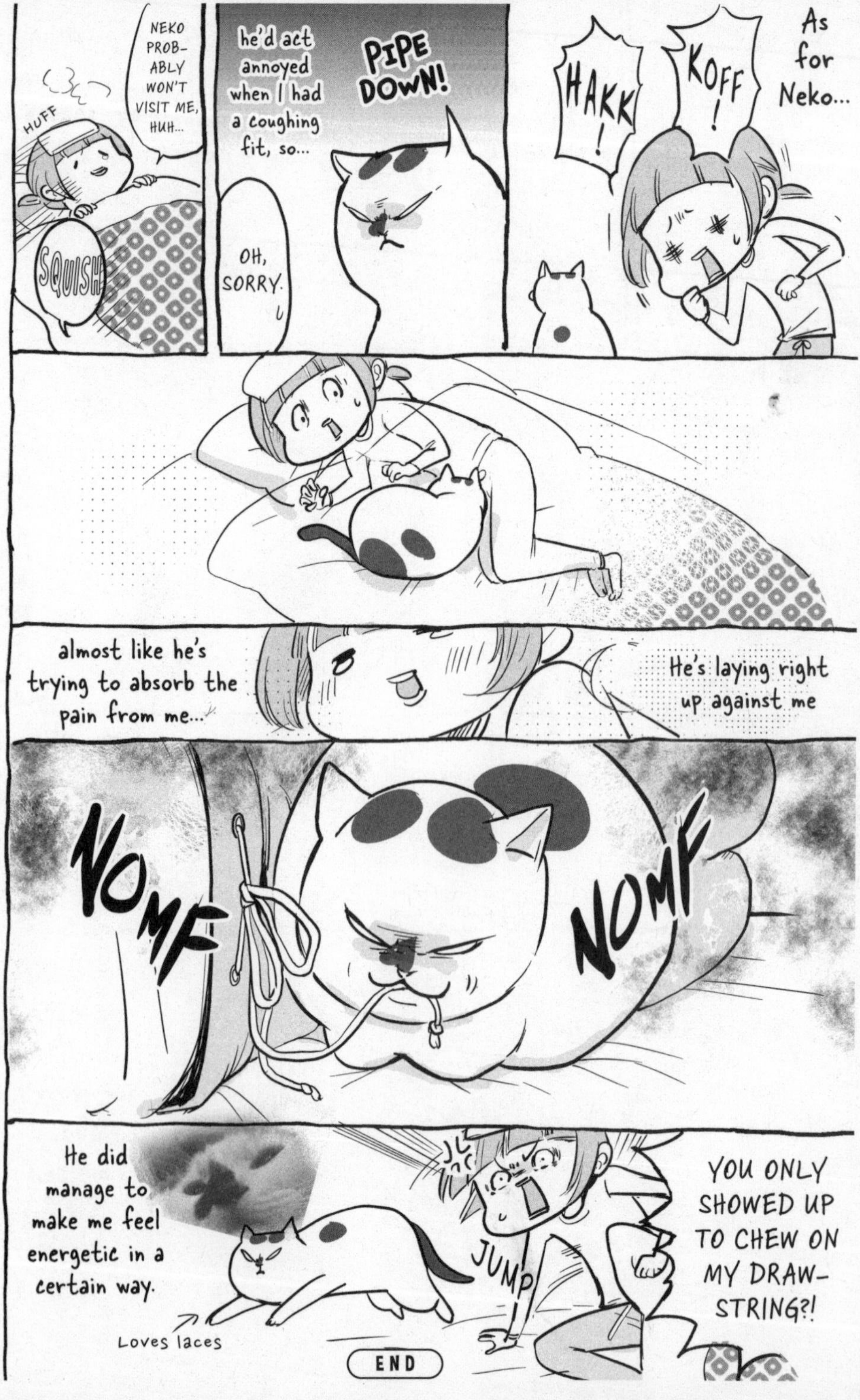
As for Neko...
KOFF!
HAKK!
he'd act annoyed when I had a coughing fit, so...
PIPE DOWN!
OH, SORRY.
NEKO PROB-ABLY WON'T VISIT ME, HUH...
HUFF
SQUISH
He's laying right up against me
almost like he's trying to absorb the pain from me...
NOMF
NOMF
YOU ONLY SHOWED UP TO CHEW ON MY DRAW-STRING?!
JUMP
He did manage to make me feel energetic in a certain way.
Loves laces
END

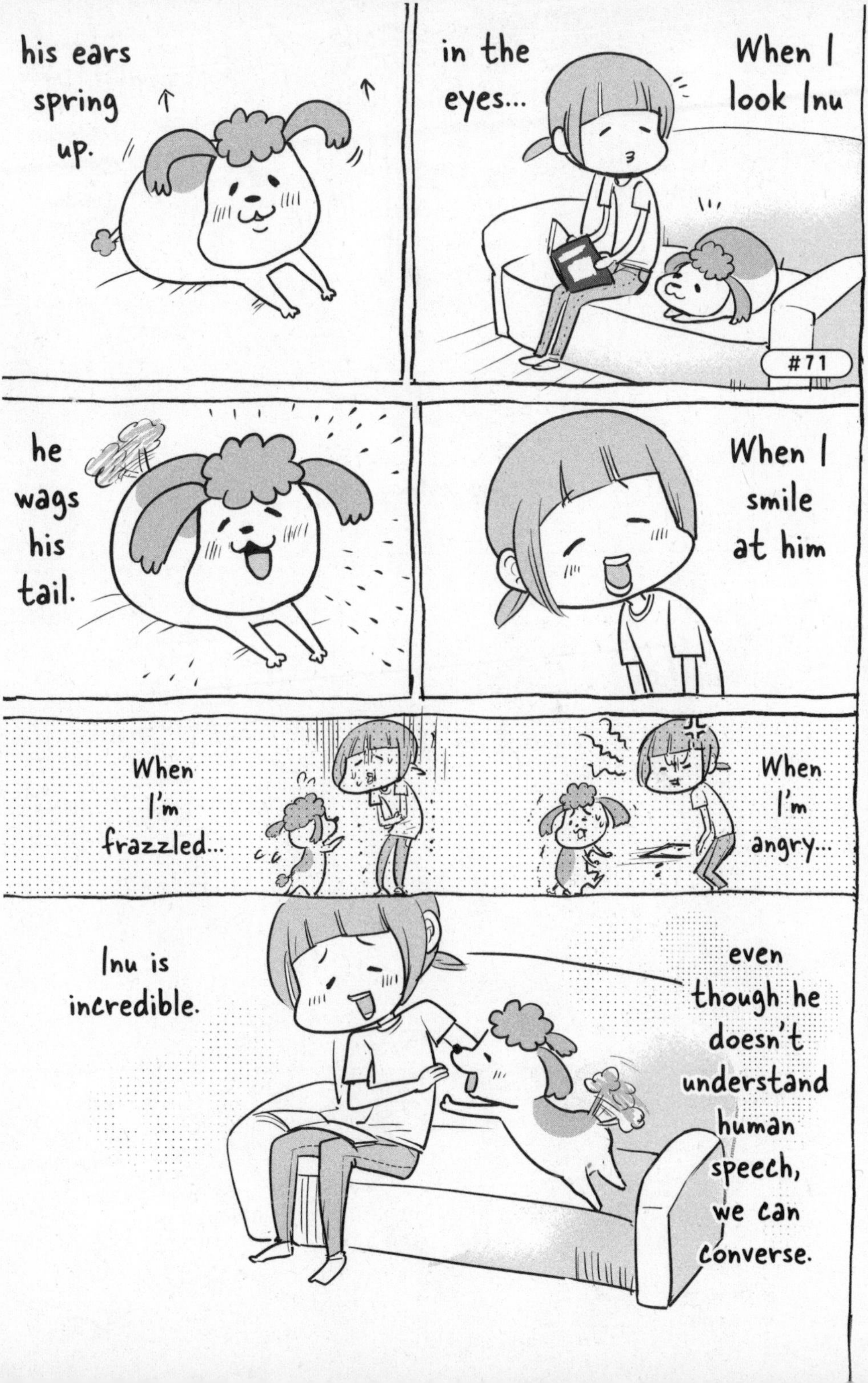
#71
When I look Inu
in the eyes...
his ears spring up.
When I smile at him
he wags his tail.
When I'm angry...
When I'm frazzled...
even though he doesn't understand human speech, we can converse.
Inu is incredible.

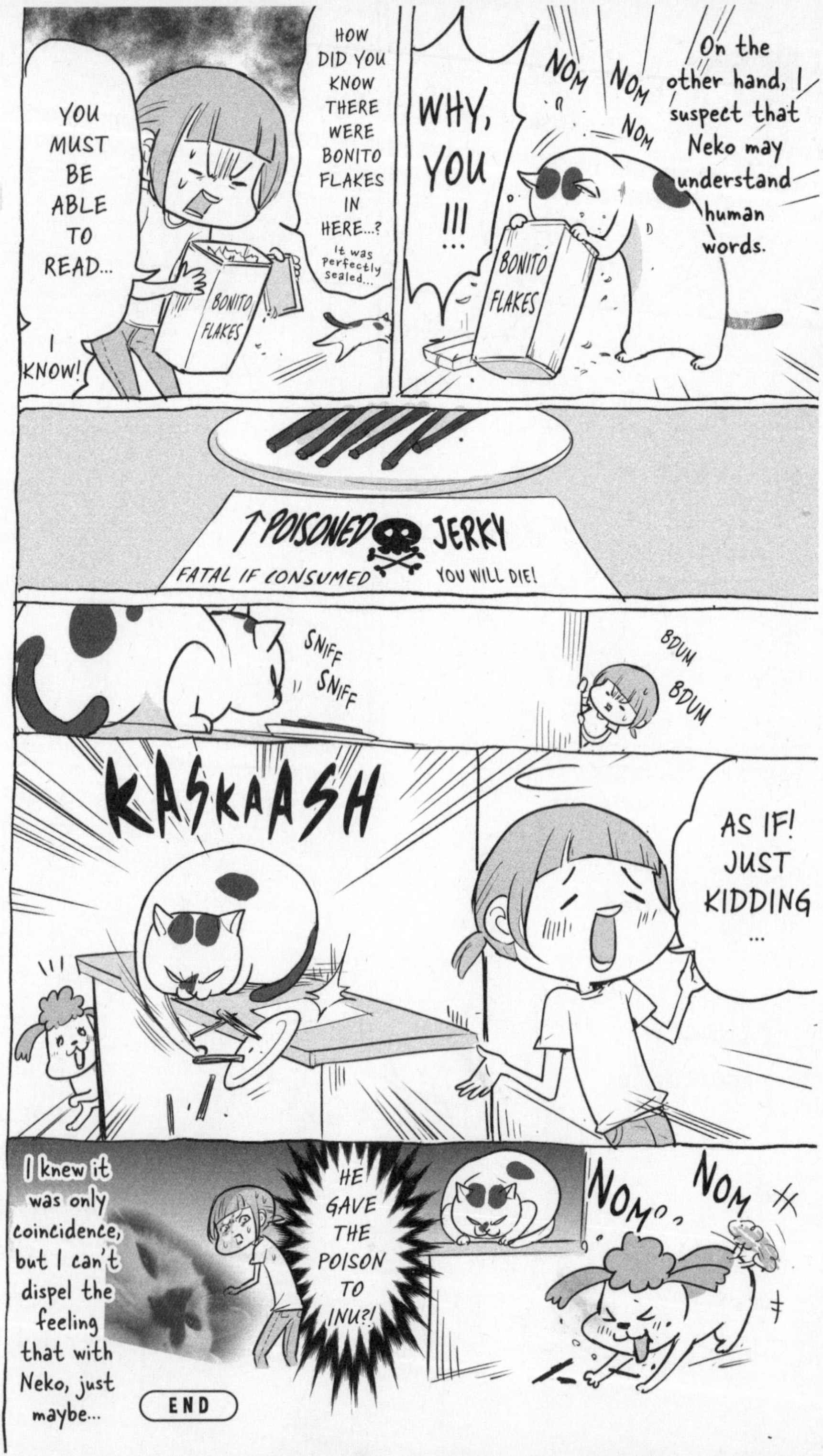
On the other hand, I suspect that Neko may understand human words.
NOM NOM NOM
WHY, YOU !!! ...
BONITO FLAKES
HOW DID YOU KNOW THERE WERE BONITO FLAKES IN HERE...?
It was Perfectly sealed...
YOU MUST BE ABLE TO READ...
I KNOW!
BONITO FLAKES
↑POISONED JERKY
FATAL IF CONSUMED
YOU WILL DIE!
BDUM BDUM
SNIFF SNIFF
AS IF! JUST KIDDING ...
KASKAASH
NOM NOM
HE GAVE THE POISON TO INU?!
I knew it was only coincidence, but I can't dispel the feeling that with Neko, just maybe...
END

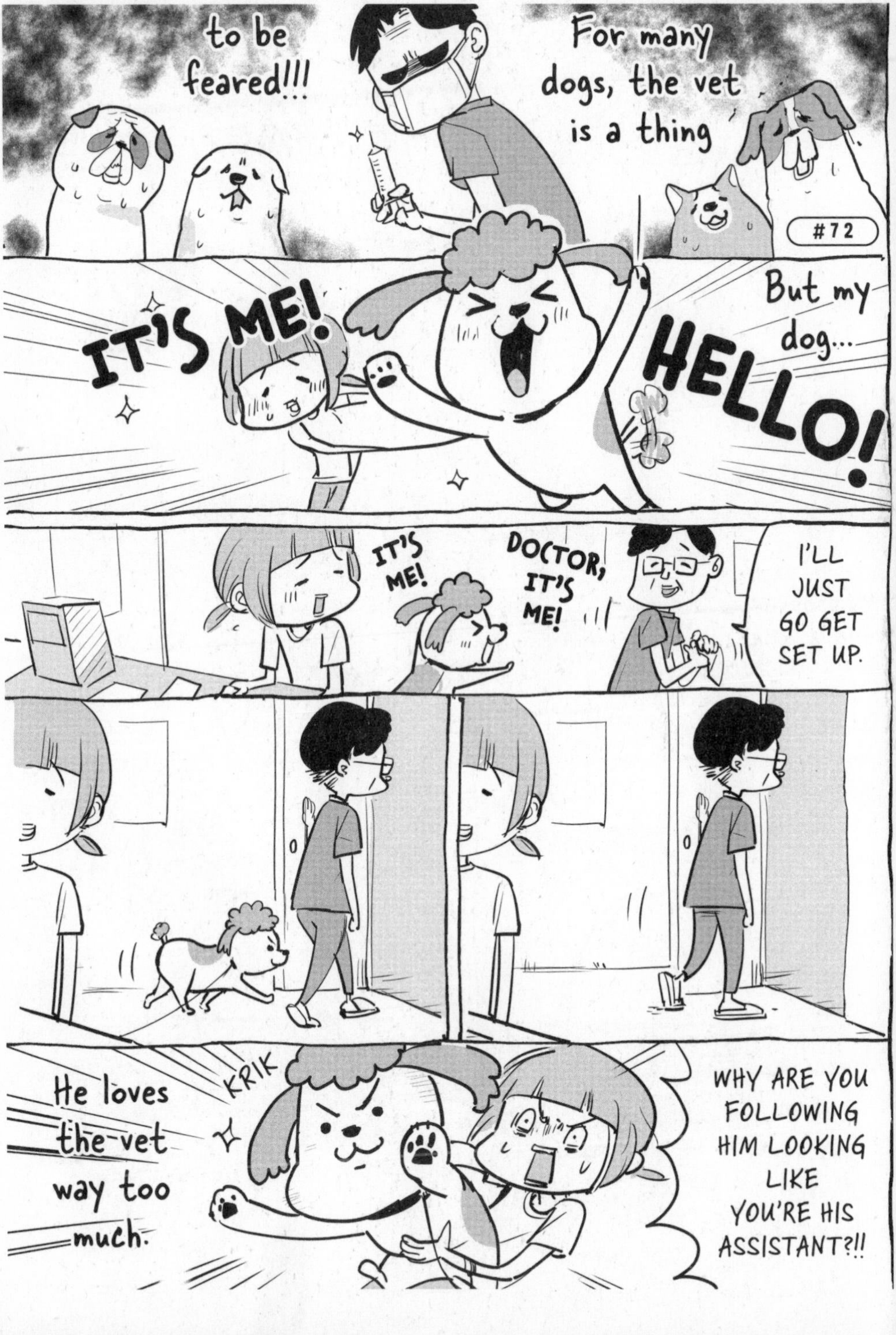
For many dogs, the vet is a thing
to be feared!!!
#72
But my dog...
HELLO!
IT'S ME!
I'LL JUST GO GET SET UP.
DOCTOR, IT'S ME!
IT'S ME!
WHY ARE YOU FOLLOWING HIM LOOKING LIKE YOU'RE HIS ASSISTANT?!!
KRIK
He loves the vet way too much.

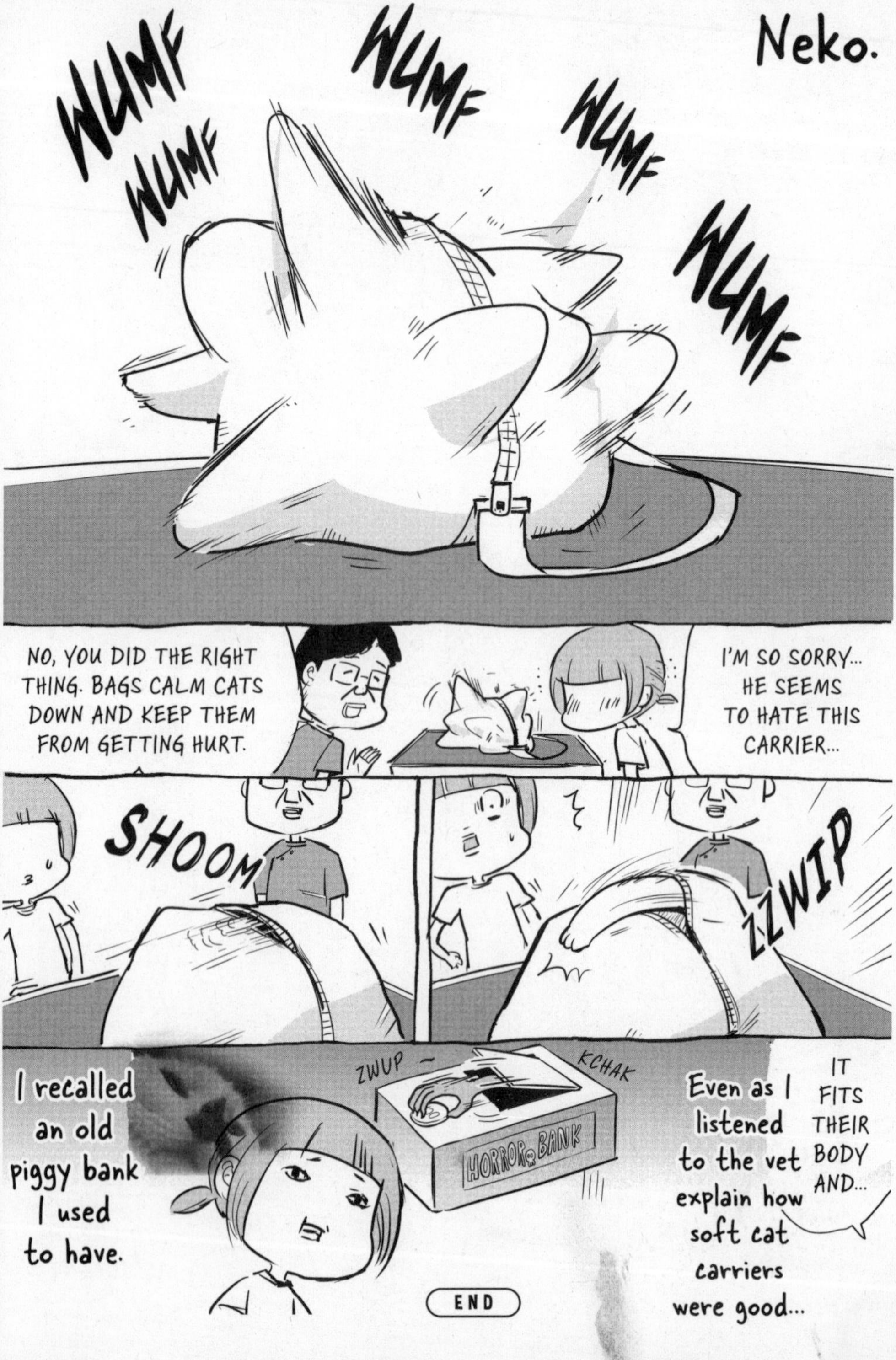
WUMF
WUMF
WUMF
WUMF
WUMF
I'M SO SORRY... HE SEEMS TO HATE THIS CARRIER...
NO, YOU DID THE RIGHT THING. BAGS CALM CATS DOWN AND KEEP THEM FROM GETTING HURT.
ZZWIP
SHOOM
IT FITS THEIR BODY AND...
Even as I listened to the vet explain how soft cat carriers were good...
KCHAK
ZWUP
HORROR BANK
I recalled an old piggy bank I used to have.
END

It's me!

Newly-Drawn 4-Panel Strip

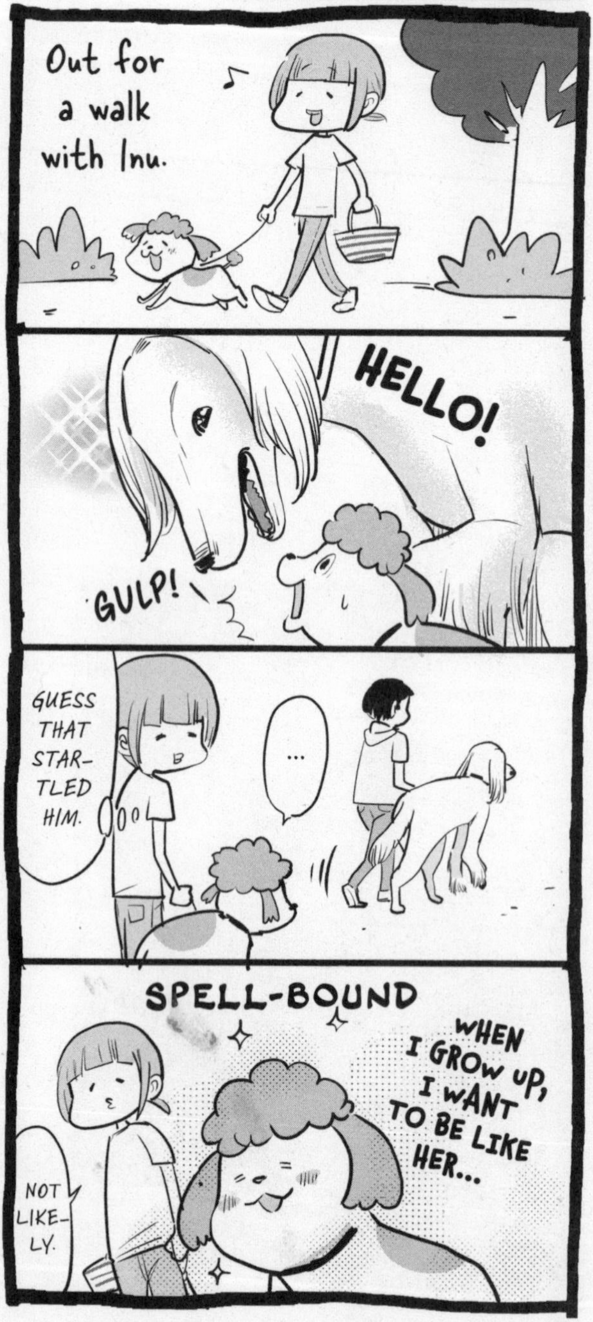
Out for a walk with Inu.
HELLO!
GULP!
GUESS THAT STAR-TLED HIM.
...
SPELL-BOUND
WHEN I GROW UP, I WANT TO BE LIKE HER...
NOT LIKE-LY.

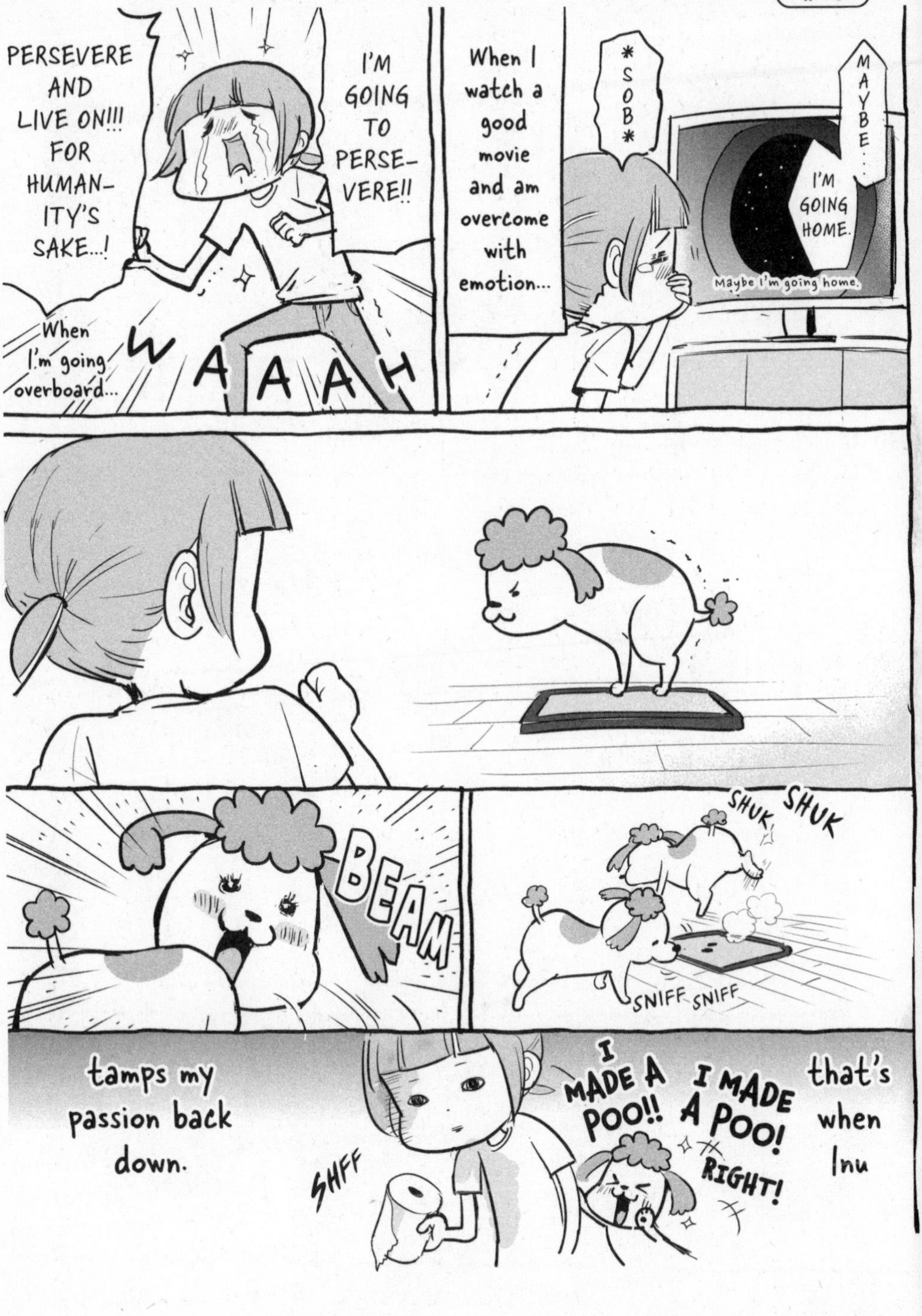
MAYBE...
I'M GOING HOME.
Maybe I'm going home.
SOB
When I watch a good movie and am overcome with emotion...
I'M GOING TO PERSEVERE!!
PERSEVERE AND LIVE ON!!! FOR HUMANITY'S SAKE...!
When I'm going overboard...
WAAAH
SHUK SHUK
SNIFF SNIFF
BEAM
that's when Inu
I MADE A POO!!
I MADE A POO!
RIGHT!
SHFF
tamps my passion back down.

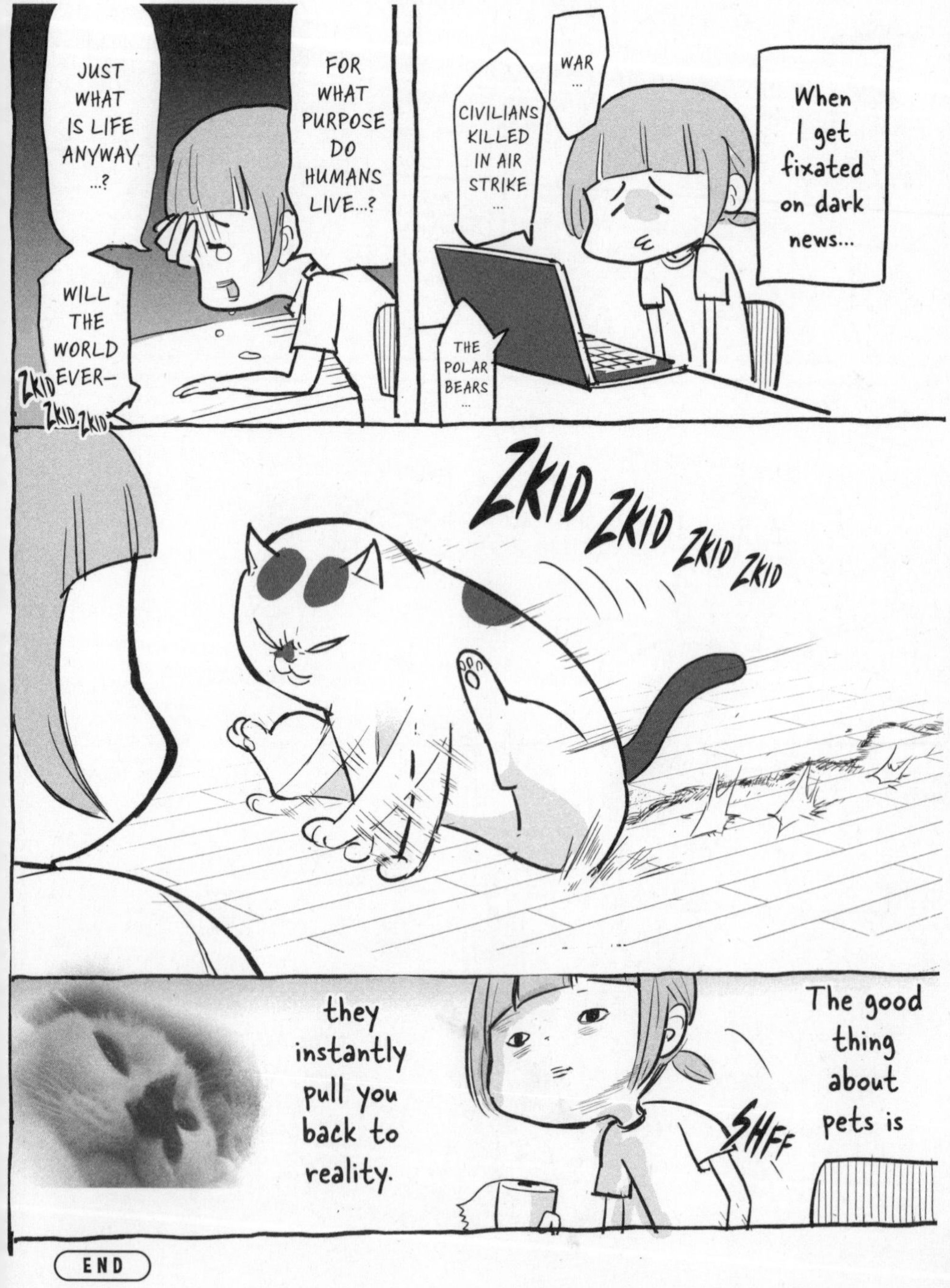
When I get fixated on dark news...
WAR ...
CIVILIANS KILLED IN AIR STRIKE ...
THE POLAR BEARS ...
FOR WHAT PURPOSE DO HUMANS LIVE...?
JUST WHAT IS LIFE ANYWAY ...?
WILL THE WORLD EVER—
ZKID ZKID ZKID
ZKID ZKID ZKID ZKID
The good thing about pets is
SHFF
they instantly pull you back to reality.

END

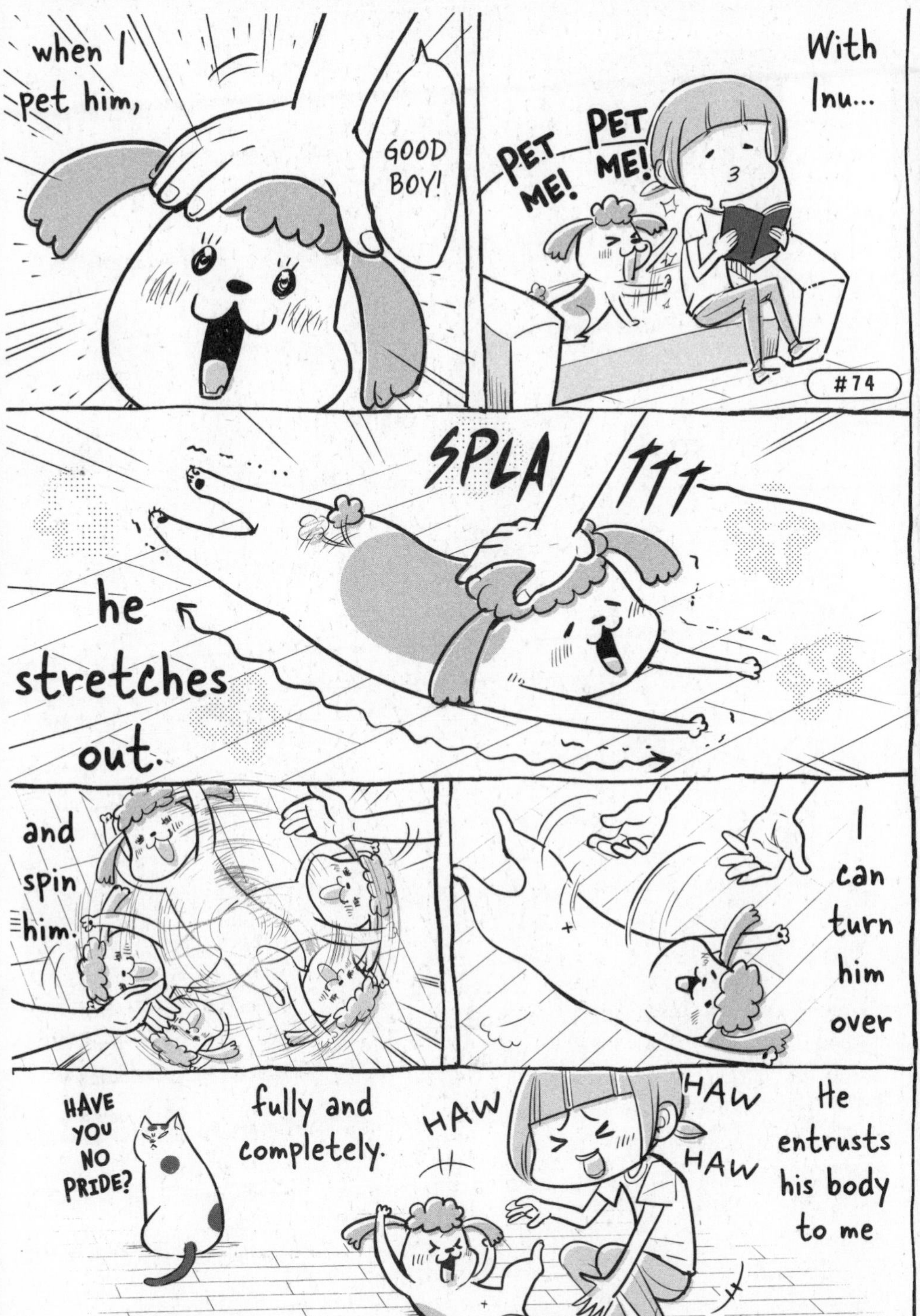
With Inu...
PET ME!
PET ME!
#74
GOOD BOY!
when I pet him,
SPLATTT
he stretches out.
I can turn him over
and spin him.
He entrusts his body to me
HAW
HAW
HAW
fully and completely.
HAVE YOU NO PRIDE?

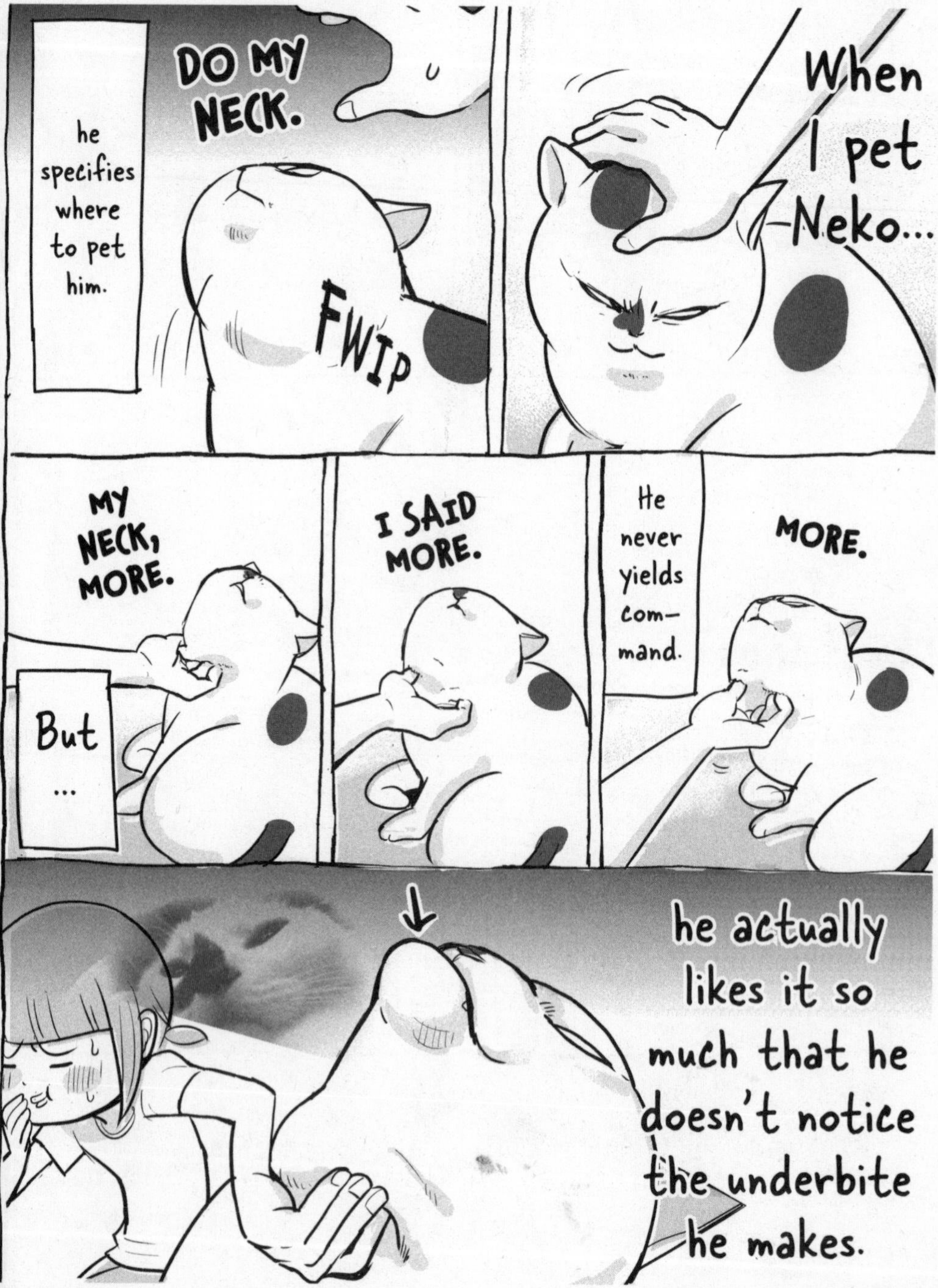
When I pet Neko...
DO MY NECK.
he specifies where to pet him.
FWIP
MORE.
He never yields com-mand.
I SAID MORE.
MY NECK, MORE.
But ...
he actually likes it so much that he doesn't notice the underbite he makes.

END

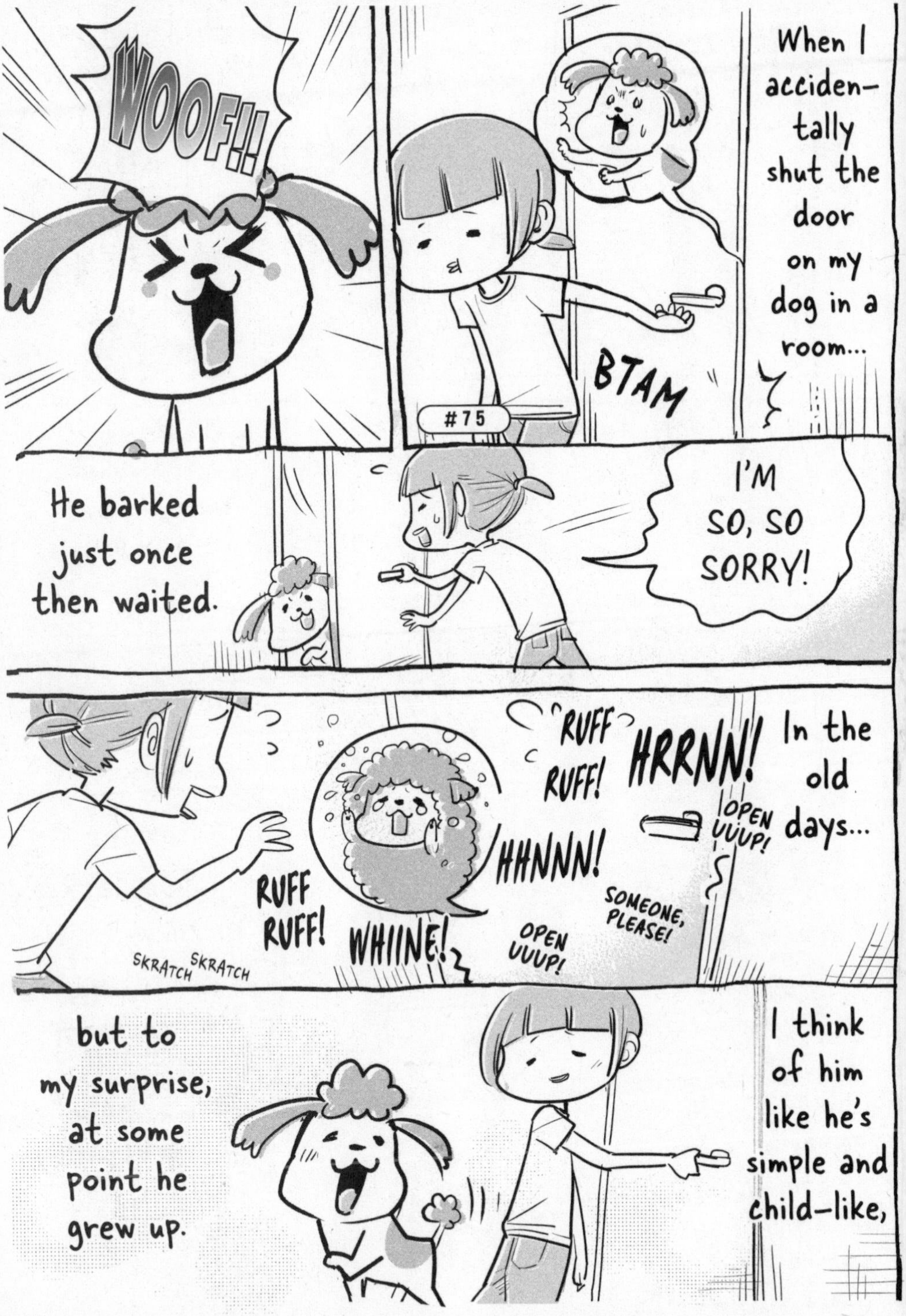
#75
When I accidentally shut the door on my dog in a room...
BTAM
WOOF!!
I'M SO, SO SORRY!
He barked just once then waited.
In the old days...
HRRNN!
RUFF RUFF!
OPEN UUUP!
HHNNN!
SOMEONE, PLEASE!
OPEN UUUP!
WHIINE!
RUFF RUFF!
SKRATCH SKRATCH
I think of him like he's simple and child-like,
but to my surprise, at some point he grew up.

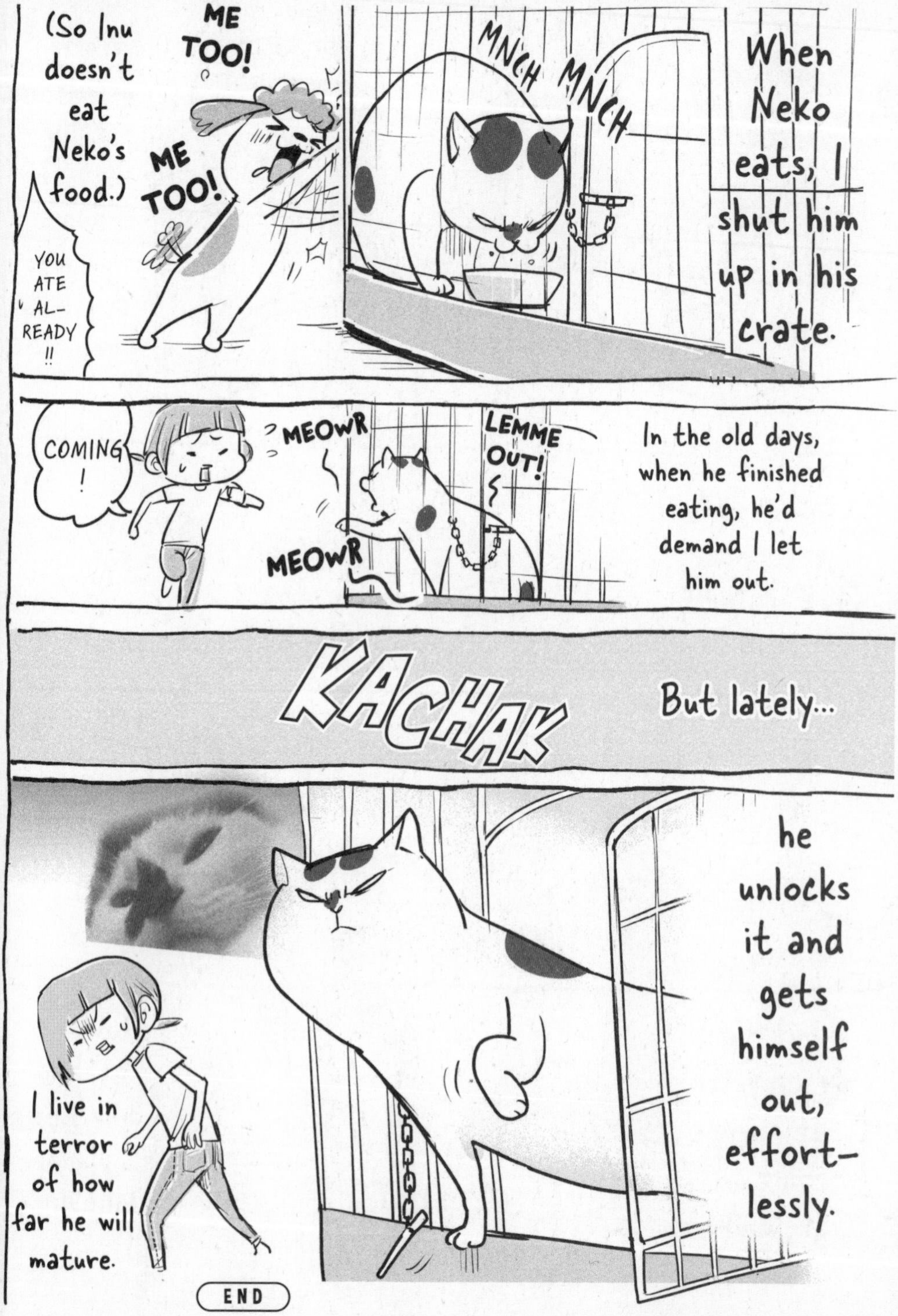
When Neko eats, I shut him up in his crate.
MNCH MNCH
ME TOO!
ME TOO!
(So Inu doesn't eat Neko's food.)
YOU ATE AL-READY!!
In the old days, when he finished eating, he'd demand I let him out.
LEMME OUT!
MEOWR
MEOWR
COMING!
But lately...
KACHAK
he unlocks it and gets himself out, effort-lessly.
I live in terror of how far he will mature.
END

More About #73

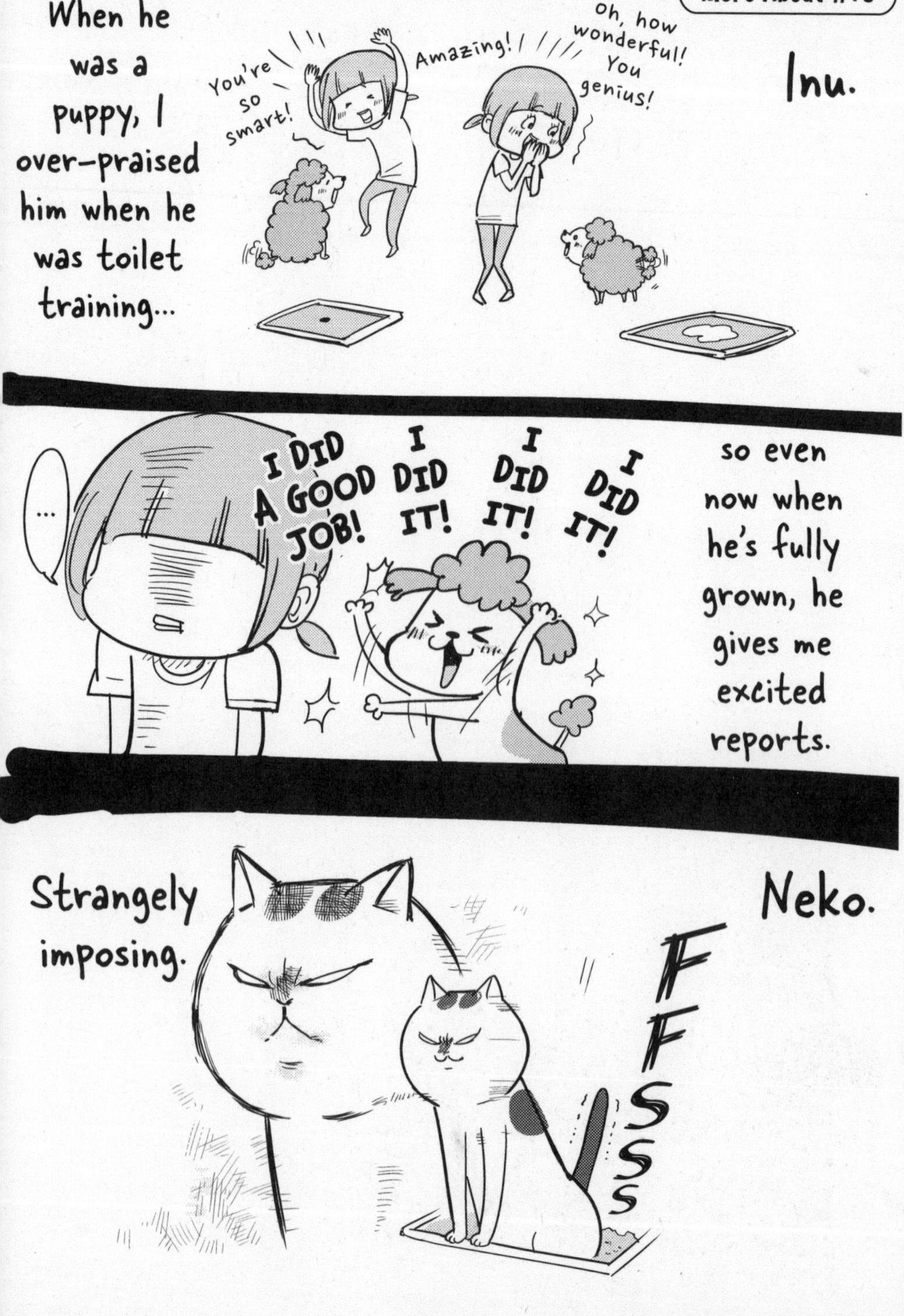
Inu.
Oh, how wonderful! You genius!
Amazing!
You're so smart!
When he was a puppy, I over-praised him when he was toilet training...
so even now when he's fully grown, he gives me excited reports.
I DID IT!
I DID IT!
I DID IT!
I DID A GOOD JOB!
...
Neko.
FFSSS
Strangely imposing.

Soft like mochi~

Newly-Drawn 4-Panel Strip

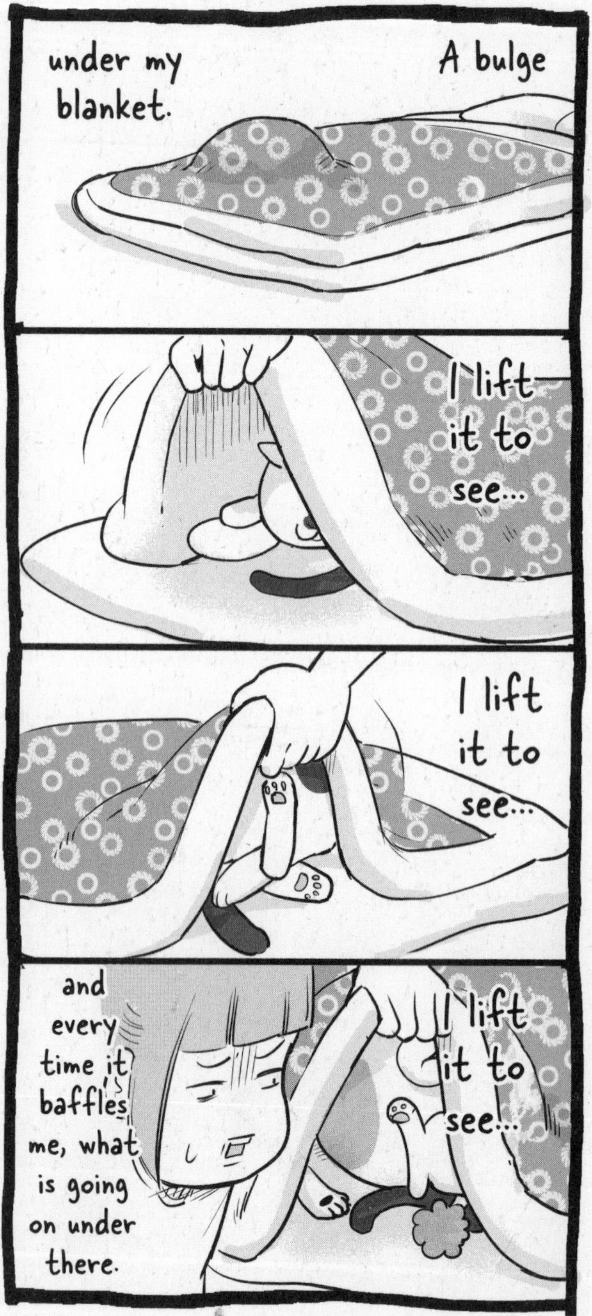
A bulge
under my blanket.
I lift it to see...
I lift it to see...
I lift it to see...
and every time it baffles me, what is going on under there.

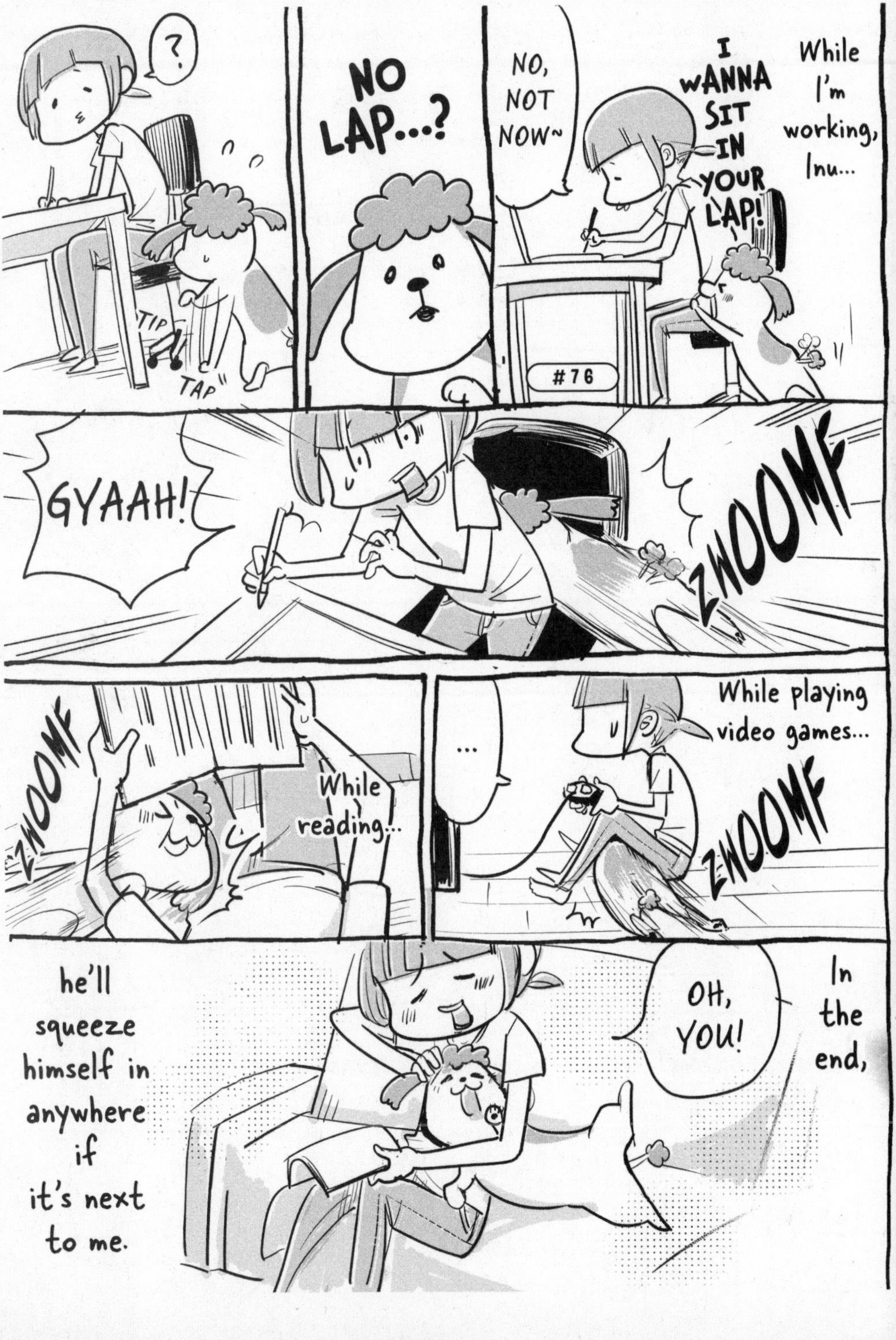
While I'm working, Inu...
I WANNA SIT IN YOUR LAP!
NO, NOT NOW~
#76
NO LAP...?
?
TIP TAP
ZWOOMF
GYAAH!
While playing video games...
ZWOOMF
...
While reading...
ZWOOMF
In the end,
OH, YOU!
he'll squeeze himself in anywhere if it's next to me.

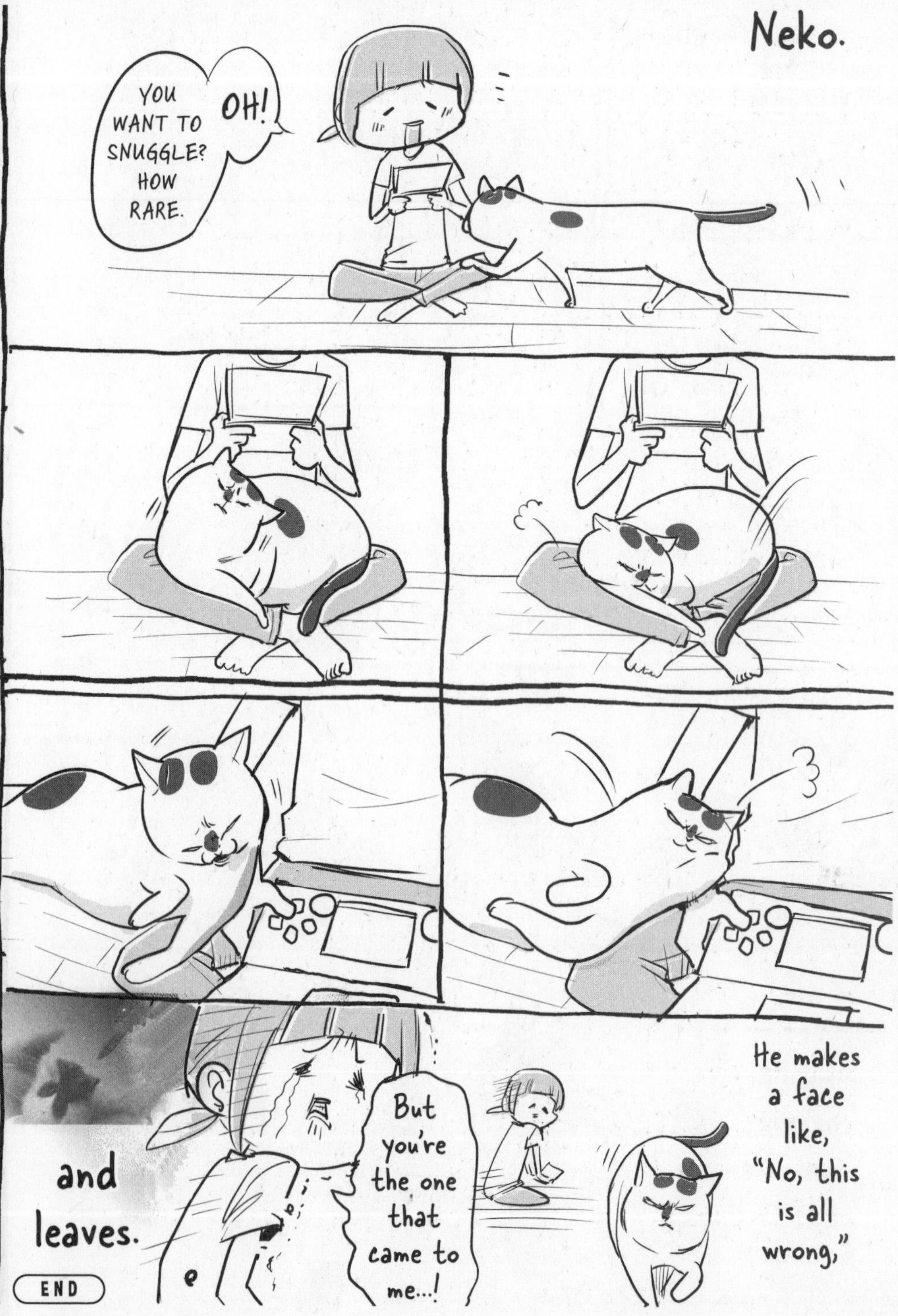
Neko.
OH!
YOU WANT TO SNUGGLE? HOW RARE.
He makes a face like, "No, this is all wrong,"
But you're the one that came to me...!
and leaves.
END

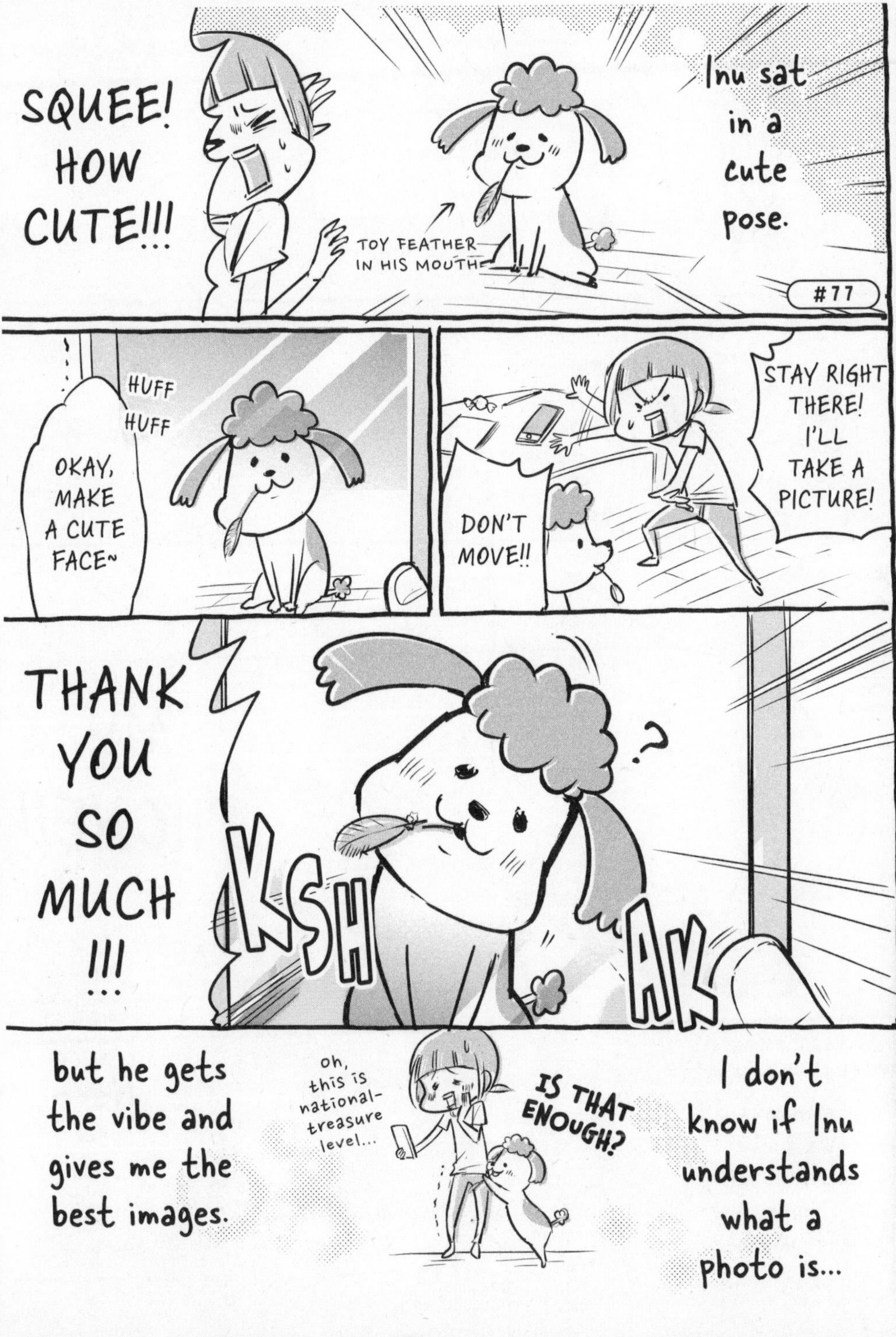
#77
Inu sat in a cute pose.
SQUEE! HOW CUTE!!!...
TOY FEATHER IN HIS MOUTH
STAY RIGHT THERE! I'LL TAKE A PICTURE!
DON'T MOVE!!
HUFF HUFF
OKAY, MAKE A CUTE FACE~
?
KSHAK
THANK YOU SO MUCH!!!...
I don't know if Inu understands what a photo is...
IS THAT ENOUGH?
oh, this is national-treasure level...
but he gets the vibe and gives me the best images.

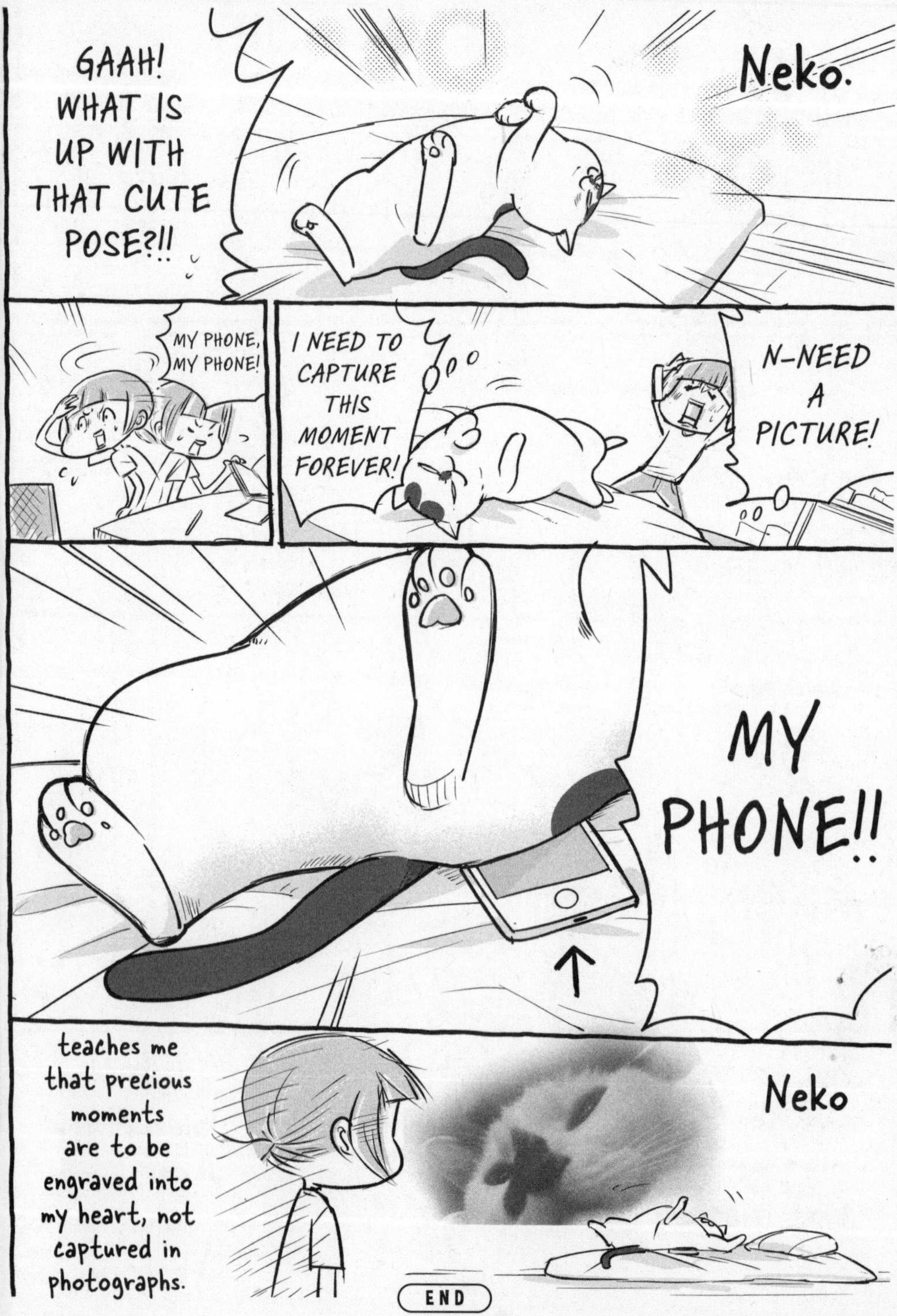
Neko.
GAAH! WHAT IS UP WITH THAT CUTE POSE?!!
N-NEED A PICTURE!
I NEED TO CAPTURE THIS MOMENT FOREVER!
MY PHONE, MY PHONE!
MY PHONE!!..
Neko
teaches me that precious moments are to be engraved into my heart, not captured in photographs.
END

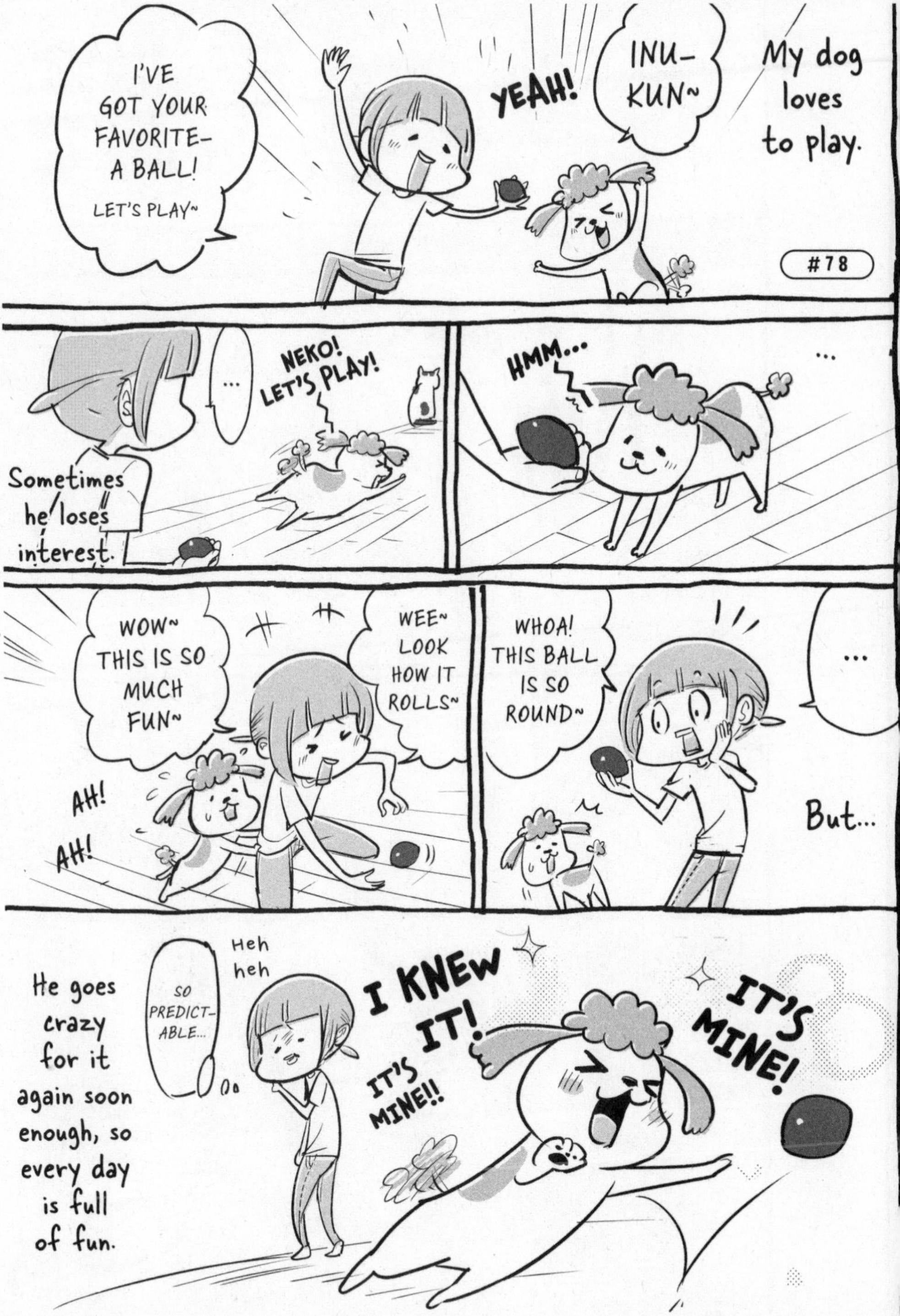
My dog loves to play.
#78
INU-KUN~
YEAH!
I'VE GOT YOUR FAVORITE— A BALL!
LET'S PLAY~
...
HMM...
...
NEKO! LET'S PLAY!
Sometimes he loses interest.
...
But...
WHOA! THIS BALL IS SO ROUND~
WEE~ LOOK HOW IT ROLLS~
WOW~ THIS IS SO MUCH FUN~
AH!
AH!
IT'S MINE!
I KNEW IT!
IT'S MINE!!
Heh heh
SO PREDICTABLE...
He goes crazy for it again soon enough, so every day is full of fun.

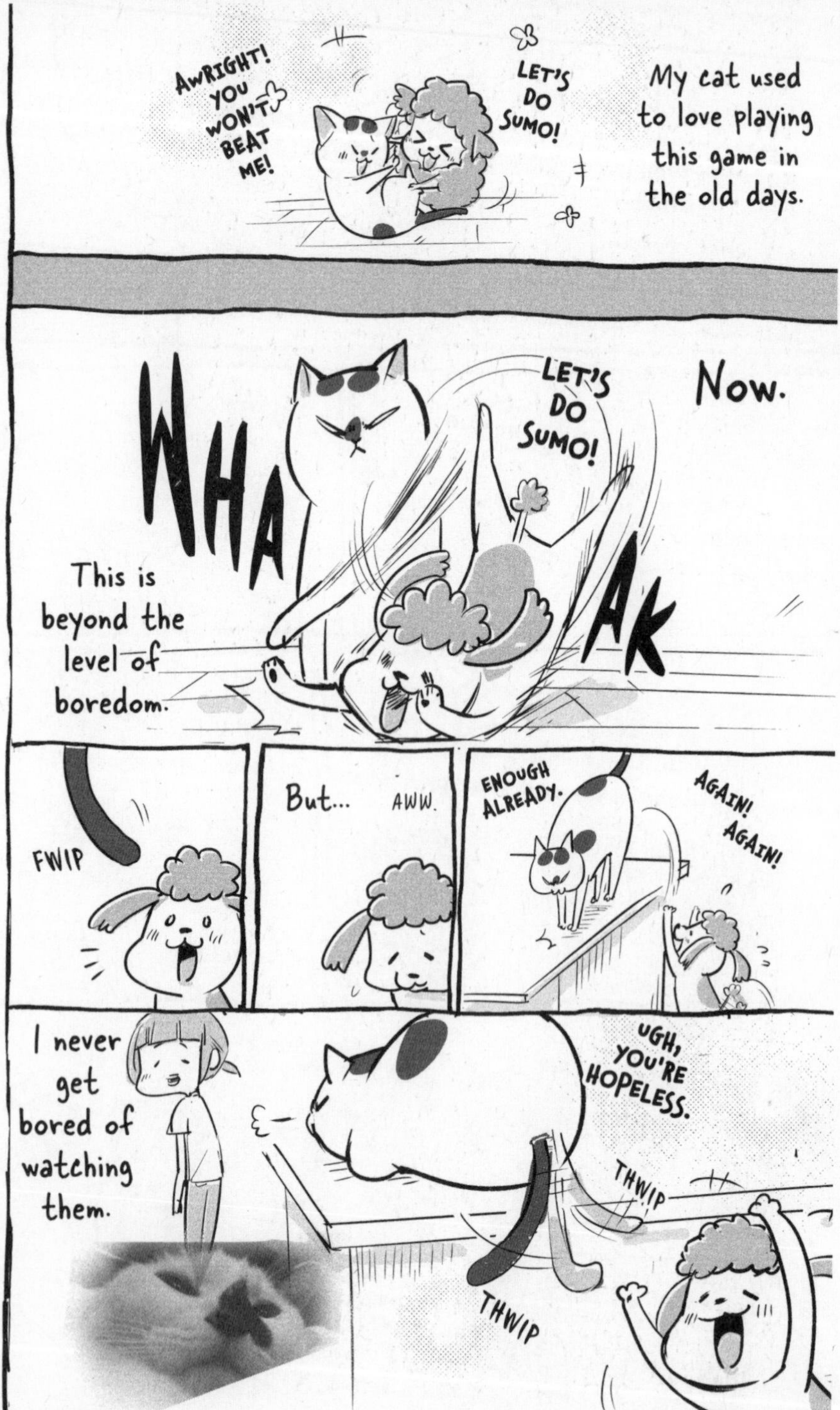
My cat used to love playing this game in the old days.
LET'S DO SUMO!
AWRIGHT! YOU WON'T BEAT ME!
Now.
LET'S DO SUMO!
WHAAK
This is beyond the level of boredom.
ENOUGH ALREADY.
AGAIN! AGAIN!
But...
AWW.
FWIP
UGH, YOU'RE HOPELESS.
THWIP
THWIP
I never get bored of watching them.
END

Please don't look at me like that.

Newly-Drawn 4-Panel Strip

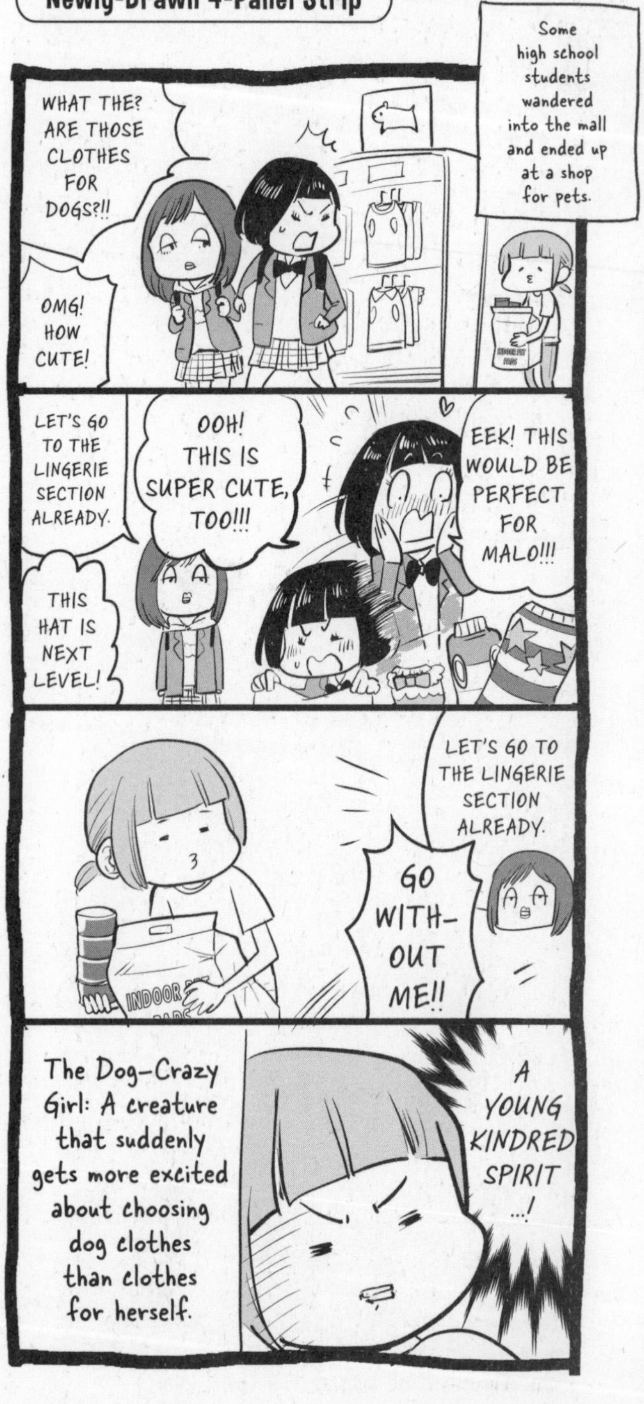

Some high school students wandered into the mall and ended up at a shop for pets.
WHAT THE? ARE THOSE CLOTHES FOR DOGS?!!
OMG! HOW CUTE!
EEK! THIS WOULD BE PERFECT FOR MALO!!!
OOH! THIS IS SUPER CUTE, TOO!!!
LET'S GO TO THE LINGERIE SECTION ALREADY.
THIS HAT IS NEXT LEVEL!
LET'S GO TO THE LINGERIE SECTION ALREADY.
GO WITH-OUT ME!!
A YOUNG KINDRED SPIRIT ...!
The Dog-Crazy Girl: A creature that suddenly gets more excited about choosing dog clothes than clothes for herself.

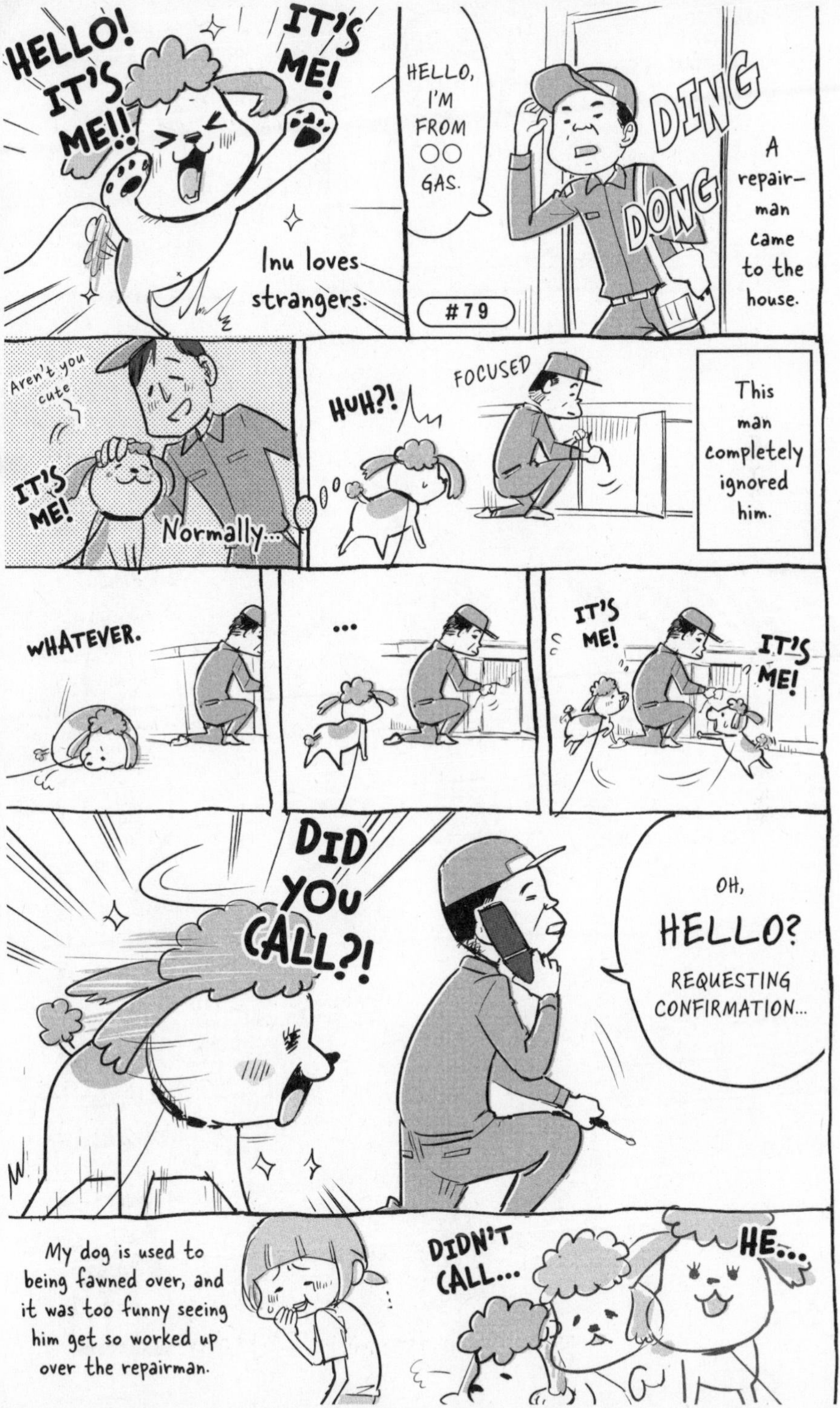

A repairman came to the house.
DING
DONG
HELLO, I'M FROM ○○ GAS.
#79
IT'S ME!
HELLO! IT'S ME!!
Inu loves strangers.
This man completely ignored him.
FOCUSED
HUH?!
Aren't you cute
IT'S ME!
Normally...
IT'S ME!
IT'S ME!
...
WHATEVER.
OH, HELLO? REQUESTING CONFIRMATION...
DID YOU CALL?!
HE...
DIDN'T CALL...
My dog is used to being fawned over, and it was too funny seeing him get so worked up over the repairman.

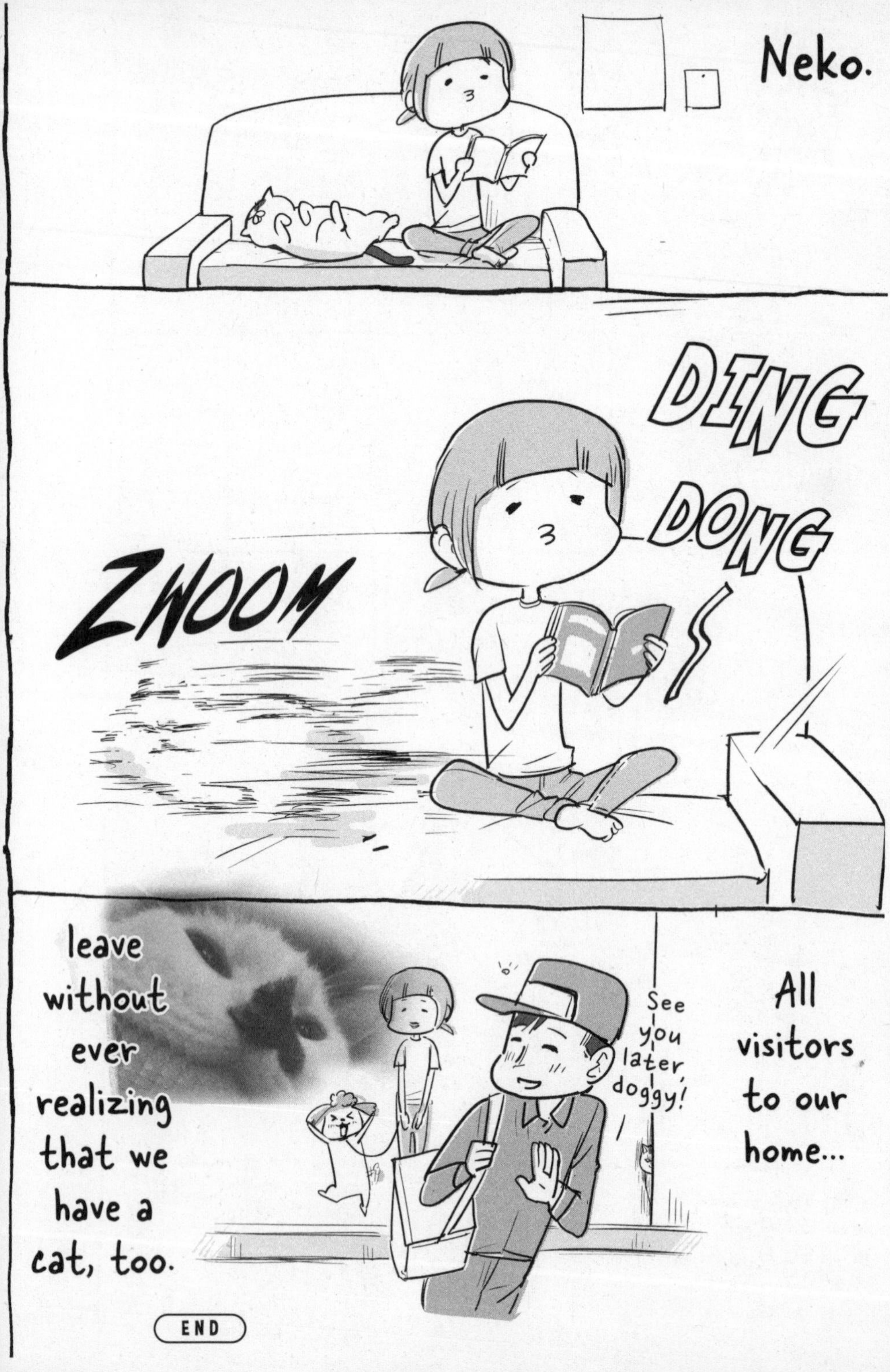
Neko.
DING DONG
ZWOOM
All visitors to our home...
See you later doggy!
leave without ever realizing that we have a cat, too.
END

#80

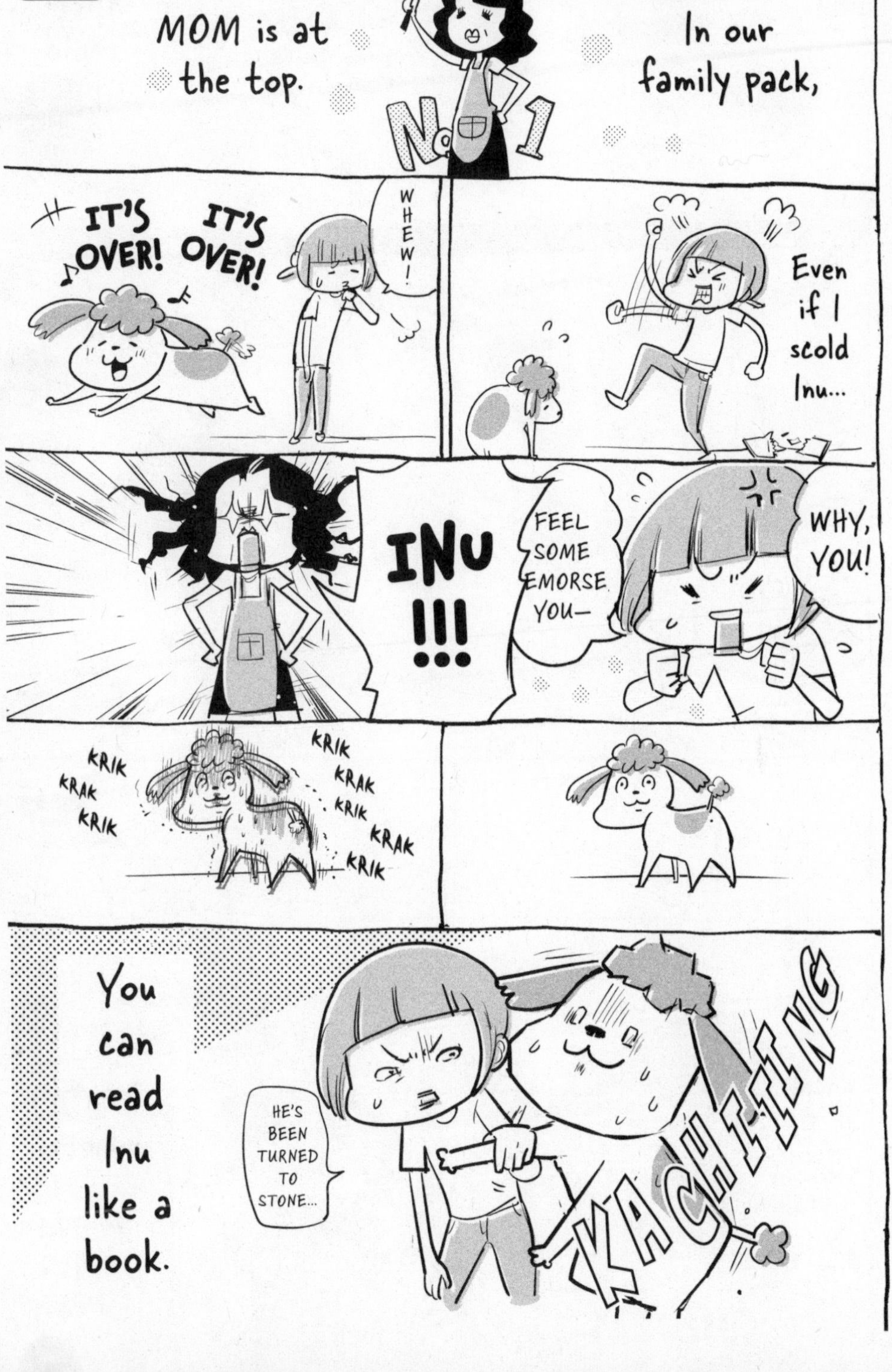
In our family pack,
MOM is at the top.
No 1
Even if I scold Inu...
WHEW!
IT'S OVER! IT'S OVER!
WHY, YOU!
FEEL SOME EMORSE YOU—
INU!!!
KRIK
KRAK
KRIK
KRAK
KRIK
KRAK
KRIK
KRIK
KRAK
KRIK
KACHIIING
You can read Inu like a book.
HE'S BEEN TURNED TO STONE...

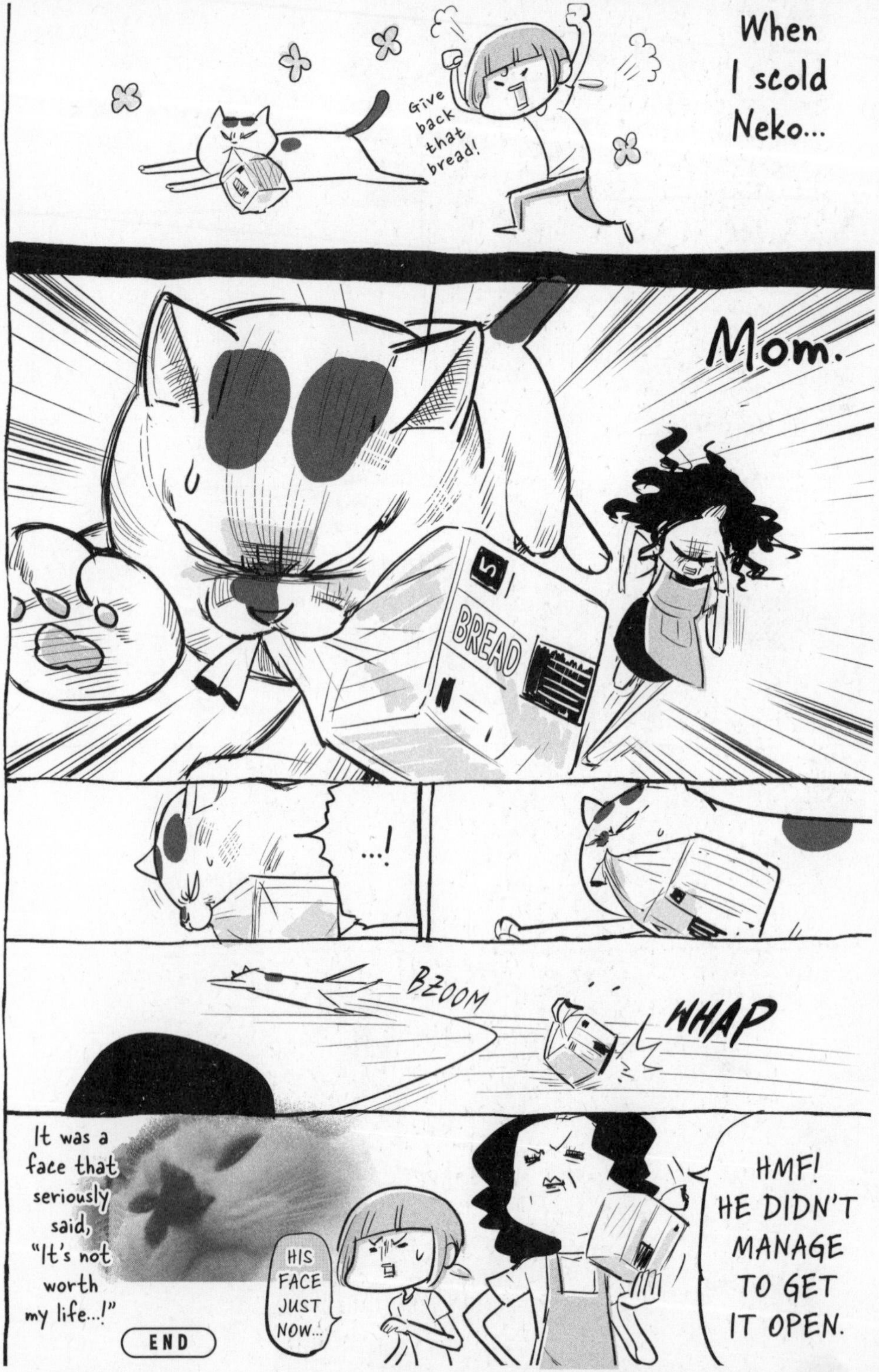
When I scold Neko...
Give back that bread!
Mom.
BREAD
...!
WHAP
BZOOM
HMF! HE DIDN'T MANAGE TO GET IT OPEN.
HIS FACE JUST NOW...
It was a face that seriously said, "It's not worth my life...!"
END

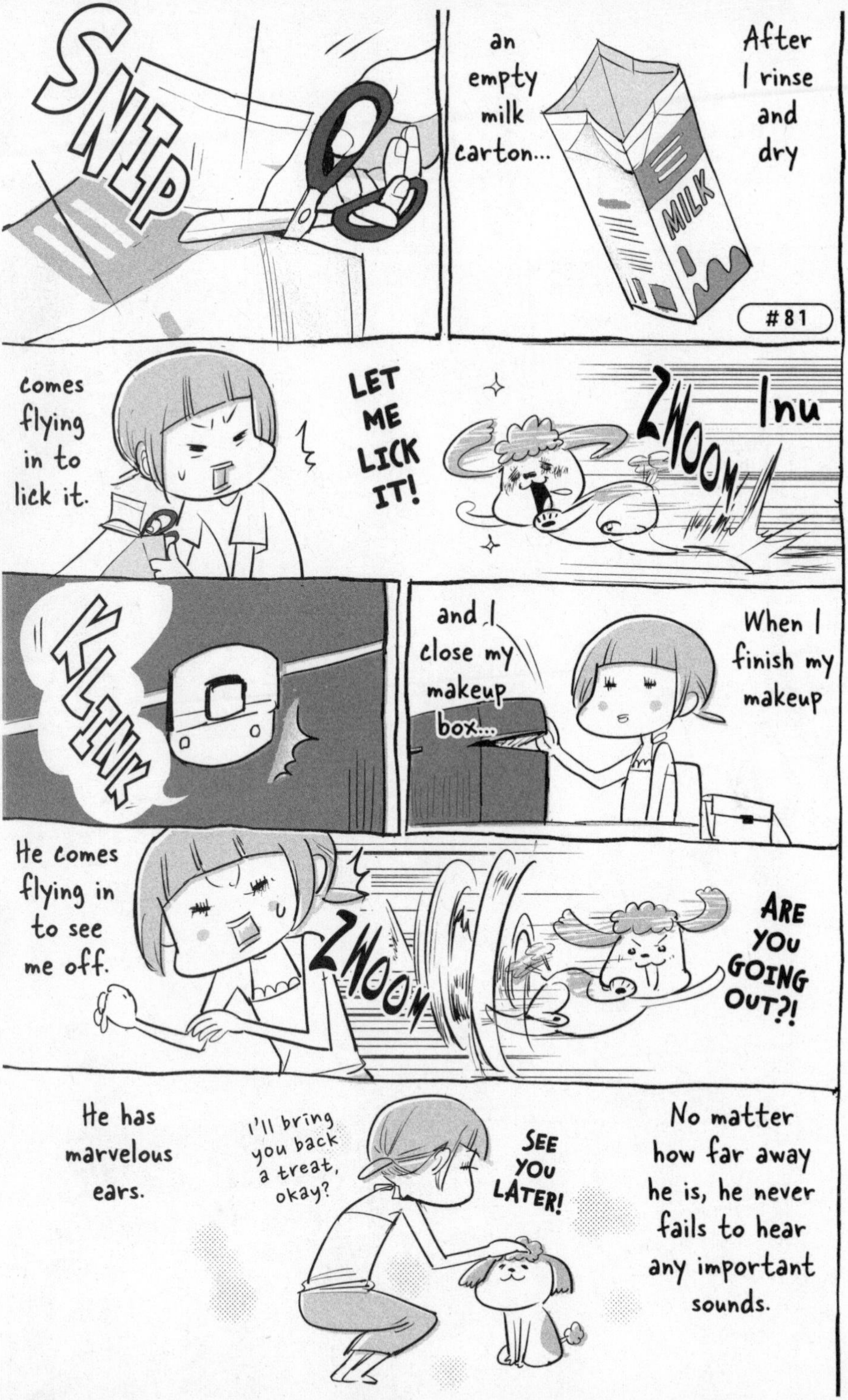

#81
After I rinse and dry
an empty milk carton...
MILK
SNIP
Inu
ZWOOM!
LET ME LICK IT!
comes flying in to lick it.
When I finish my makeup
and I close my makeup box...
KLINK
ARE YOU GOING OUT?!
ZWOOM
He comes flying in to see me off.
No matter how far away he is, he never fails to hear any important sounds.
SEE YOU LATER!
I'll bring you back a treat, okay?
He has marvelous ears.

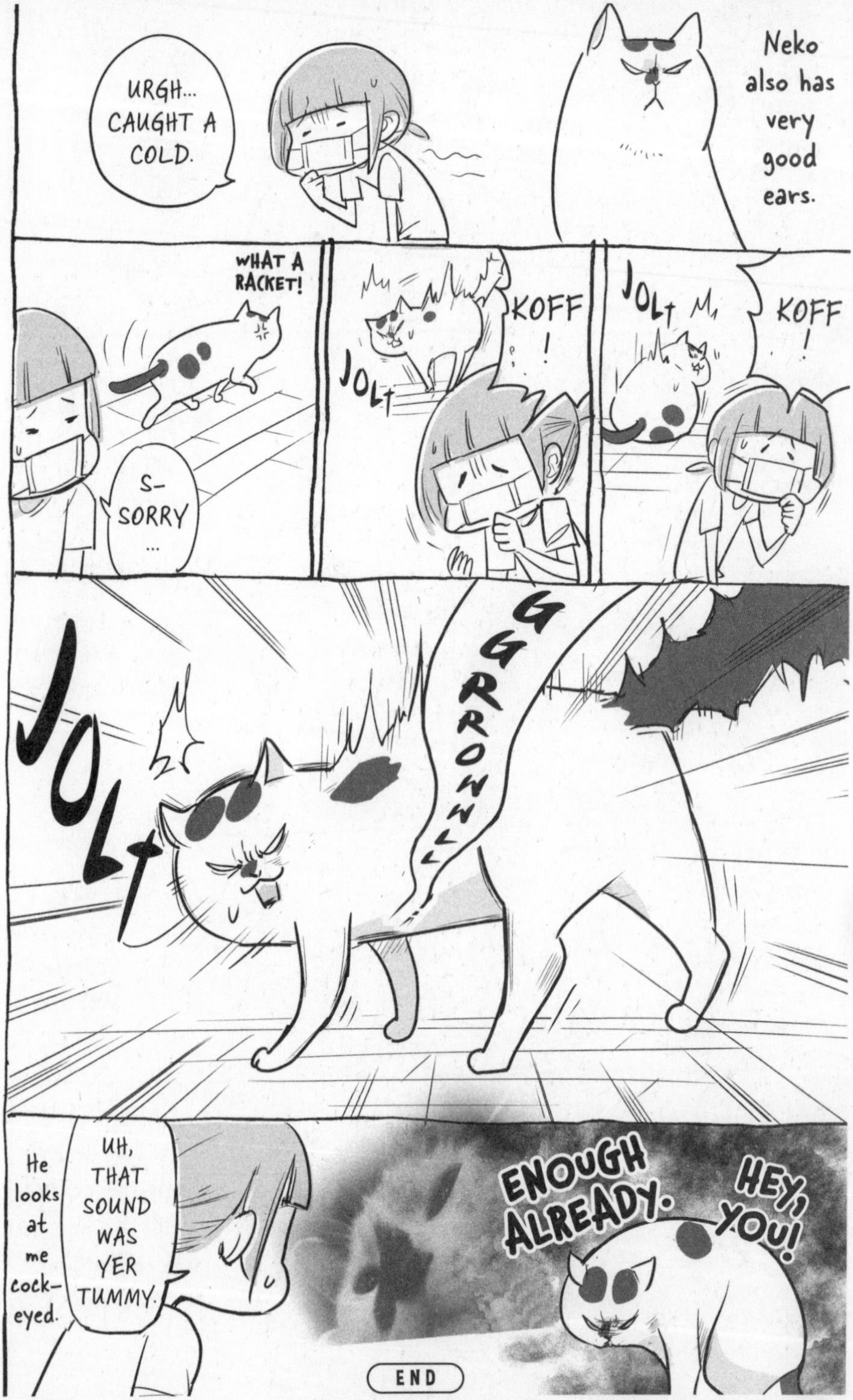

Neko also has very good ears.
URGH... CAUGHT A COLD.
JOLT
KOFF!
KOFF!
JOLT
WHAT A RACKET!
S-SORRY...
GGRROWWLL
JOLT
HEY, YOU!
ENOUGH ALREADY.
UH, THAT SOUND WAS YER TUMMY.
He looks at me cock-eyed.
END

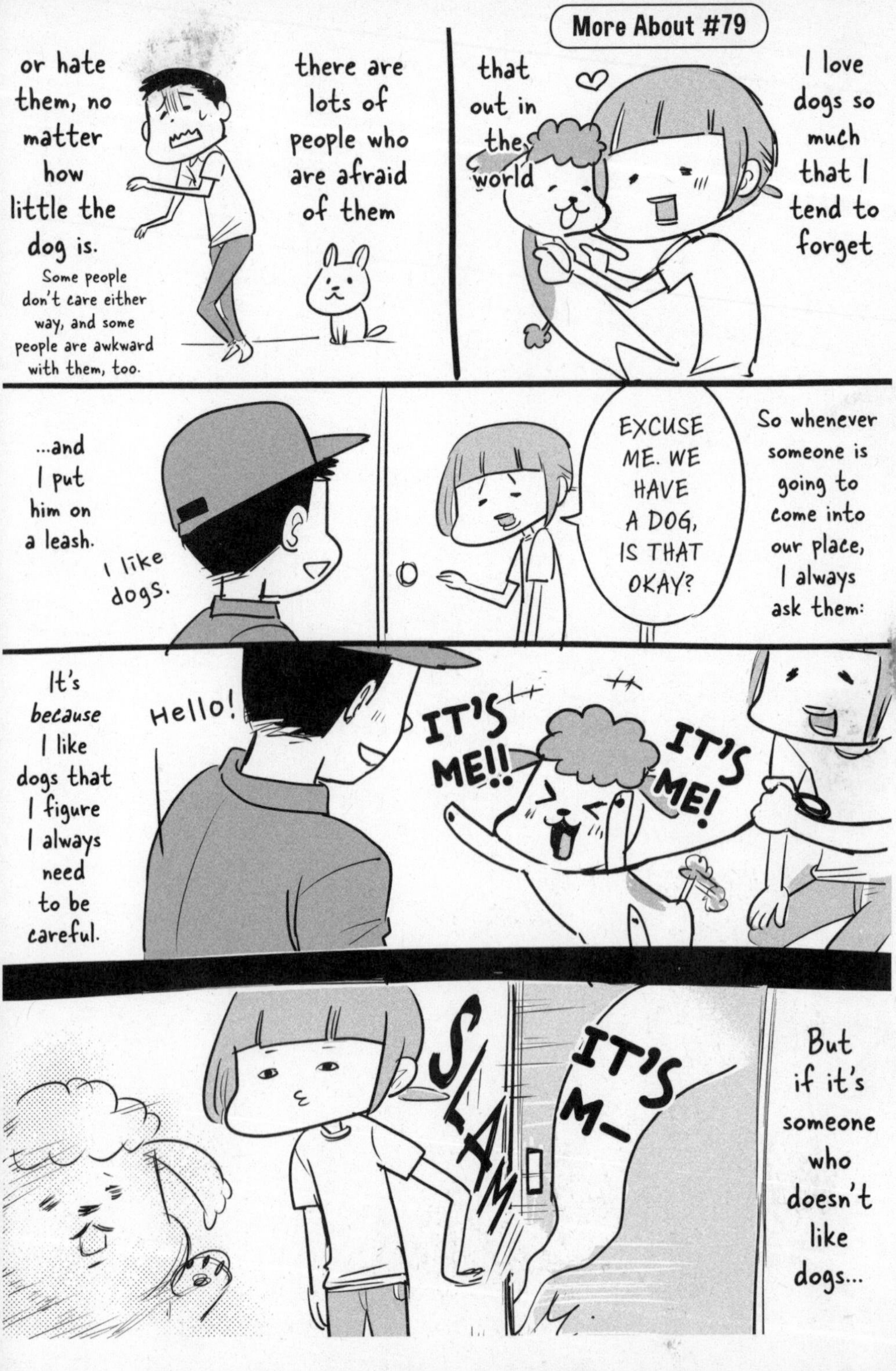
More About #79
I love dogs so much that I tend to forget
that out in the world
there are lots of people who are afraid of them
or hate them, no matter how little the dog is.
Some people don't care either way, and some people are awkward with them, too.
So whenever someone is going to come into our place, I always ask them:
EXCUSE ME. WE HAVE A DOG, IS THAT OKAY?
I like dogs.
...and I put him on a leash.
IT'S ME!
IT'S ME!!
Hello!
It's *because* I like dogs that I figure I always need to be careful.
But if it's someone who doesn't like dogs...
IT'S M—
SLAM

Inu and Neko mercilessly making a playground of my work desk.

Newly-Drawn 4-Panel Strip

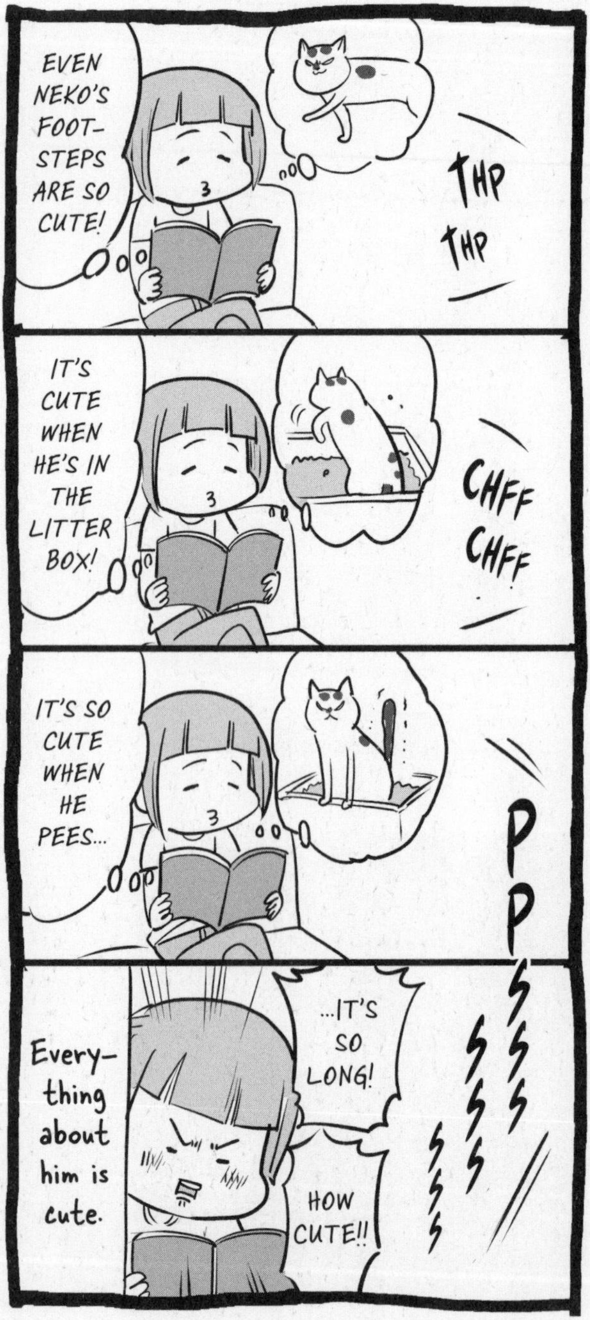
THP
THP
EVEN NEKO'S FOOT-STEPS ARE SO CUTE!
CHFF
CHFF
IT'S CUTE WHEN HE'S IN THE LITTER BOX!
PPSSS
IT'S SO CUTE WHEN HE PEES...
SSSS
SSS
...IT'S SO LONG!
HOW CUTE!!
Every-thing about him is cute.

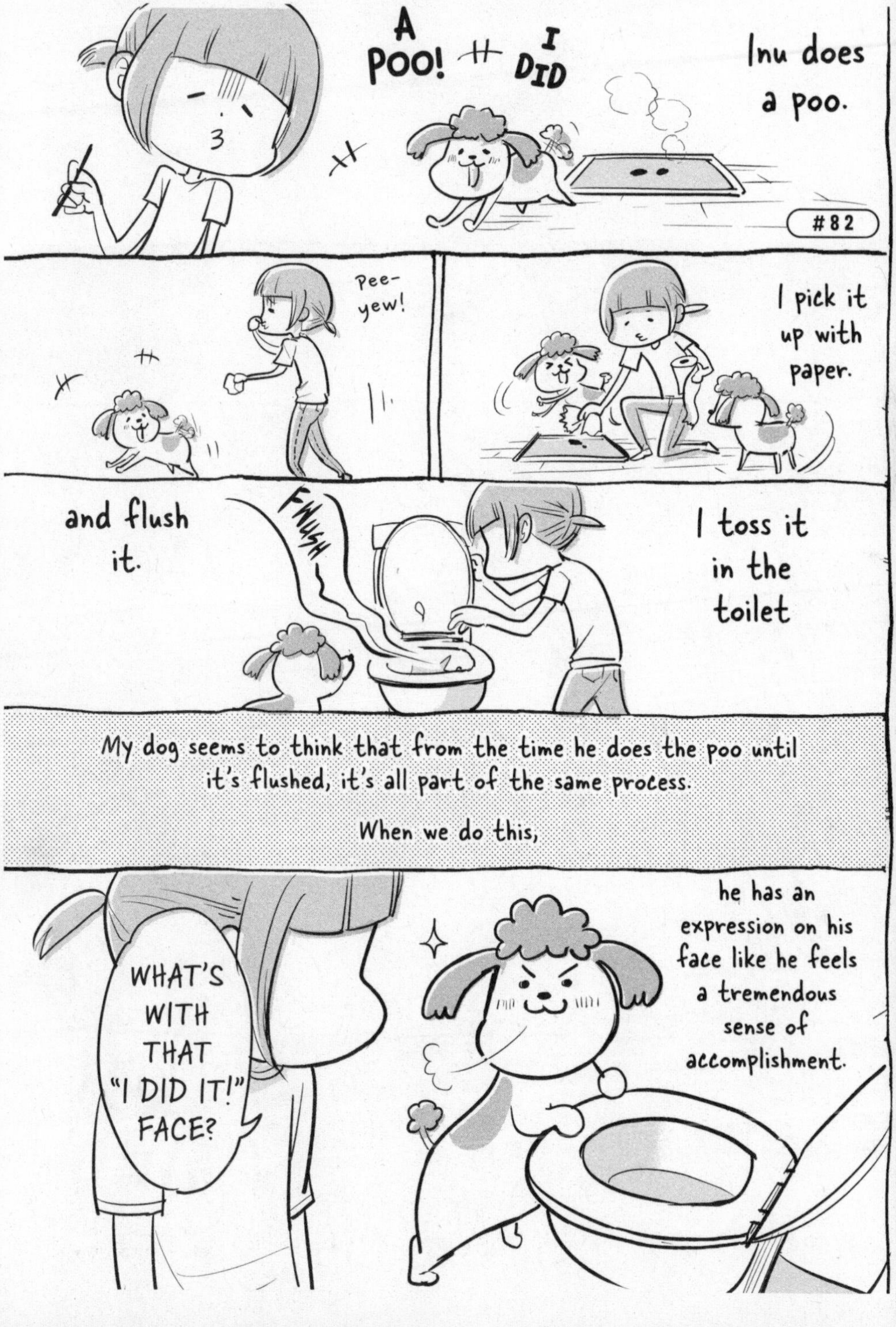
#82
Inu does a poo.
I DID A POO!
I pick it up with paper.
Pee-yew!
I toss it in the toilet
FWUSH
and flush it.
My dog seems to think that from the time he does the poo until it's flushed, it's all part of the same process.
When we do this,
he has an expression on his face like he feels a tremendous sense of accomplishment.
WHAT'S WITH THAT "I DID IT!" FACE?

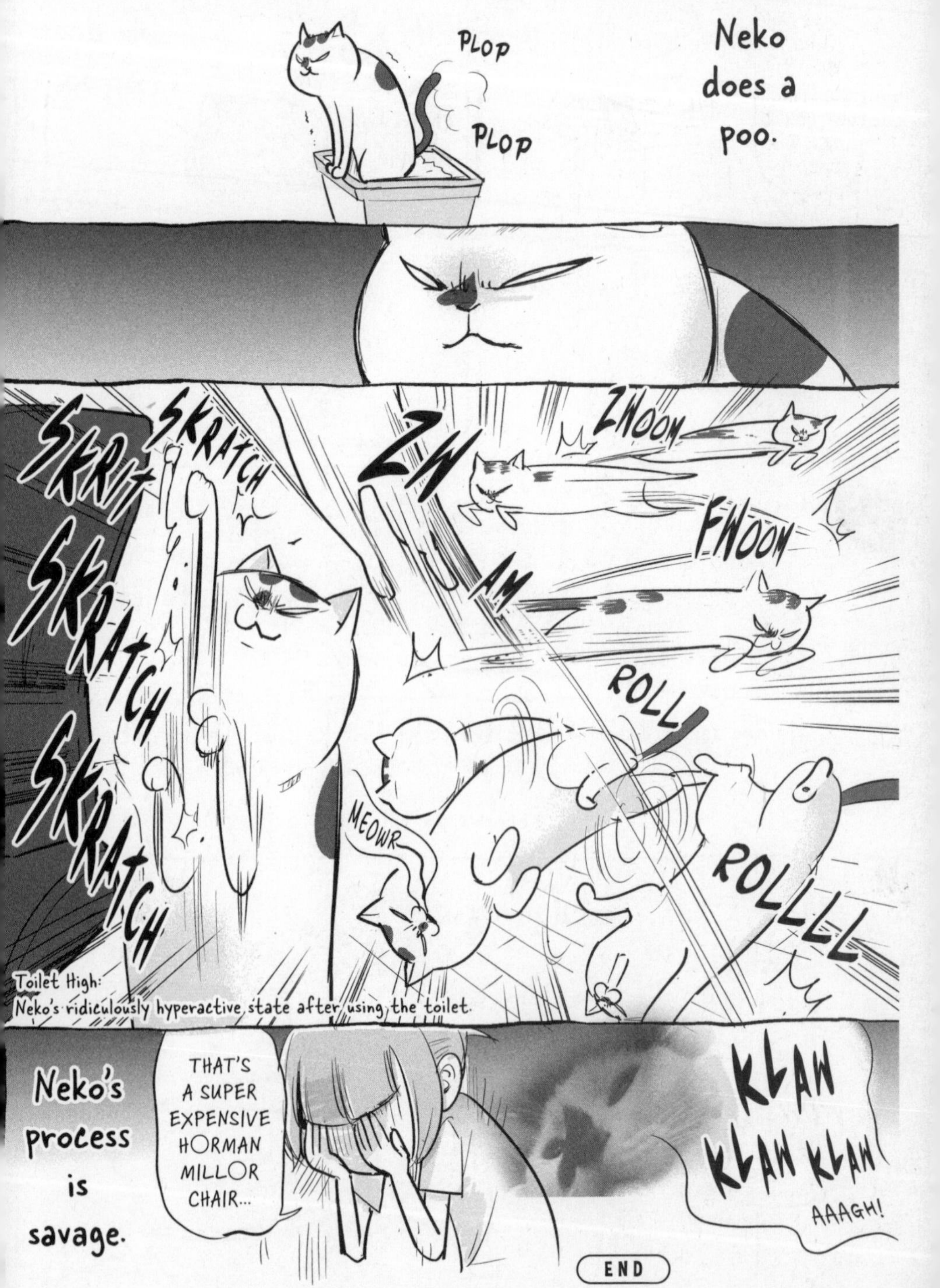
Neko does a poo.
PLOP
PLOP
ZWOOM
FWOOM
ZWAM
ROLL
ROLLLLL
MEOWR
SKRATCH
SKRIT SKRATCH SKRATCH
Toilet High:
Neko's ridiculously hyperactive state after using the toilet.
KLAW
KLAW KLAW
AAAGH!
THAT'S A SUPER EXPENSIVE HORMAN MILLOR CHAIR...
Neko's process is savage.
END

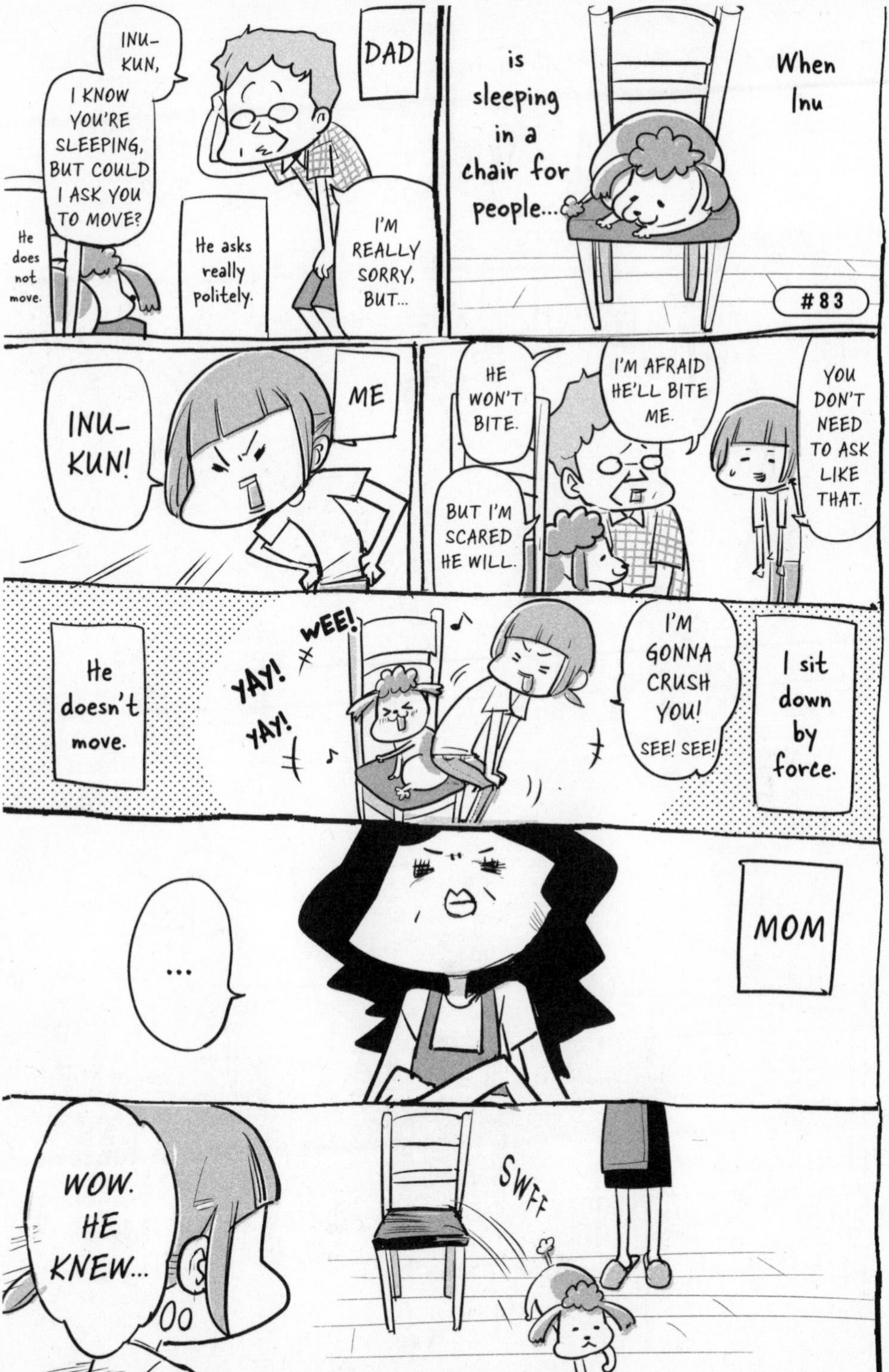

When Inu
is sleeping in a chair for people...
#83
DAD
INU-KUN,
I KNOW YOU'RE SLEEPING, BUT COULD I ASK YOU TO MOVE?
I'M REALLY SORRY, BUT...
He asks really politely.
He does not move.
YOU DON'T NEED TO ASK LIKE THAT.
I'M AFRAID HE'LL BITE ME.
HE WON'T BITE.
BUT I'M SCARED HE WILL.
ME
INU-KUN!
I sit down by force.
I'M GONNA CRUSH YOU! SEE! SEE!
WEE!
YAY! YAY!
He doesn't move.
MOM
...
SWFF
WOW. HE KNEW...

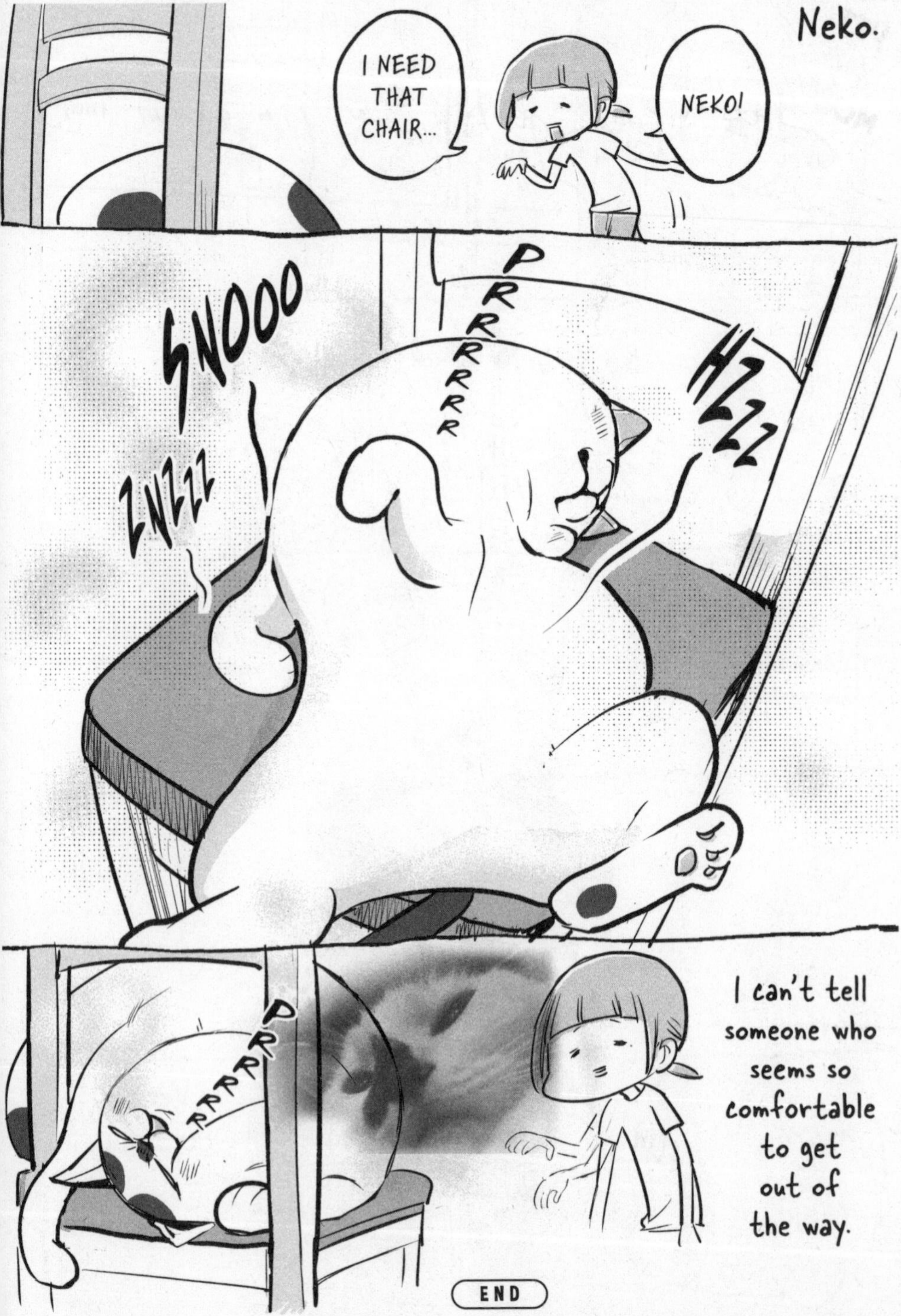
Neko.
NEKO!
I NEED THAT CHAIR...
PRRRRRRR
HZZZ
SNOOO
ZNZZZ
I can't tell someone who seems so comfortable to get out of the way.
PRRRRRR
END

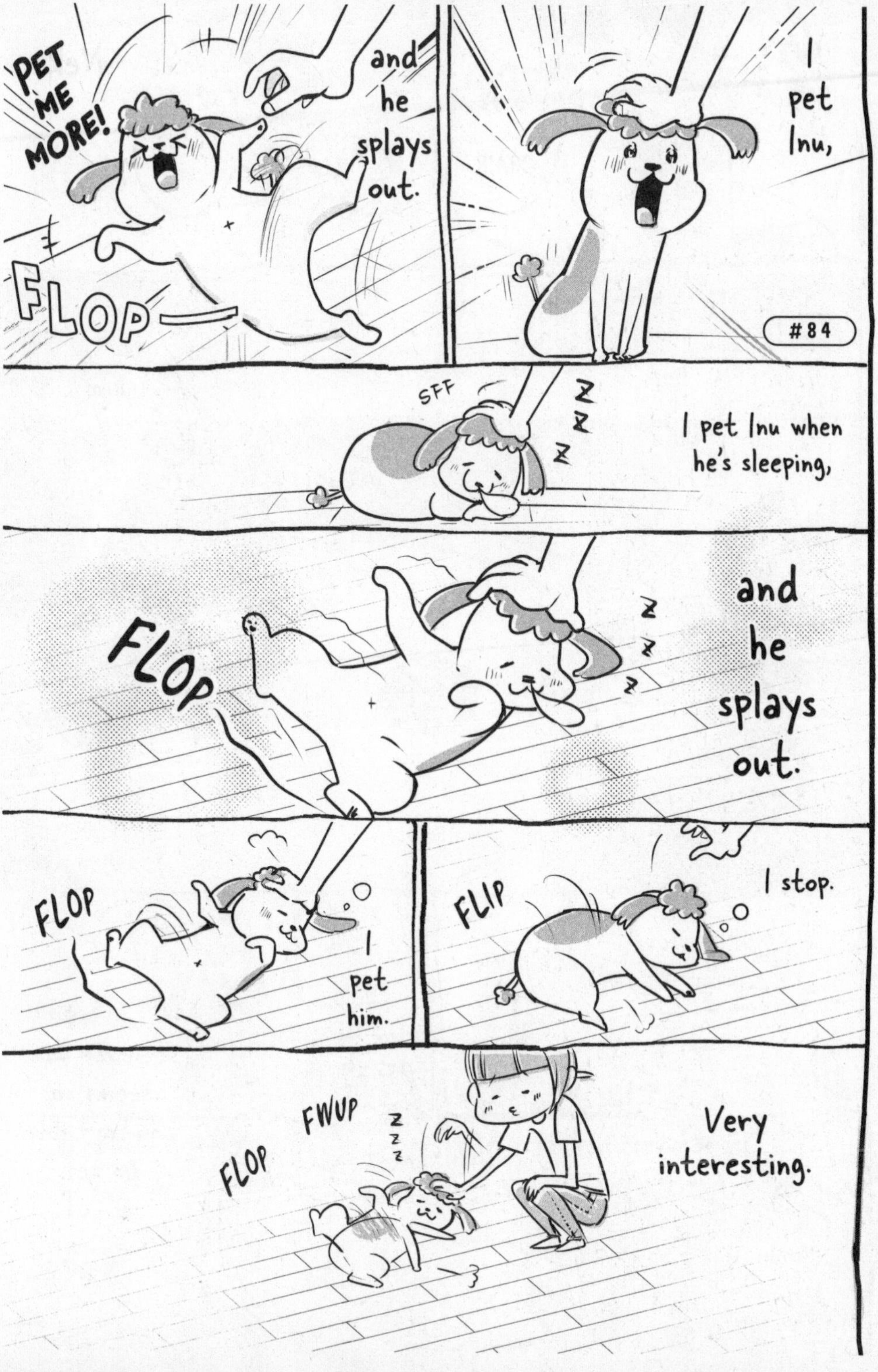
I pet Inu,
#84
and he splays out.
PET ME MORE!
FLOP—
SFF
ZZZ
I pet Inu when he's sleeping,
and he splays out.
ZZZ
FLOP
I stop.
FLIP
I pet him.
FLOP
Very interesting.
ZZZ
FWUP
FLOP

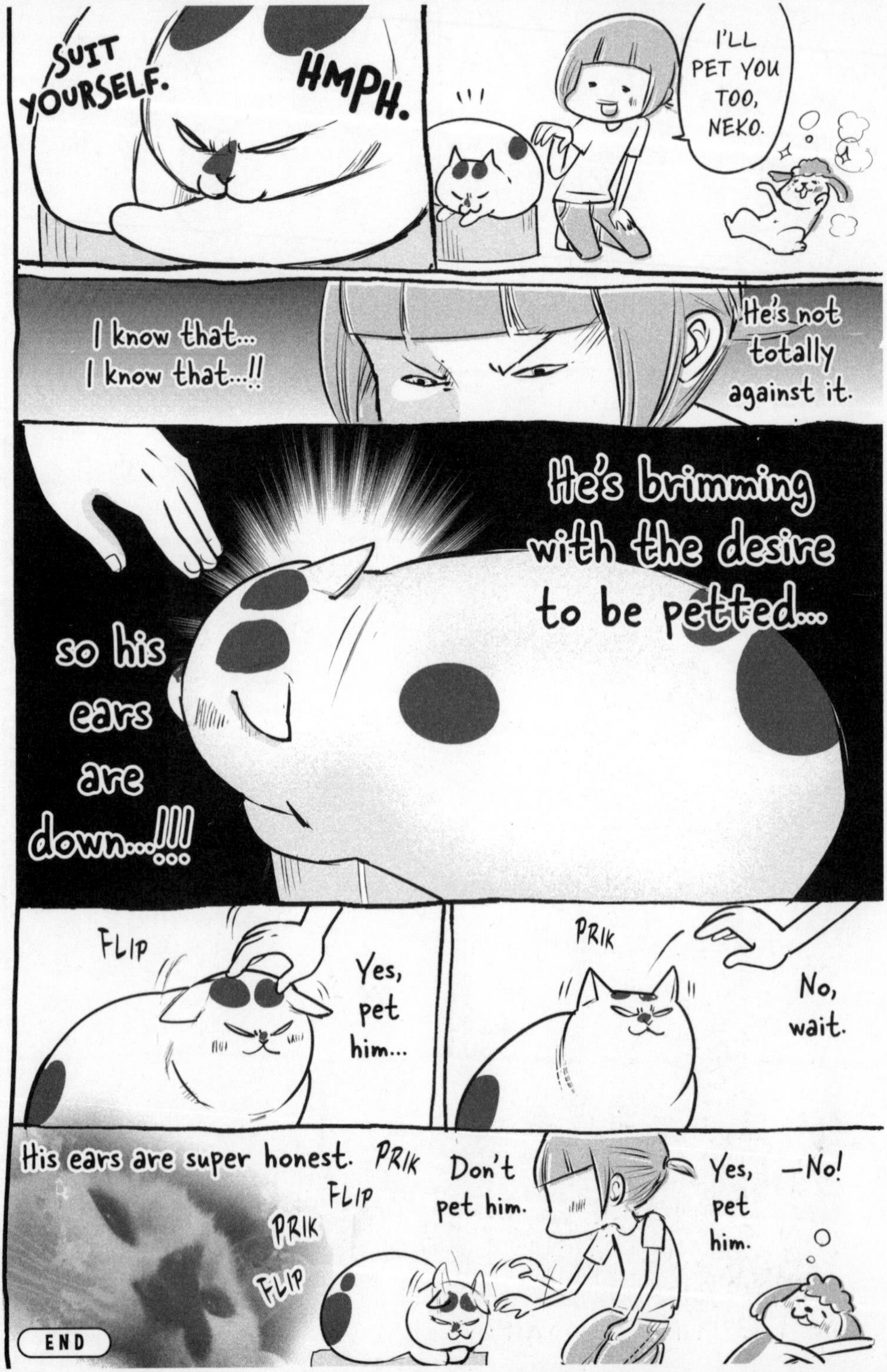
I'LL PET YOU TOO, NEKO.
SUIT YOURSELF.
HMPH.
He's not totally against it.
I know that... I know that...!!
He's brimming with the desire to be petted...
so his ears are down...!!!
PRIK
No, wait.
FLIP
Yes, pet him...
—No!
Yes, pet him.
Don't pet him.
His ears are super honest.
PRIK
FLIP
PRIK
FLIP
END

Aah, I don't feel like doing anything at all.

Newly-Drawn 4-Panel Strip

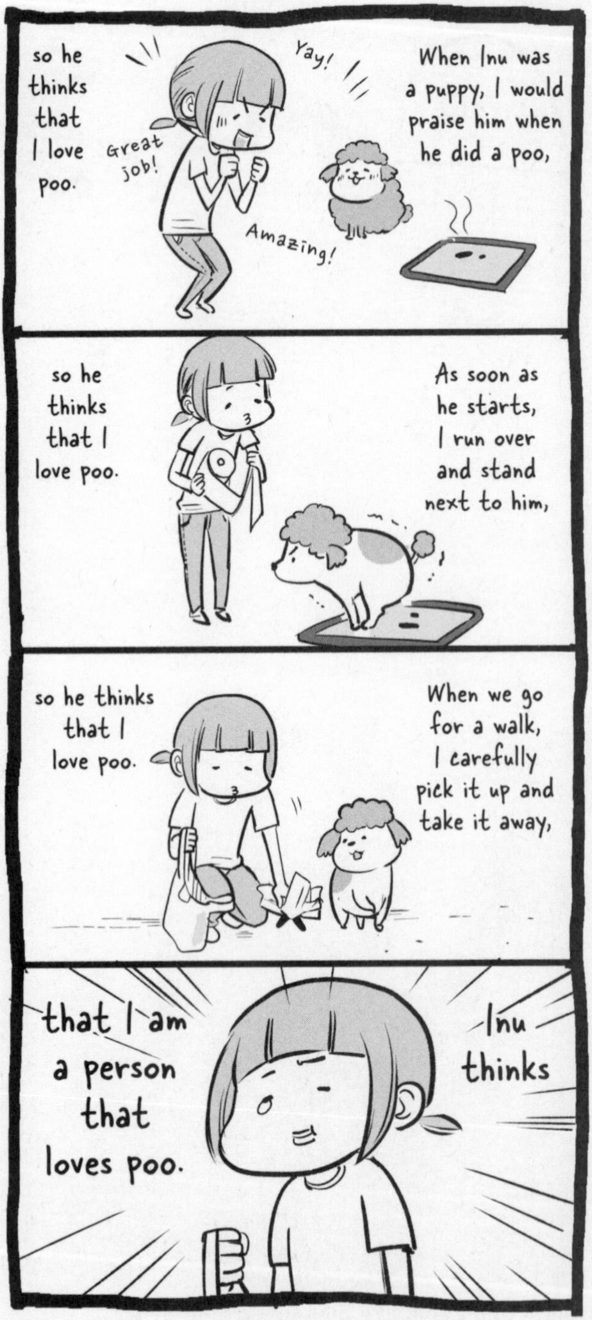

When Inu was a puppy, I would praise him when he did a poo,
Yay!
Great job!
Amazing!
so he thinks that I love poo.
As soon as he starts, I run over and stand next to him,
so he thinks that I love poo.
When we go for a walk, I carefully pick it up and take it away,
so he thinks that I love poo.
Inu thinks
that I am a person that loves poo.

★ Fellow Dog Owners

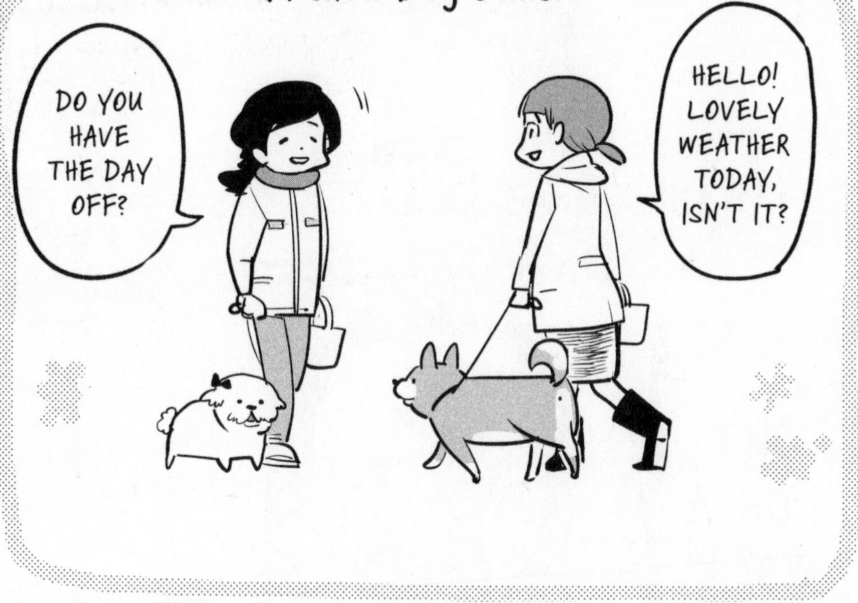
HELLO! LOVELY WEATHER TODAY, ISN'T IT?
DO YOU HAVE THE DAY OFF?

★ Fellow Shy Dog Owners

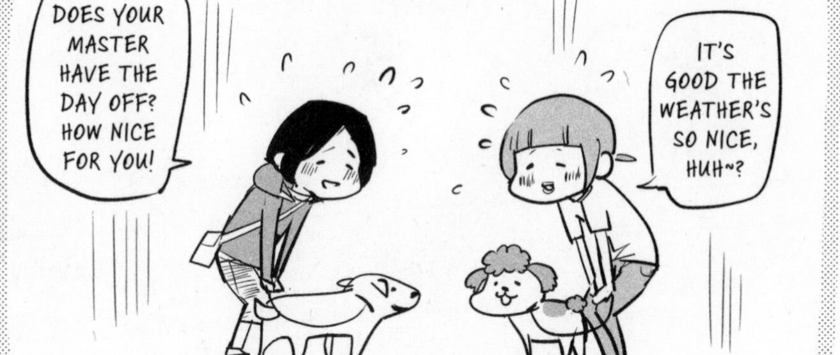
IT'S GOOD THE WEATHER'S SO NICE, HUH~?
DOES YOUR MASTER HAVE THE DAY OFF? HOW NICE FOR YOU!

Curiously using their dogs as intermediaries to converse.

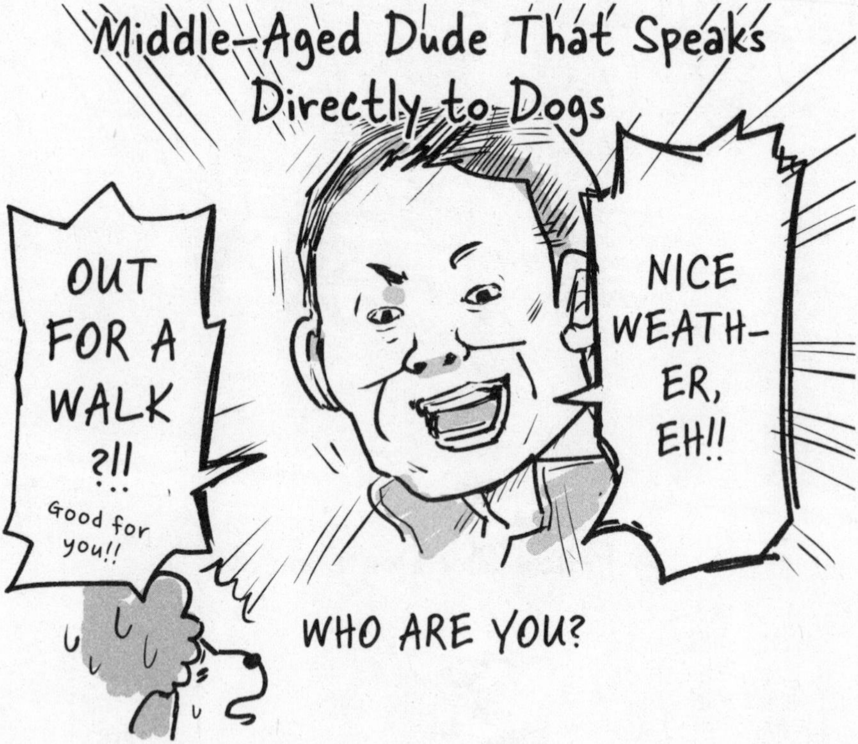
Middle-Aged Dude That Speaks Directly to Dogs
NICE WEATH- ER, EH!!
OUT FOR A WALK ?!!
Good for you!!
WHO ARE YOU?

Dog Walking

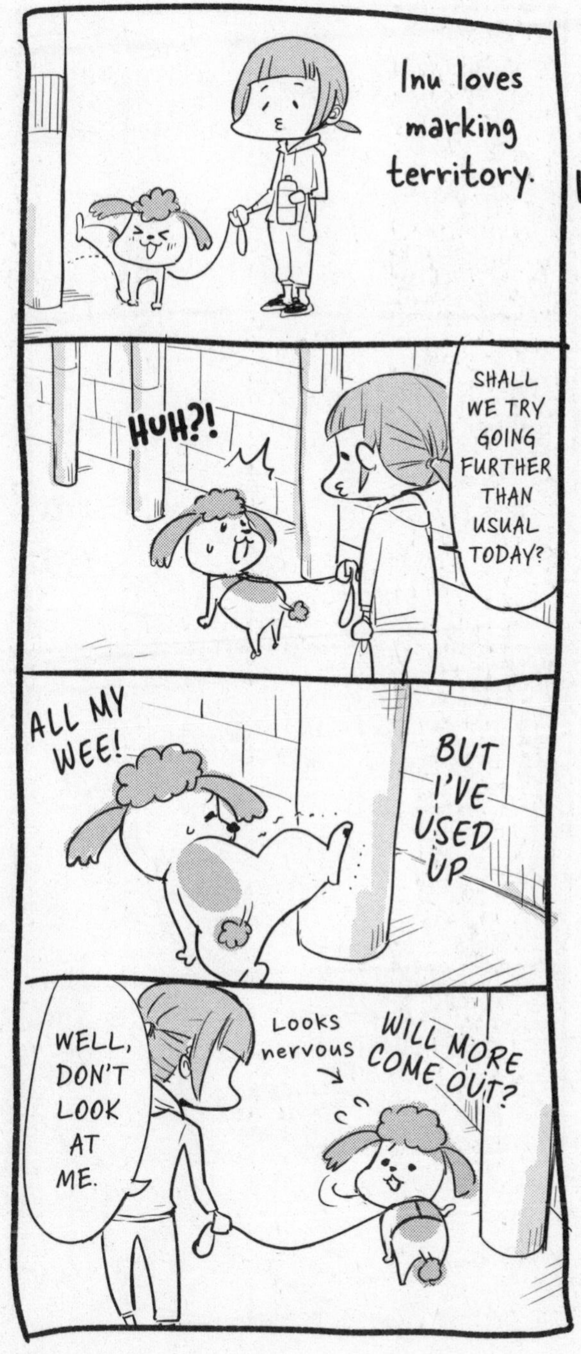
Inu loves marking territory.
SHALL WE TRY GOING FURTHER THAN USUAL TODAY?
HUH?!
BUT I'VE USED UP
ALL MY WEE!
WILL MORE COME OUT?
Looks nervous
WELL, DON'T LOOK AT ME.

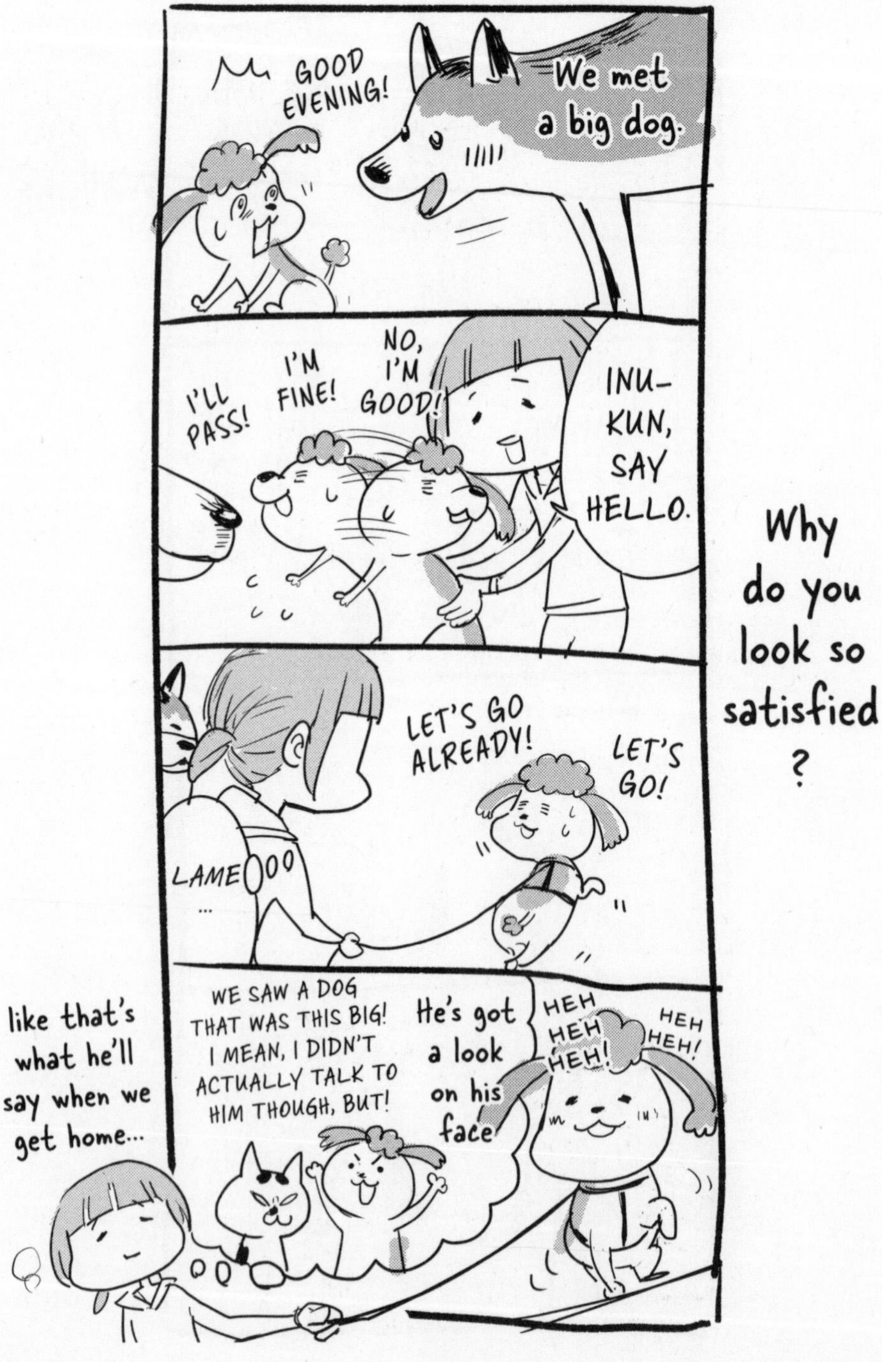
We met a big dog.
GOOD EVENING!
INU-KUN, SAY HELLO.
NO, I'M GOOD!
I'M FINE!
I'LL PASS!
LET'S GO!
LET'S GO ALREADY!
LAME ...
Why do you look so satisfied ?
HEH HEH!
HEH HEH HEH!
He's got a look on his face
WE SAW A DOG THAT WAS THIS BIG! I MEAN, I DIDN'T ACTUALLY TALK TO HIM THOUGH, BUT!
like that's what he'll say when we get home...

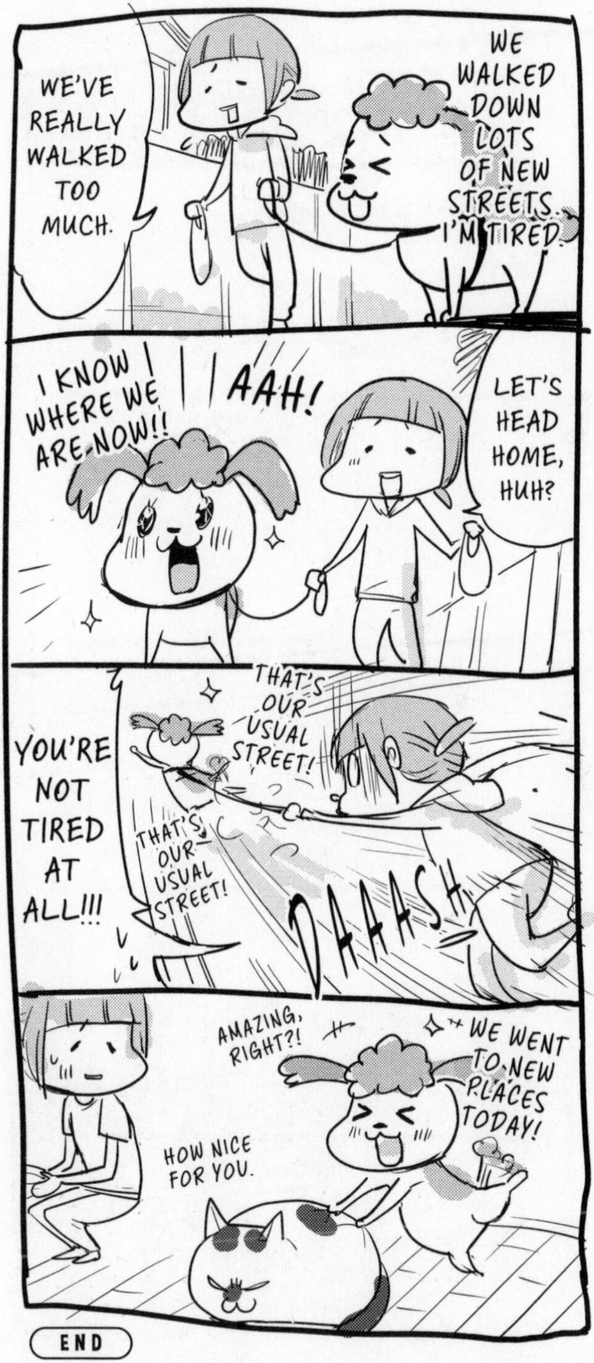
WE WALKED DOWN LOTS OF NEW STREETS. I'M TIRED.
WE'VE REALLY WALKED TOO MUCH.
LET'S HEAD HOME, HUH?
AAH!
I KNOW WHERE WE ARE NOW!!
THAT'S OUR USUAL STREET!
DAAASH
THAT'S OUR USUAL STREET!
YOU'RE NOT TIRED AT ALL!!!
WE WENT TO NEW PLACES TODAY!
AMAZING, RIGHT?!
HOW NICE FOR YOU.

Inu got super hyper and harassed Neko.

END

NEKO, LET'S PLAY!
LET'S PLAY!
LET'S PLAY!
LET'S PLAY!
LET'S PLAY!
LET'S PLAY!
LET'S PLAY!
LET'S PLAY!
LET'S PLAY!
LET'S PLAY!
LET'S PLAY!
FWING

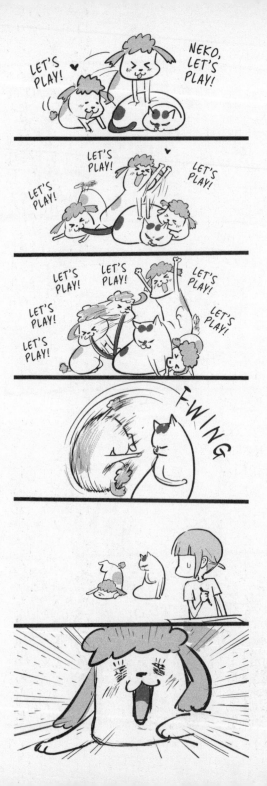

Look close and you'll see he's kicking him.

Newly-Drawn 4-Panel Strip

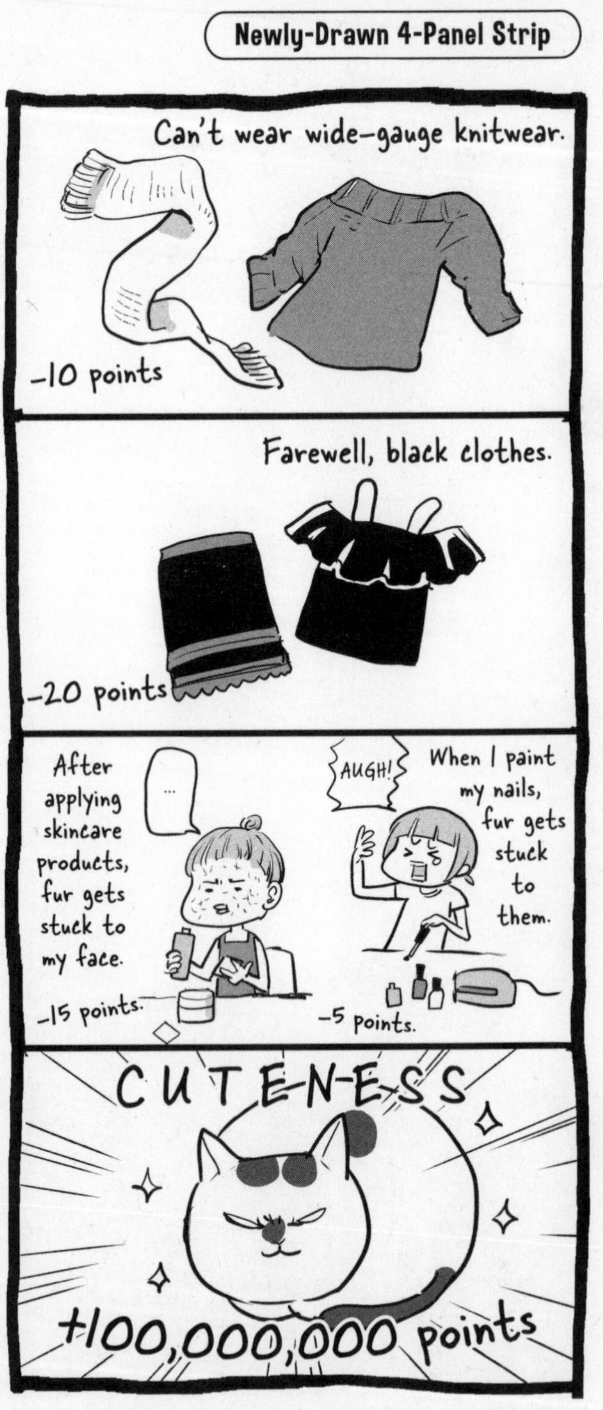
Can't wear wide-gauge knitwear.
-10 points
Farewell, black clothes.
-20 points
AUGH!
When I paint my nails, fur gets stuck to them.
-5 points.
...
After applying skincare products, fur gets stuck to my face.
-15 points.
CUTENESS
+100,000,000 points

#85

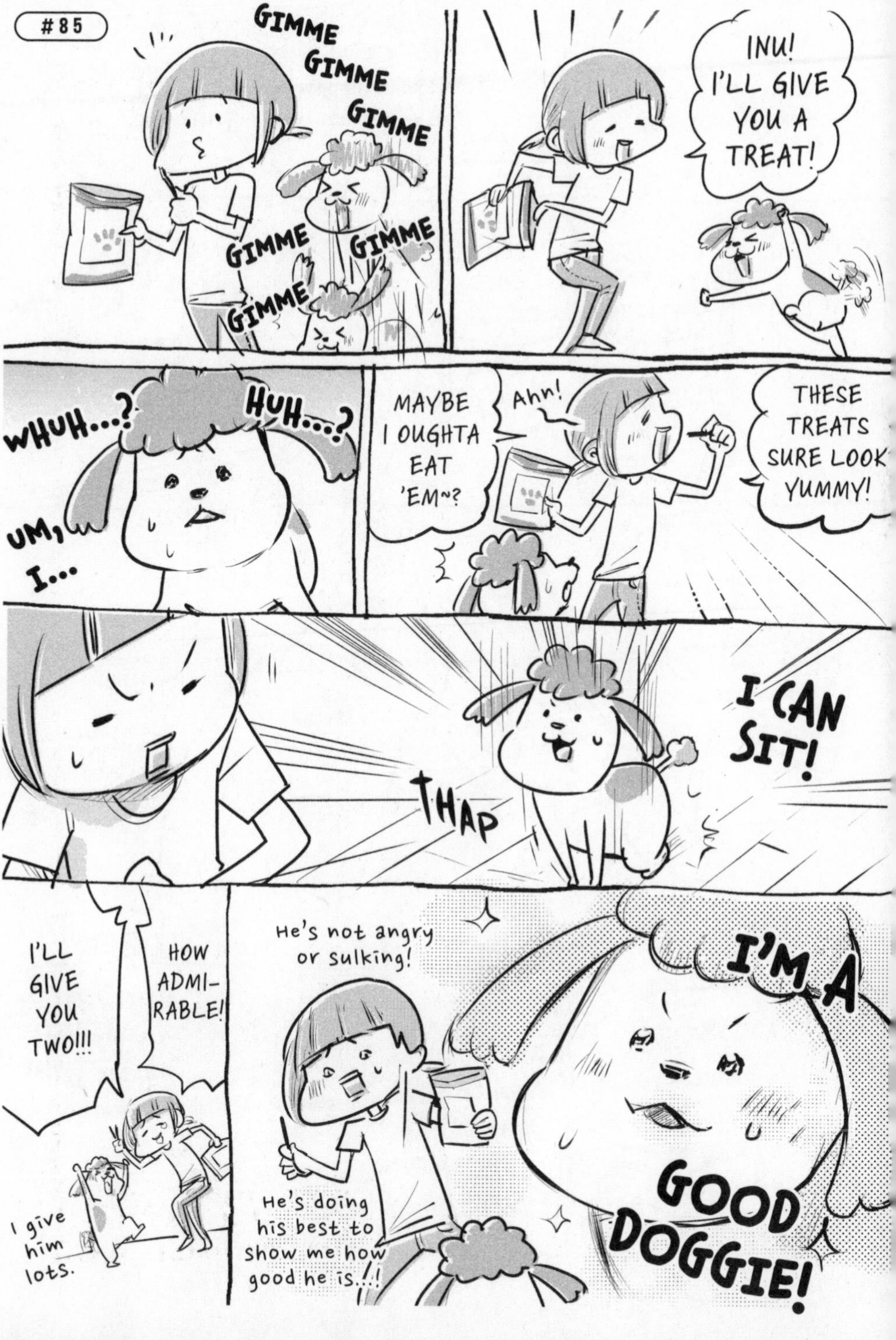
INU! I'LL GIVE YOU A TREAT!
GIMME
GIMME
GIMME
GIMME
GIMME
GIMME
THESE TREATS SURE LOOK YUMMY!
Ahn!
MAYBE I OUGHTA EAT 'EM~?
HUH...?
WHUH...?
UM, I...
I CAN SIT!
THAP
He's not angry or sulking!
I'M A GOOD DOGGIE!
He's doing his best to show me how good he is...!
HOW ADMI-RABLE!
I'LL GIVE YOU TWO!!!
I give him lots.

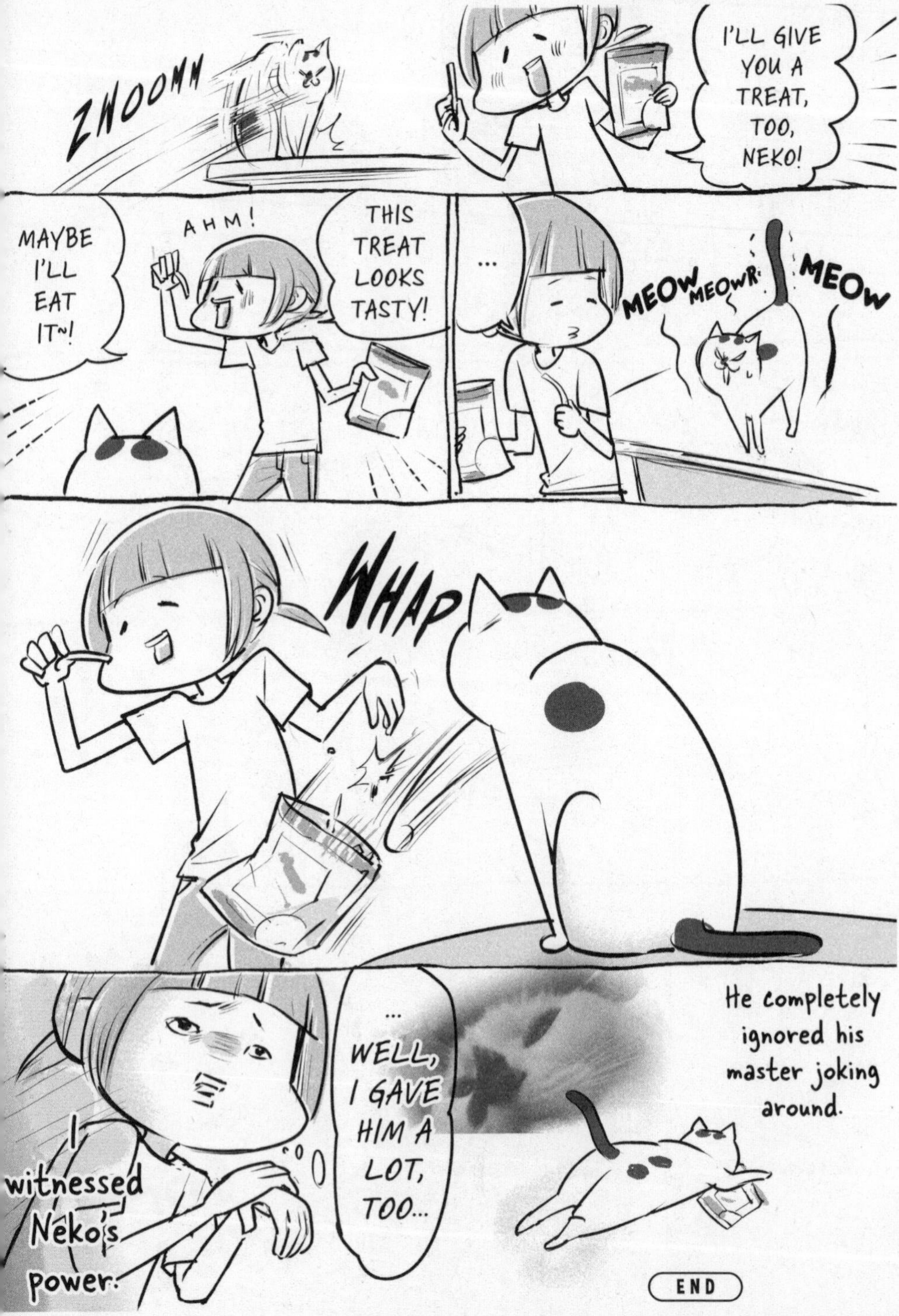
I'LL GIVE YOU A TREAT, TOO, NEKO!
ZWOOMM
MEOW
MEOWR
MEOW
...
THIS TREAT LOOKS TASTY!
AHM!
MAYBE I'LL EAT IT~!
WHAP
He completely ignored his master joking around.
... WELL, I GAVE HIM A LOT, TOO...
I witnessed Neko's power.
END

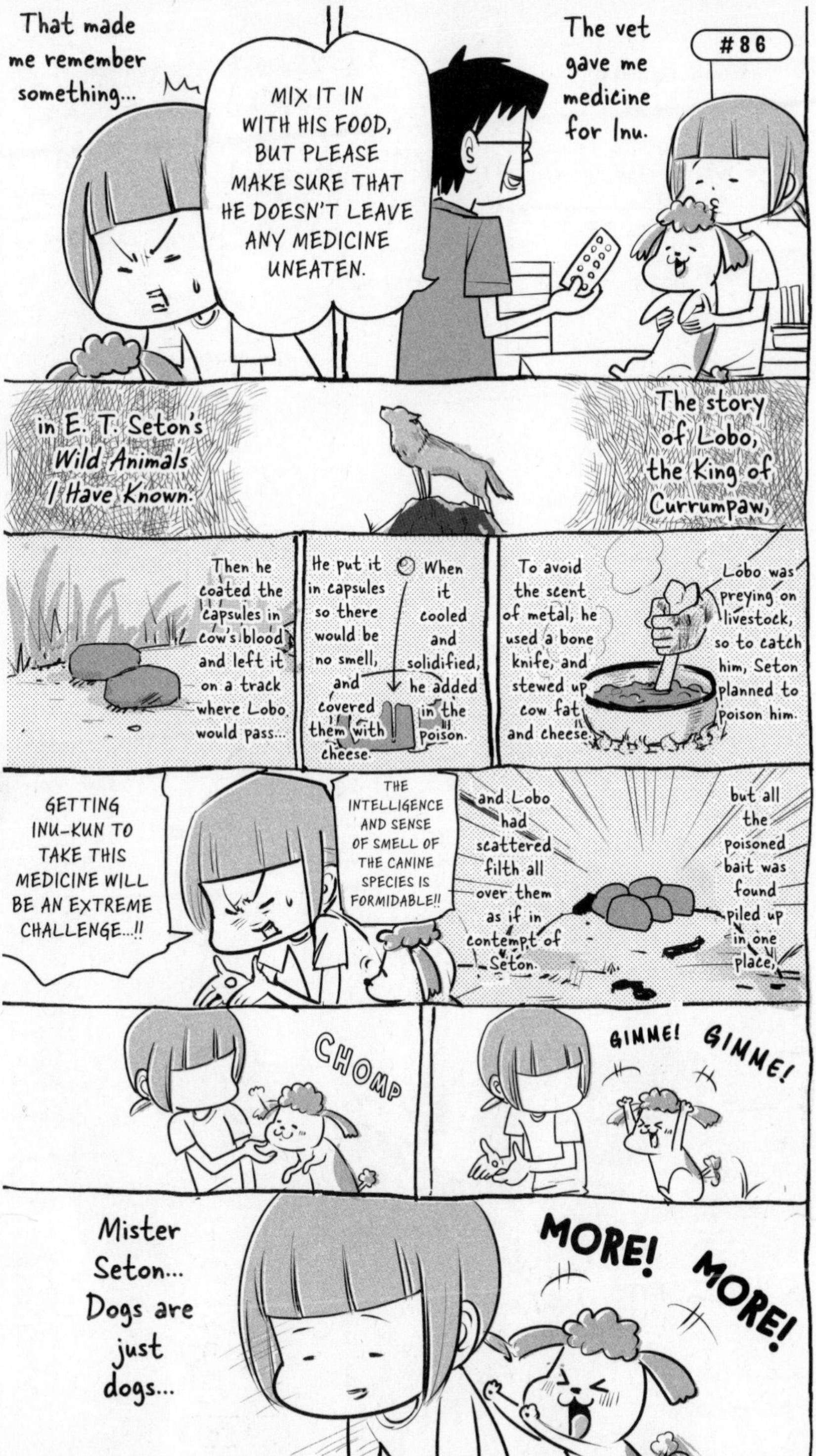
#86
The vet gave me medicine for Inu.
MIX IT IN WITH HIS FOOD, BUT PLEASE MAKE SURE THAT HE DOESN'T LEAVE ANY MEDICINE UNEATEN.
That made me remember something...
The story of Lobo, the King of Currumpaw,
in E. T. Seton's *Wild Animals I Have Known.*
Lobo was preying on livestock, so to catch him, Seton planned to poison him.
To avoid the scent of metal, he used a bone knife, and stewed up cow fat and cheese.
When it cooled and solidified, he added in the poison.
He put it in capsules so there would be no smell, and covered them with cheese.
Then he coated the capsules in cow's blood and left it on a track where Lobo would pass...
but all the poisoned bait was found piled up in one place,
and Lobo had scattered filth all over them as if in contempt of Seton.
THE INTELLIGENCE AND SENSE OF SMELL OF THE CANINE SPECIES IS FORMIDABLE!!
GETTING INU-KUN TO TAKE THIS MEDICINE WILL BE AN EXTREME CHALLENGE...!!
GIMME! GIMME!
CHOMP
MORE! MORE!
Mister Seton... Dogs are just dogs...

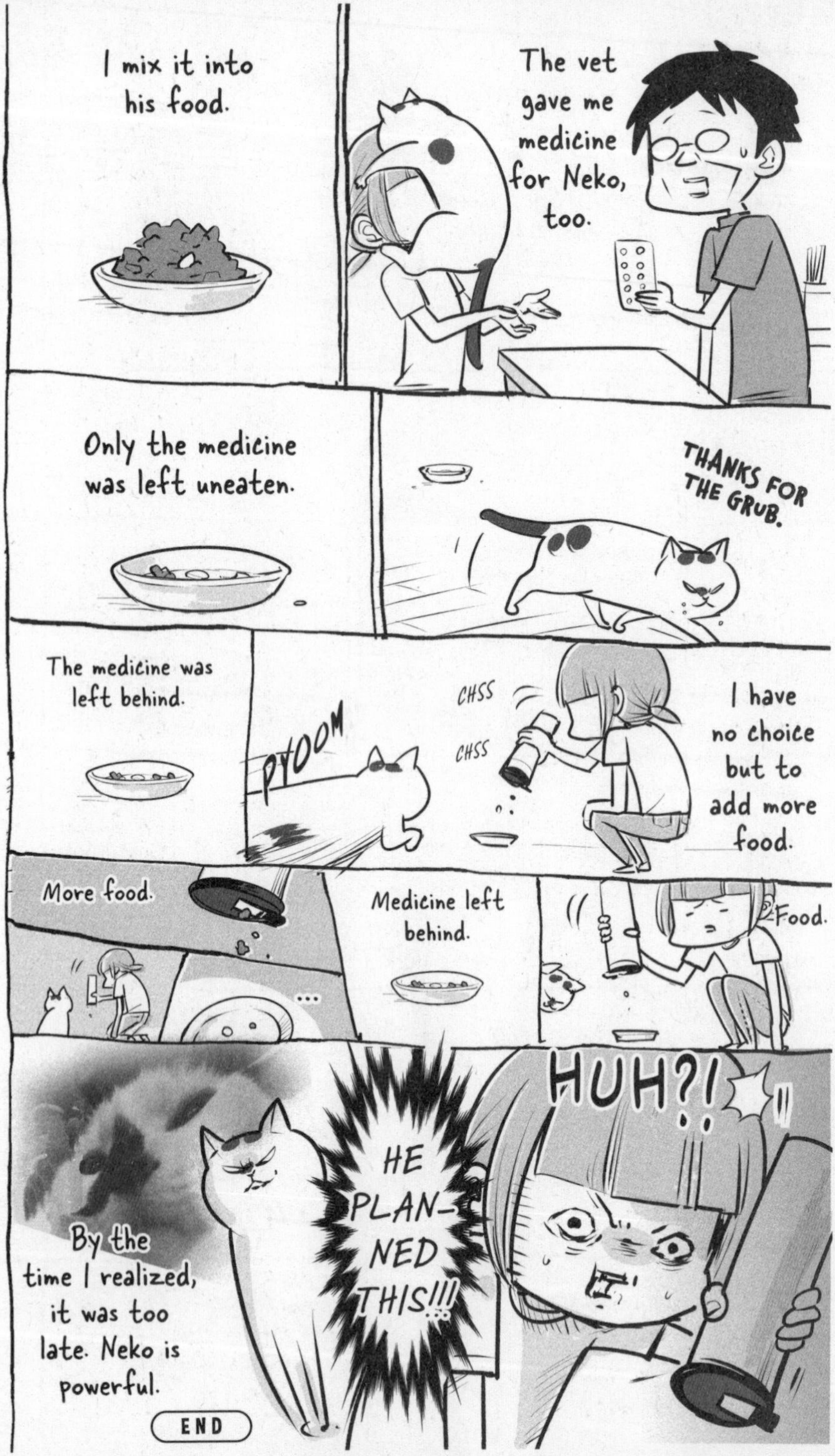
The vet gave me medicine for Neko, too.
I mix it into his food.
THANKS FOR THE GRUB.
Only the medicine was left uneaten.
I have no choice but to add more food.
CHSS
CHSS
PYOOM
The medicine was left behind.
Food.
Medicine left behind.
More food.
...
HUH?!
HE PLAN-NED THIS!!!
By the time I realized, it was too late. Neko is powerful.
END

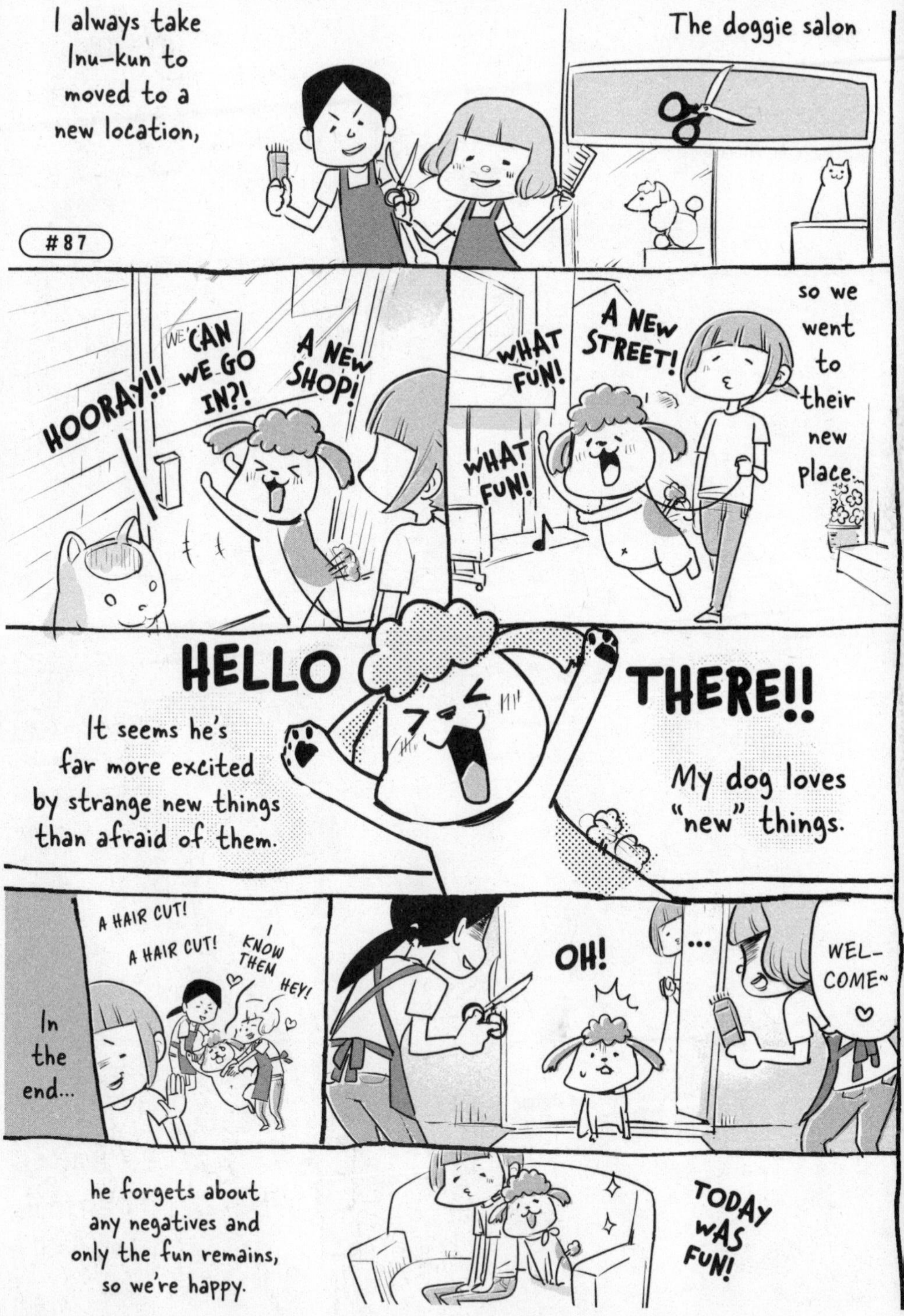
#87
The doggie salon
I always take Inu-kun to moved to a new location,
so we went to their new place.
A NEW STREET!
WHAT FUN!
WHAT FUN!
A NEW SHOP!
CAN WE GO IN?!
HOORAY!!
HELLO THERE!!
My dog loves "new" things.
It seems he's far more excited by strange new things than afraid of them.
WEL-COME~
...
OH!
In the end...
A HAIR CUT!
A HAIR CUT!
I KNOW THEM
HEY!
TODAY WAS FUN!
he forgets about any negatives and only the fun remains, so we're happy.

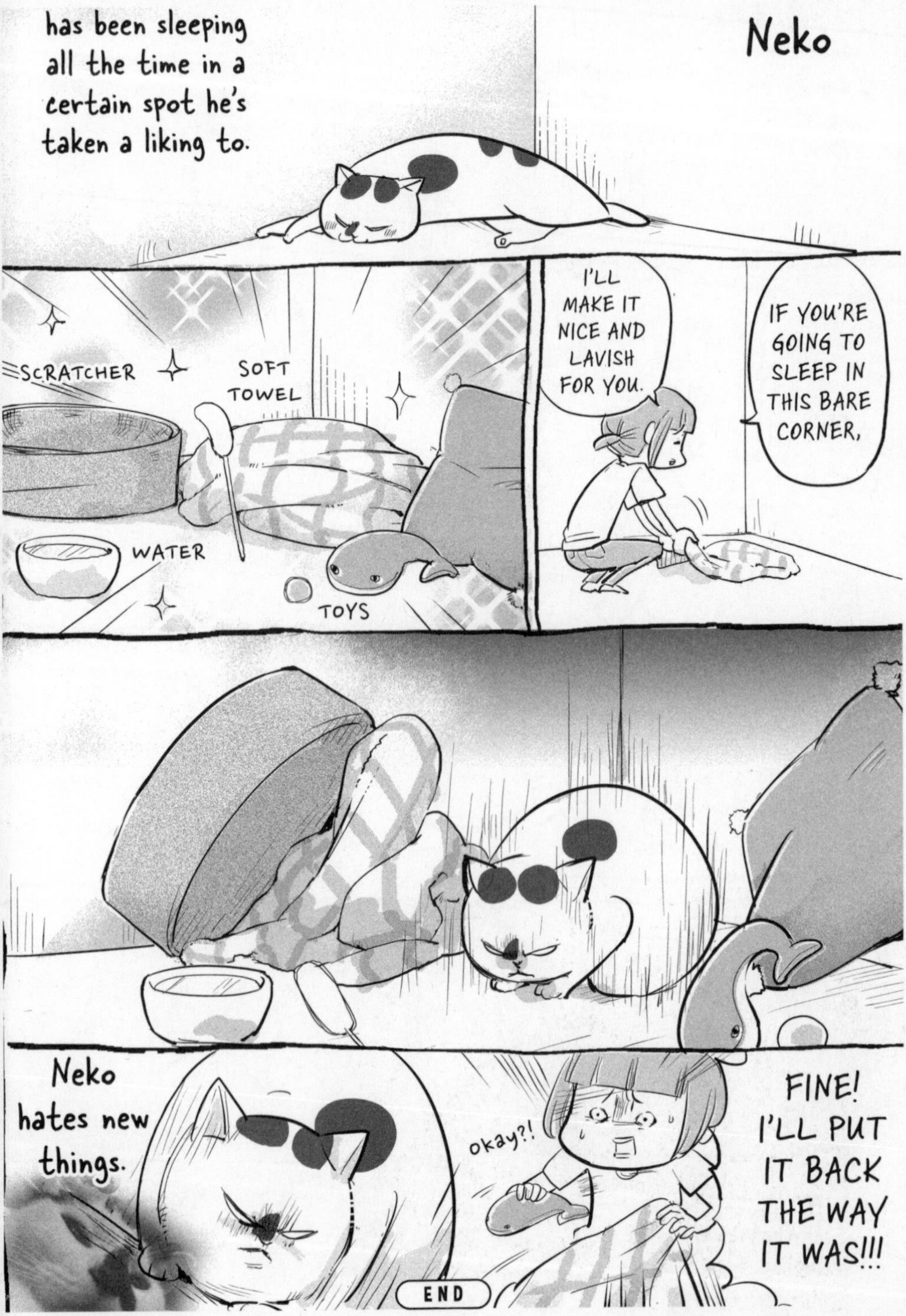
Neko
has been sleeping all the time in a certain spot he's taken a liking to.
IF YOU'RE GOING TO SLEEP IN THIS BARE CORNER,
I'LL MAKE IT NICE AND LAVISH FOR YOU.
SCRATCHER
SOFT TOWEL
WATER
TOYS
FINE! I'LL PUT IT BACK THE WAY IT WAS!!!
okay?!
Neko hates new things.
END

Rolling Stream Attack!

Newly-Drawn 4-Panel Strip

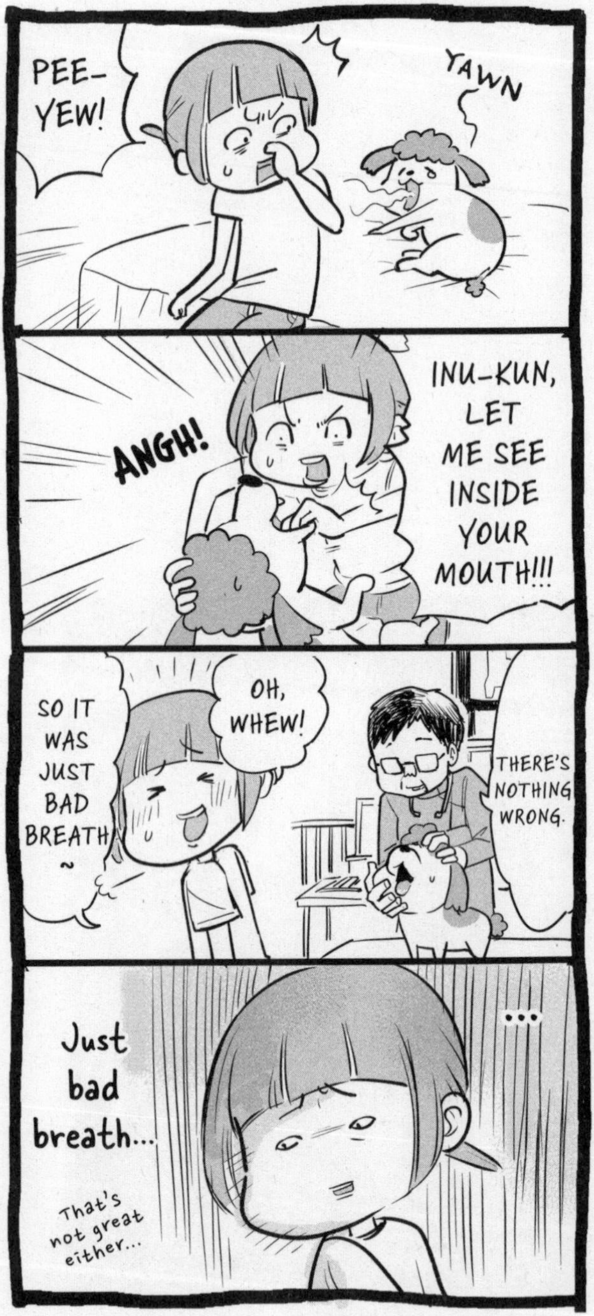
YAWN
PEE-YEW!
INU-KUN, LET ME SEE INSIDE YOUR MOUTH!!!
ANGH!
THERE'S NOTHING WRONG.
OH, WHEW!
SO IT WAS JUST BAD BREATH~
...
Just bad breath...
That's not great either...

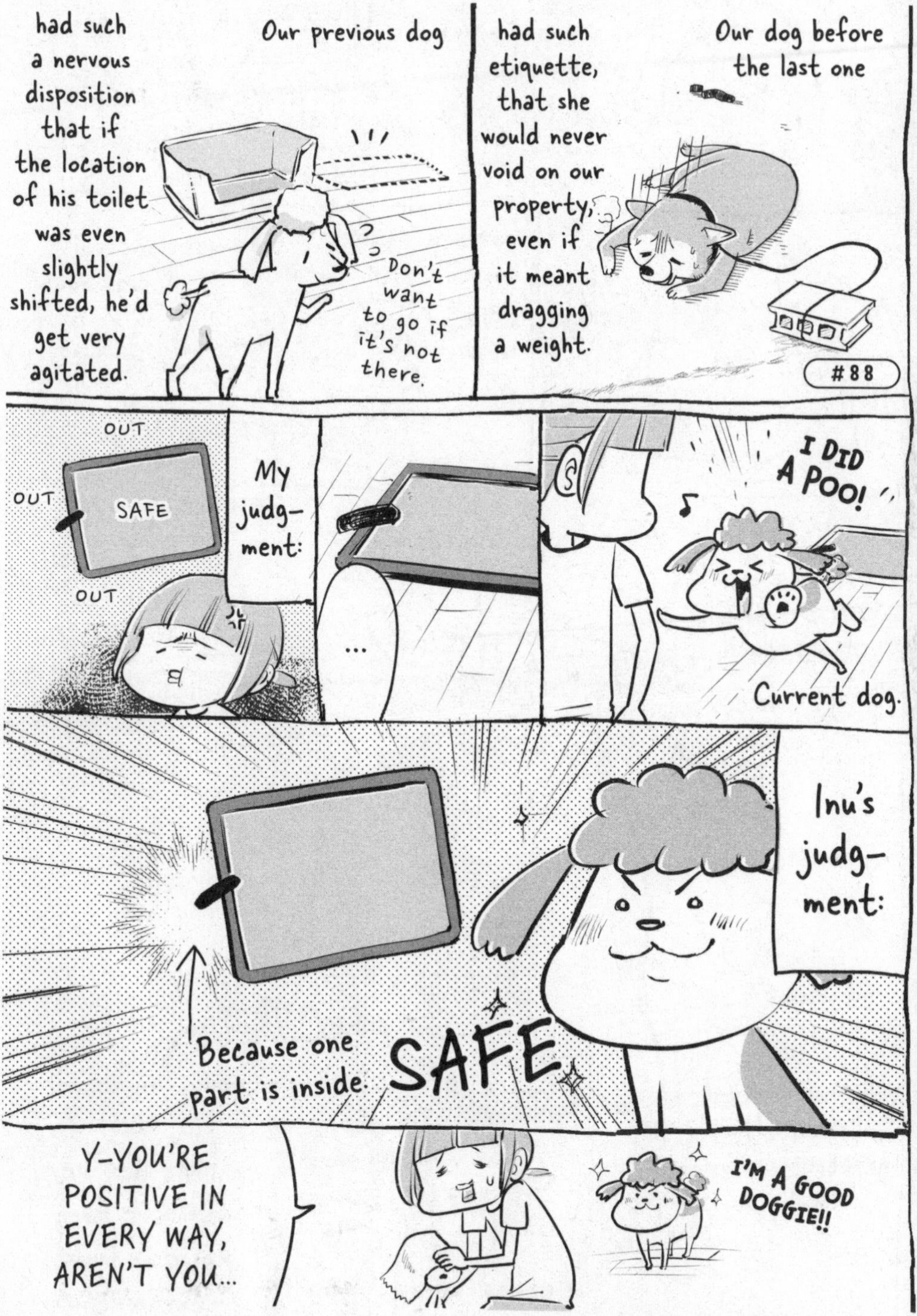
Our dog before the last one
had such etiquette, that she would never void on our property, even if it meant dragging a weight.
#88
Our previous dog
had such a nervous disposition that if the location of his toilet was even slightly shifted, he'd get very agitated.
Don't want to go if it's not there.
I DID A POO!
Current dog.
...
My judg-ment:
OUT
OUT
SAFE
OUT
Inu's judg-ment:
Because one part is inside.
SAFE
I'M A GOOD DOGGIE!!
Y-YOU'RE POSITIVE IN EVERY WAY, AREN'T YOU...

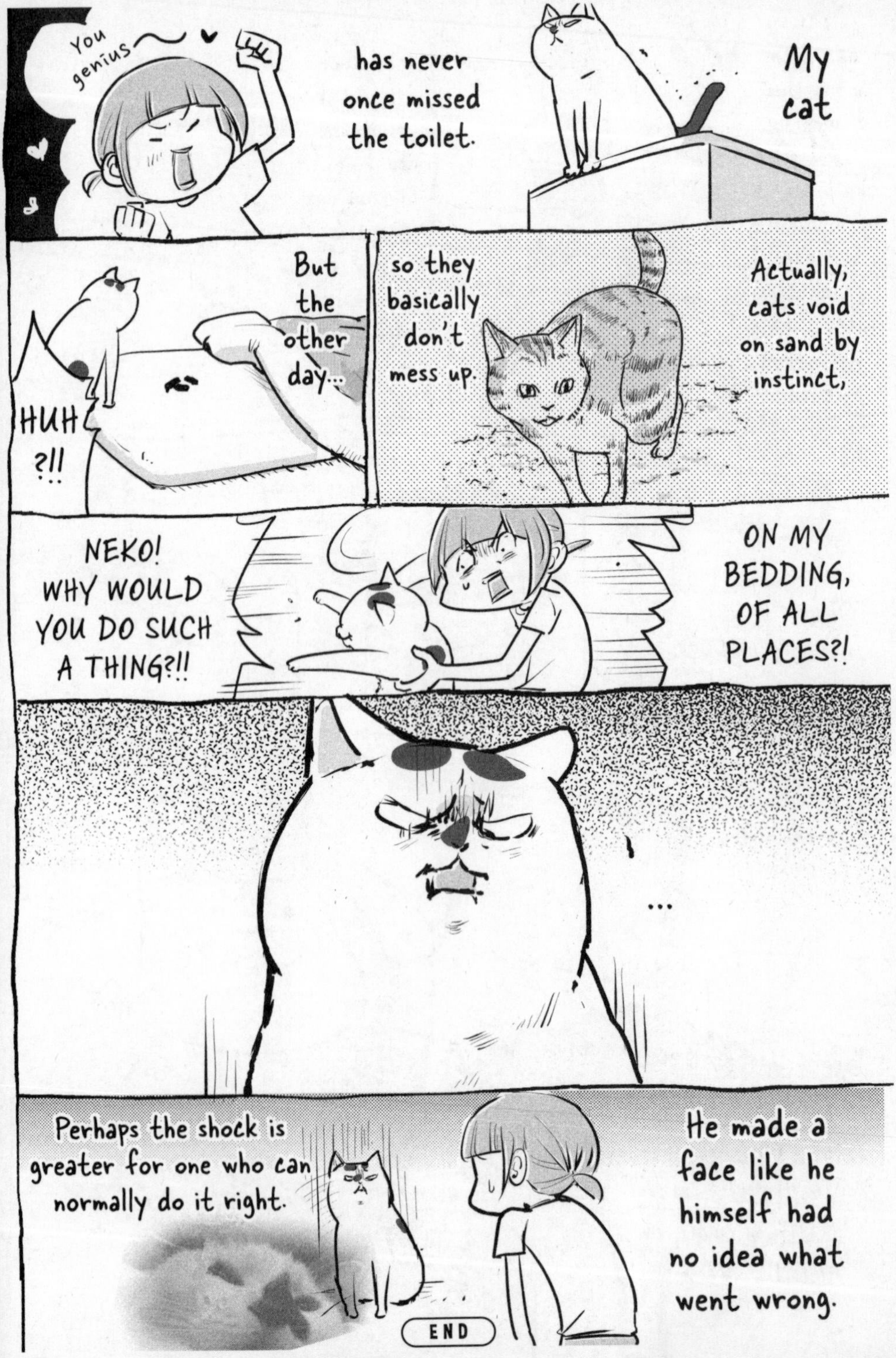
My cat
has never once missed the toilet.
You genius~ ♥
Actually, cats void on sand by instinct,
so they basically don't mess up.
But the other day...
HUH ?!!
ON MY BEDDING, OF ALL PLACES?!
NEKO! WHY WOULD YOU DO SUCH A THING?!!
...
He made a face like he himself had no idea what went wrong.
Perhaps the shock is greater for one who can normally do it right.
END

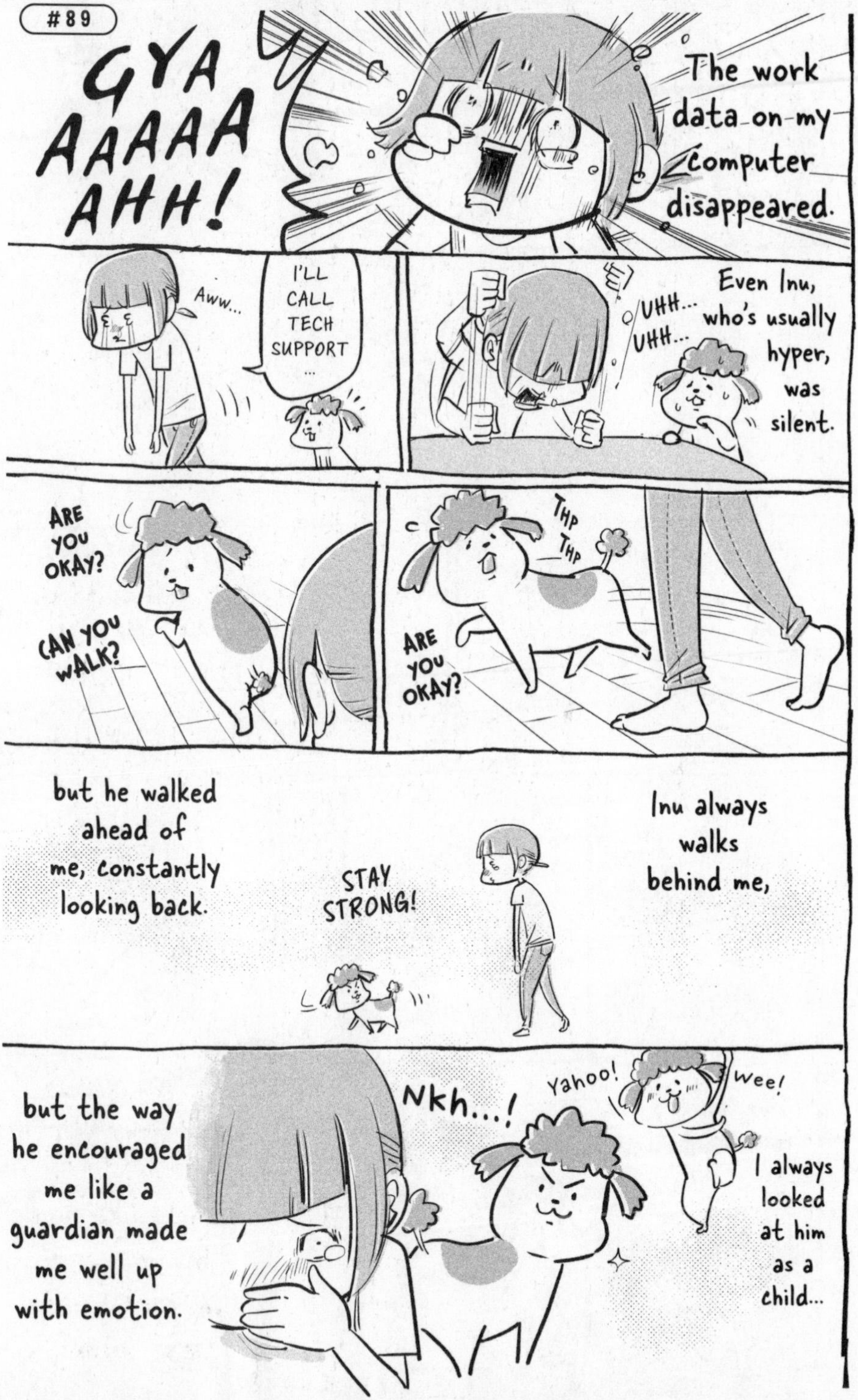
#89
The work data on my computer disappeared.
GYAAAAAAAHH!
Even Inu, who's usually hyper, was silent.
UHH... UHH...
I'LL CALL TECH SUPPORT ...
Aww...
THP THP
ARE YOU OKAY?
ARE YOU OKAY?
CAN YOU WALK?
Inu always walks behind me,
STAY STRONG!
but he walked ahead of me, constantly looking back.
I always looked at him as a child...
Wee!
Yahoo!
Nkh...!
but the way he encouraged me like a guardian made me well up with emotion.

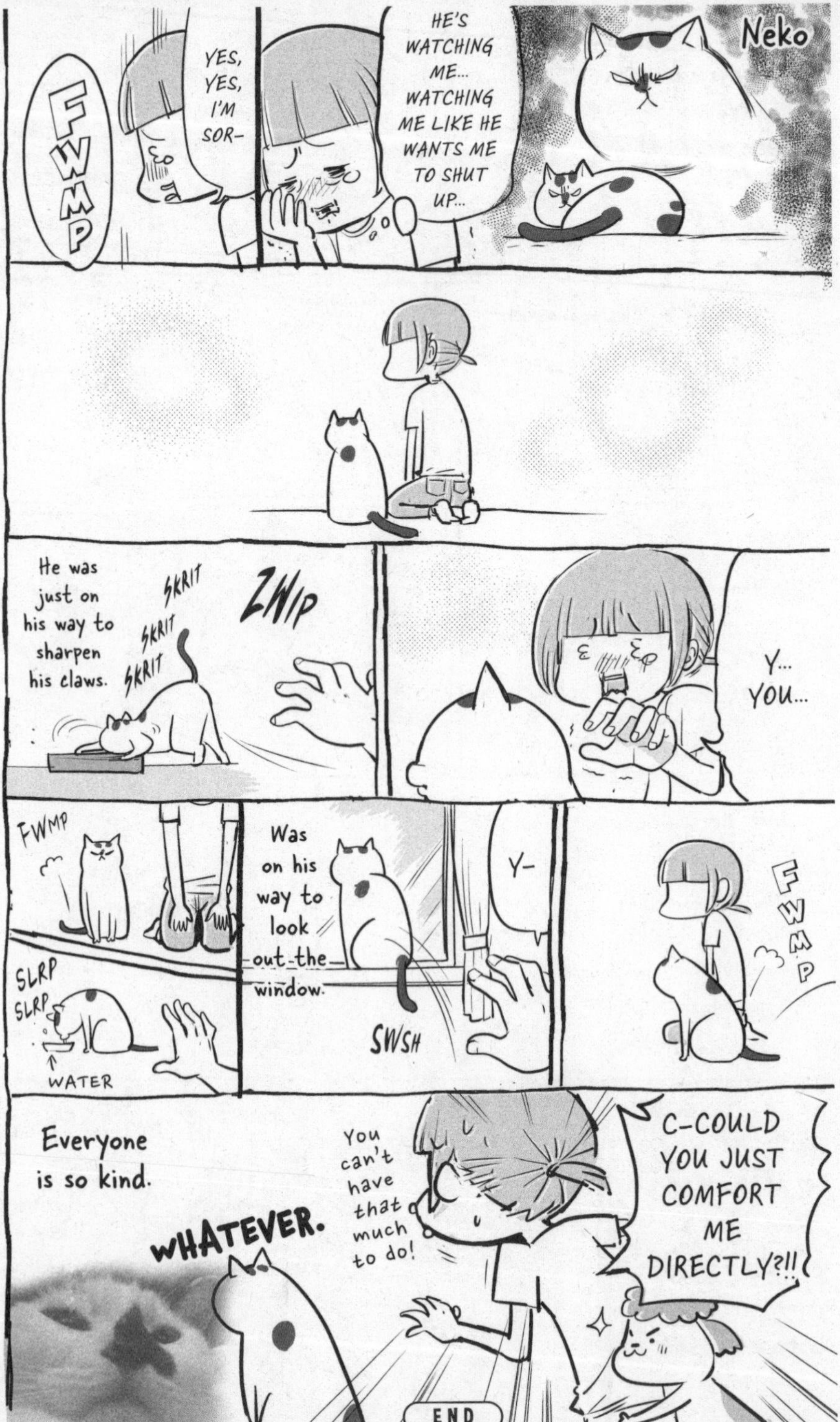

Neko
HE'S WATCHING ME... WATCHING ME LIKE HE WANTS ME TO SHUT UP...
YES, YES, I'M SOR-
FWMP
Y... YOU...
ZWIP
He was just on his way to sharpen his claws.
SKRIT SKRIT SKRIT
FWMP
Y-
SWSH
Was on his way to look out the window.
FWMP
SLRP SLRP
WATER
C-COULD YOU JUST COMFORT ME DIRECTLY?!!
You can't have that much to do!
WHATEVER.
Everyone is so kind.
END

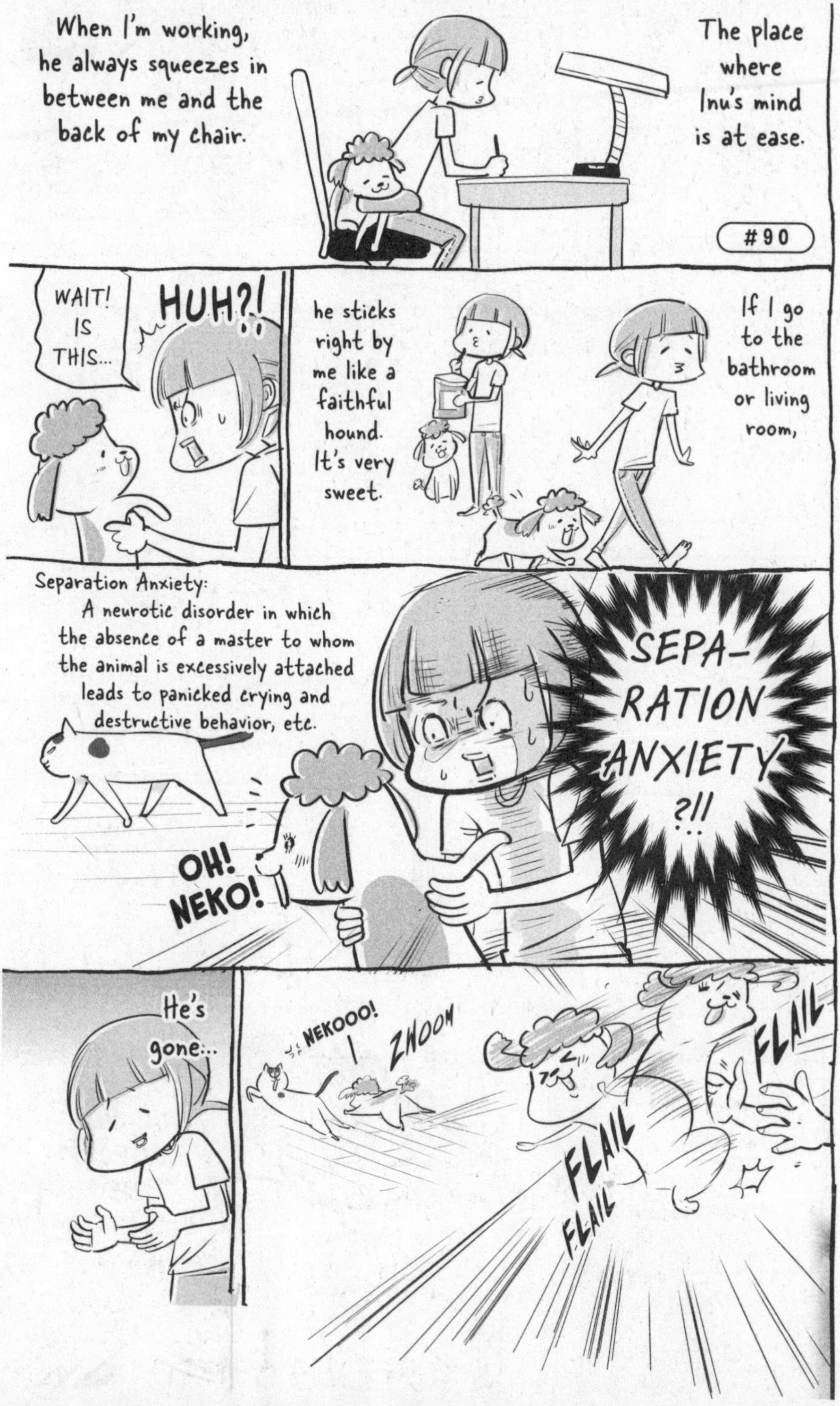

The place where Inu's mind is at ease.
When I'm working, he always squeezes in between me and the back of my chair.
#90
If I go to the bathroom or living room,
he sticks right by me like a faithful hound. It's very sweet.
HUH?!
WAIT! IS THIS...
SEPARATION ANXIETY ?!!
Separation Anxiety: A neurotic disorder in which the absence of a master to whom the animal is excessively attached leads to panicked crying and destructive behavior, etc.
OH! NEKO!
FLAIL
ZWOOM
NEKOOO!
FLAIL
FLAIL
He's gone...

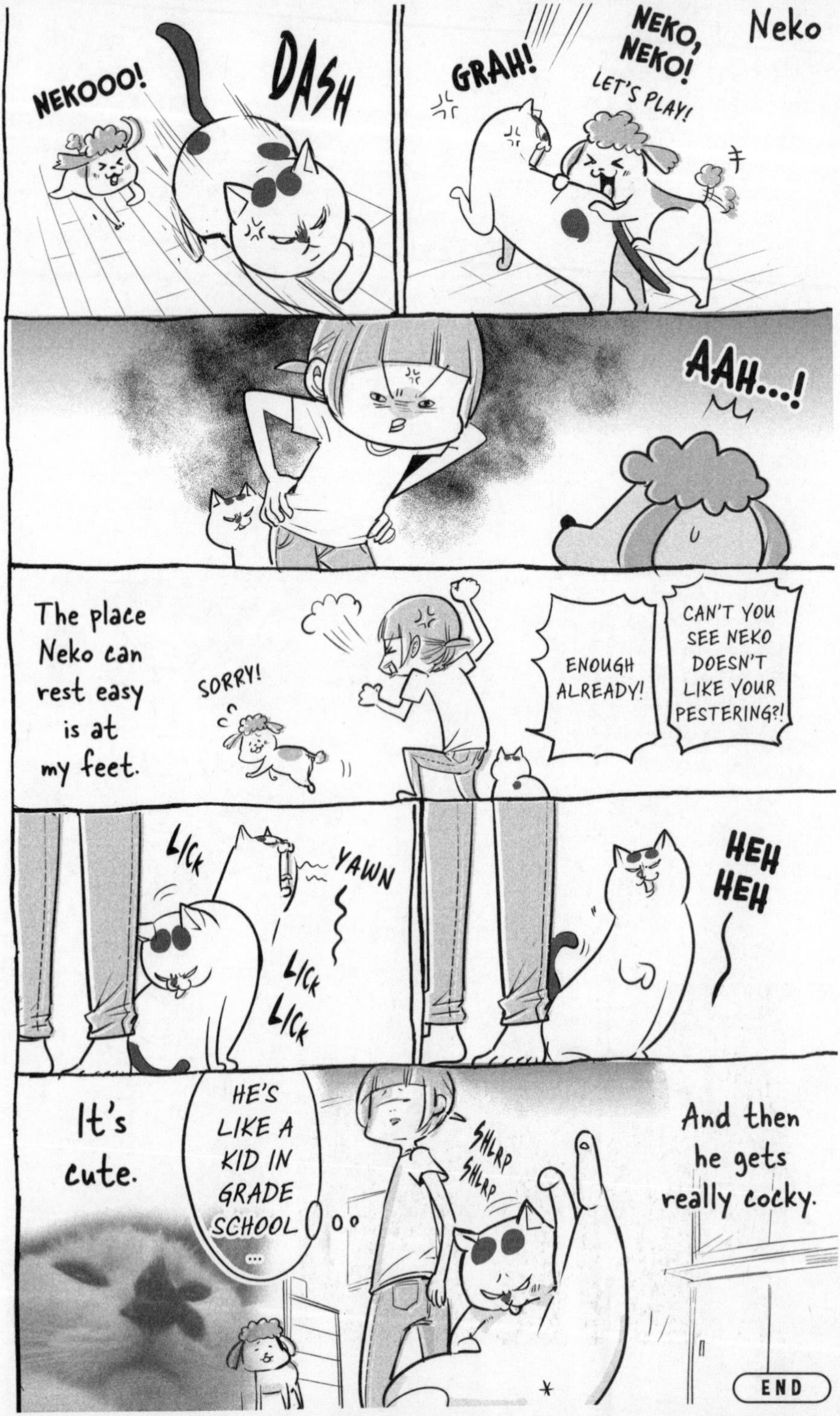
NEKO, NEKO!
LET'S PLAY!
GRAH!
DASH
NEKOOO!
AAH...!
CAN'T YOU SEE NEKO DOESN'T LIKE YOUR PESTERING?!
ENOUGH ALREADY!
SORRY!
The place Neko can rest easy is at my feet.
HEH HEH
YAWN
LICK
LICK LICK
And then he gets really cocky.
SHLRP SHLRP
HE'S LIKE A KID IN GRADE SCHOOL ...
It's cute.
END

A gourd.

Newly-Drawn 4-Panel Strip

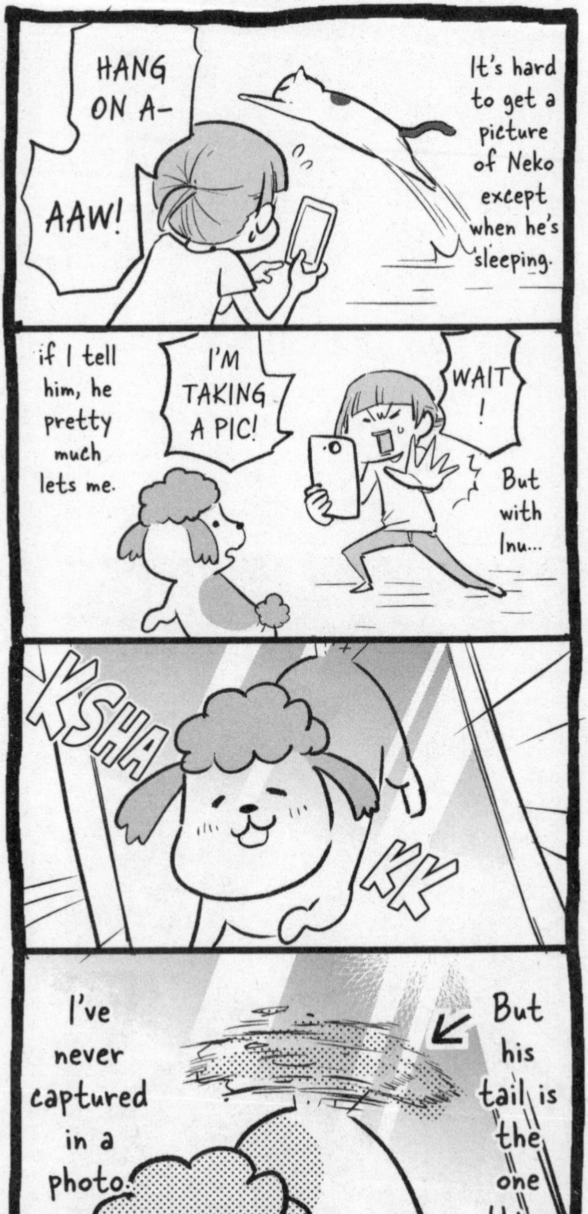
It's hard to get a picture of Neko except when he's sleeping.
HANG ON A-
AAW!
WAIT!
But with Inu...
I'M TAKING A PIC!
if I tell him, he pretty much lets me.
KSHA
KK
But his tail is the one thing
I've never captured in a photo.

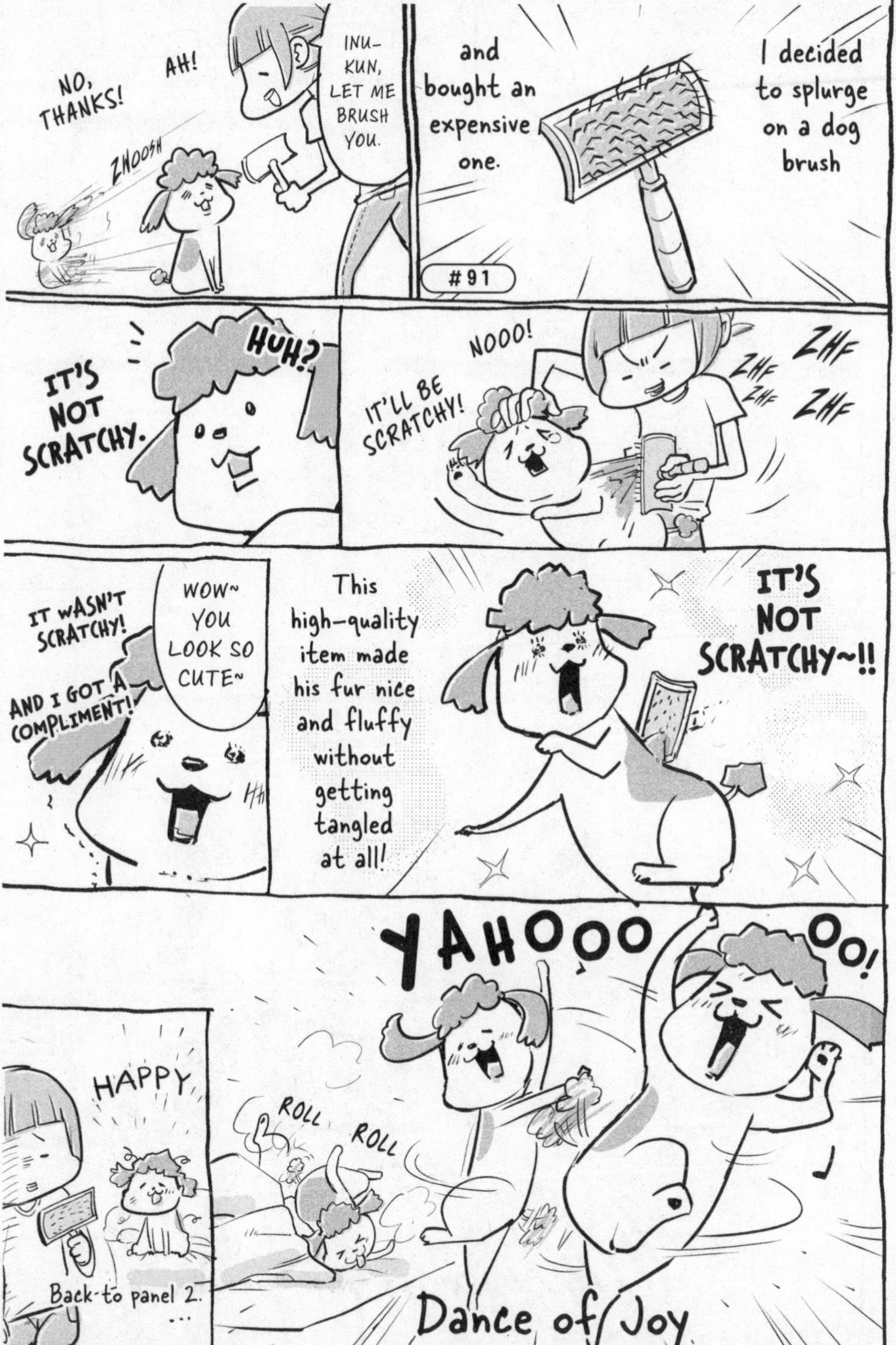
#91
I decided to splurge on a dog brush
and bought an expensive one.
INU-KUN, LET ME BRUSH YOU.
AH!
NO, THANKS!
ZWOOSH
NOOO!
IT'LL BE SCRATCHY!
ZHF ZHF ZHF ZHF
HUH?
IT'S NOT SCRATCHY.
IT'S NOT SCRATCHY~!!
This high-quality item made his fur nice and fluffy without getting tangled at all!
WOW~ YOU LOOK SO CUTE~
IT WASN'T SCRATCHY!
AND I GOT A COMPLIMENT!
YAHOOOOO!
ROLL ROLL
Dance of Joy
HAPPY
Back to panel 2.
...

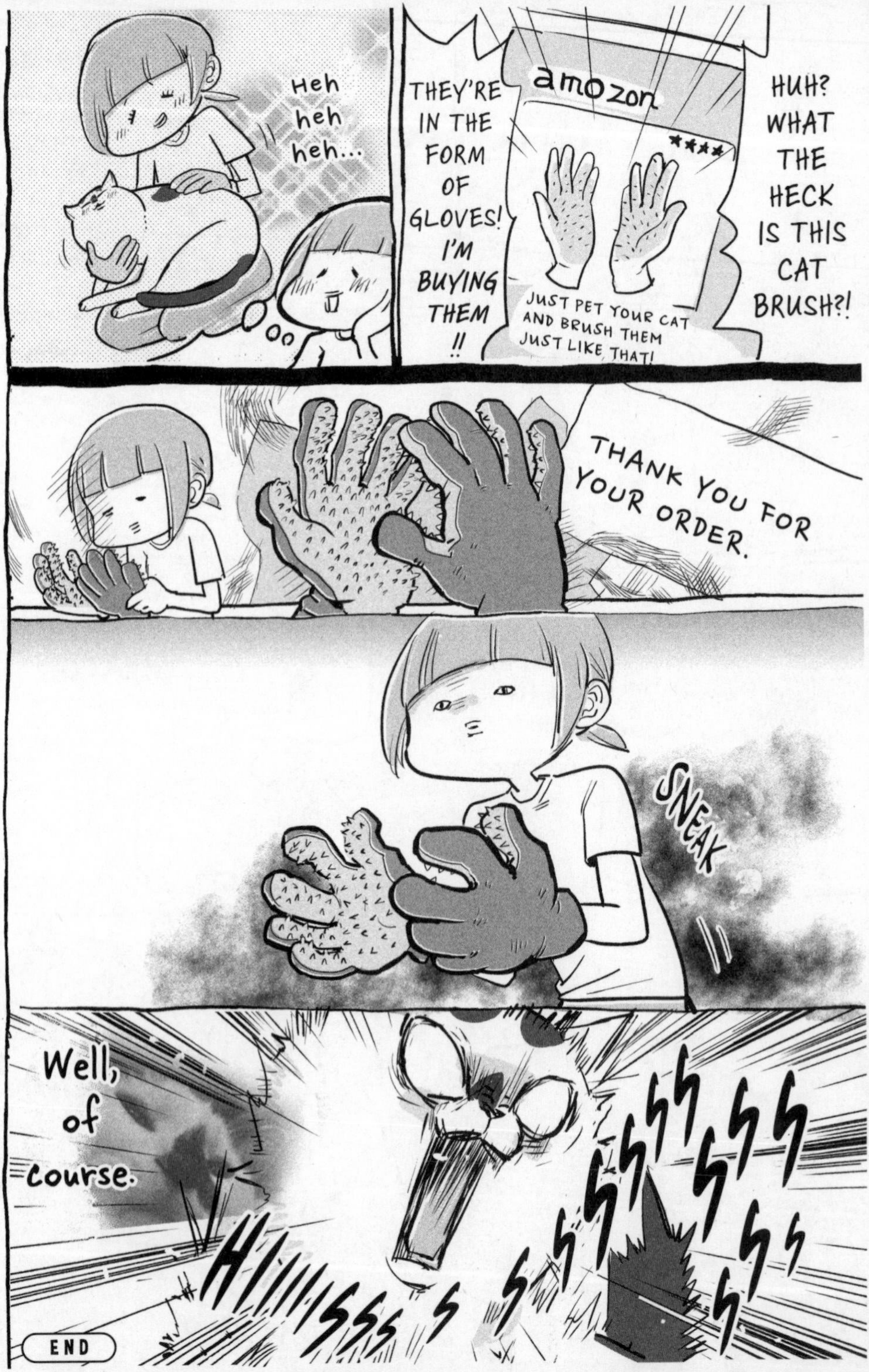
HUH? WHAT THE HECK IS THIS CAT BRUSH?!
amozon
JUST PET YOUR CAT AND BRUSH THEM JUST LIKE THAT!
THEY'RE IN THE FORM OF GLOVES! I'M BUYING THEM!!
Heh heh heh...
THANK YOU FOR YOUR ORDER.
SNEAK
HISSSSSSSSSSSSSS
Well, of course.
END

#92

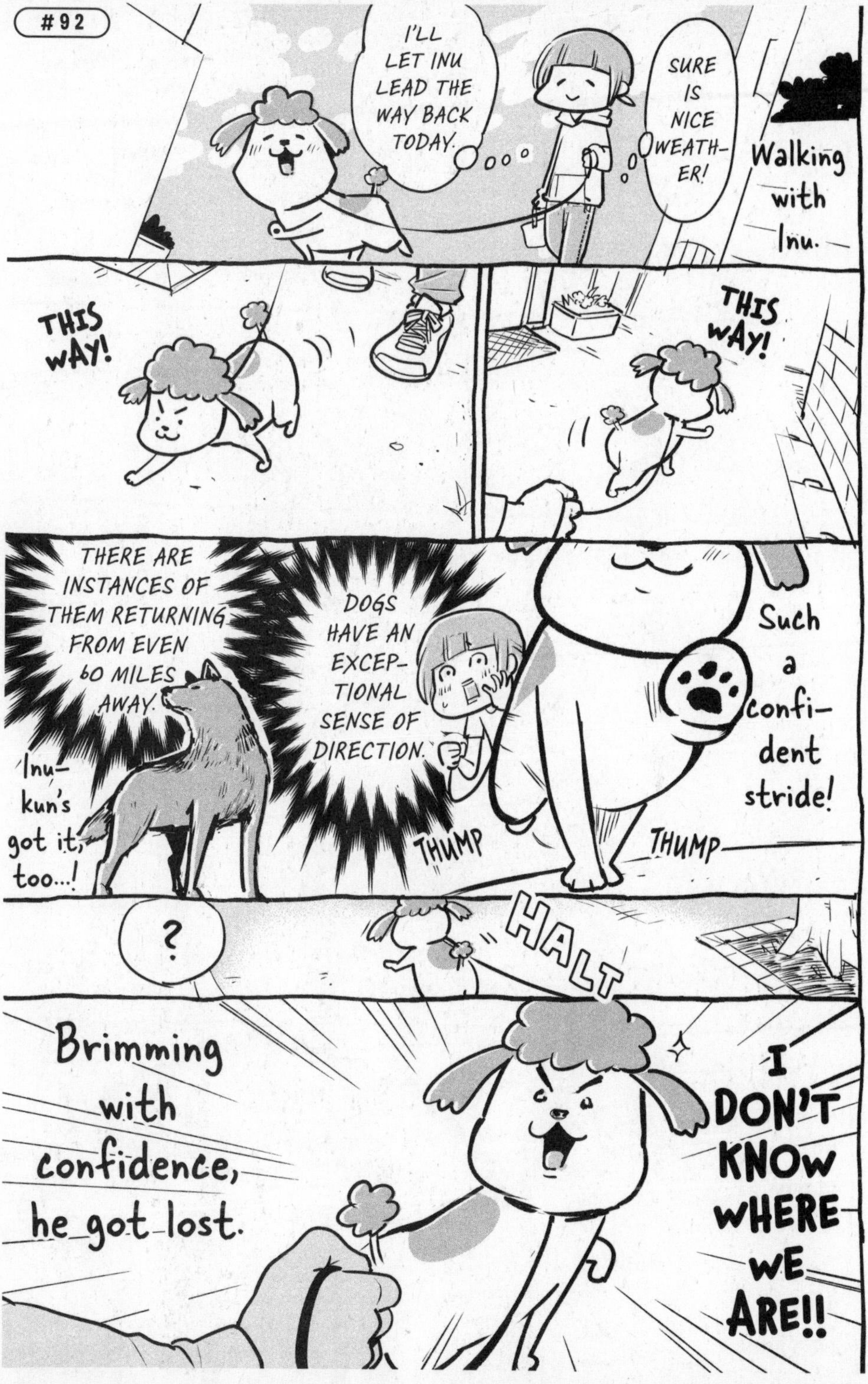

Walking with Inu.
SURE IS NICE WEATHER!
I'LL LET INU LEAD THE WAY BACK TODAY.
THIS WAY!
THIS WAY!
Such a confident stride!
THUMP
DOGS HAVE AN EXCEPTIONAL SENSE OF DIRECTION.
THERE ARE INSTANCES OF THEM RETURNING FROM EVEN 60 MILES AWAY.
THUMP
Inu-kun's got it, too...!
HALT
?
I DON'T KNOW WHERE WE ARE!!
Brimming with confidence, he got lost.

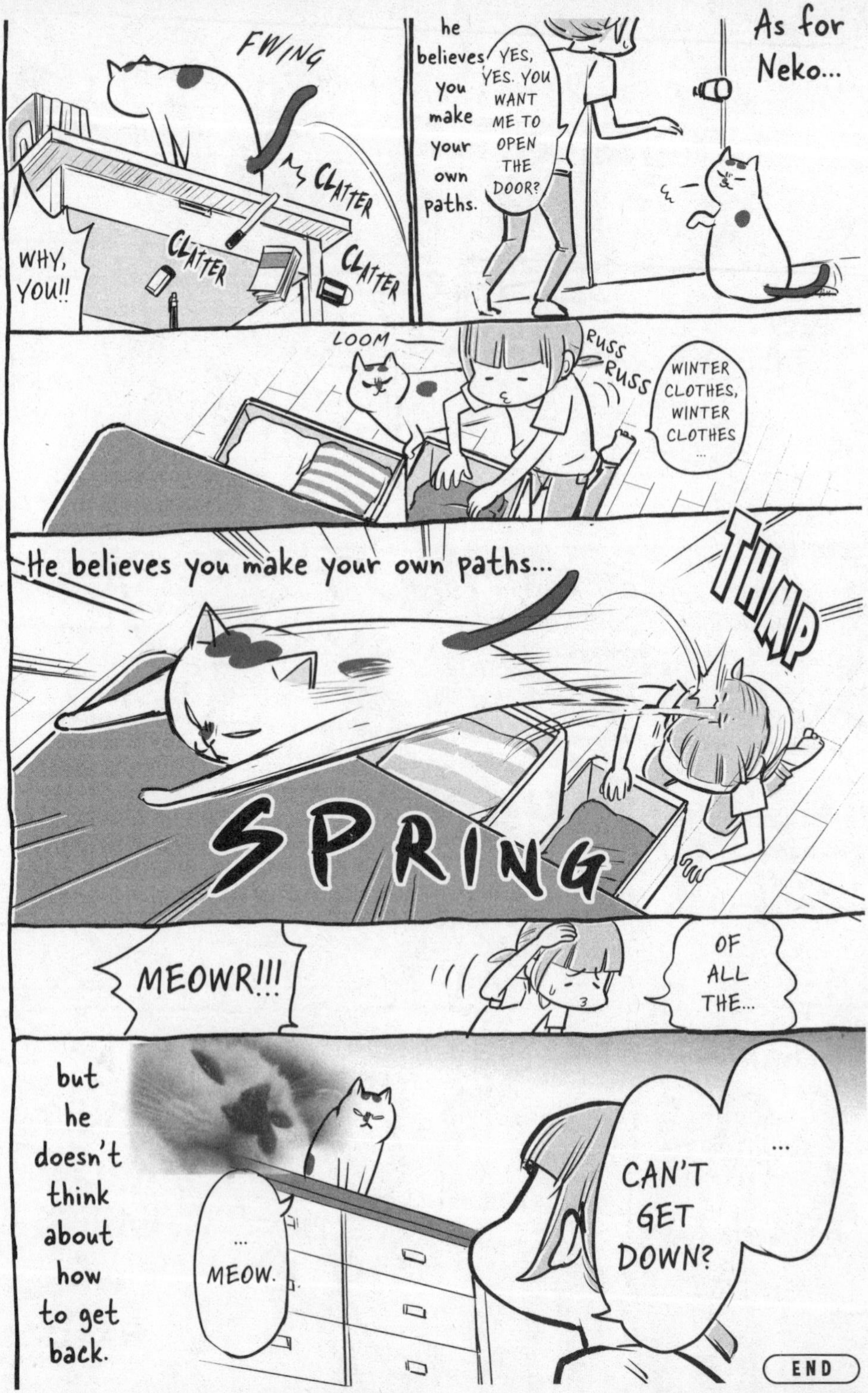
As for Neko...
he believes you make your own paths.
YES, YES. YOU WANT ME TO OPEN THE DOOR?
FWING
CLATTER
CLATTER
CLATTER
WHY, YOU!!
WINTER CLOTHES, WINTER CLOTHES ...
RUSS RUSS
LOOM
THMP
He believes you make your own paths...
SPRING
OF ALL THE...
MEOWR!!!
... CAN'T GET DOWN?
... MEOW.
but he doesn't think about how to get back.
END

#93

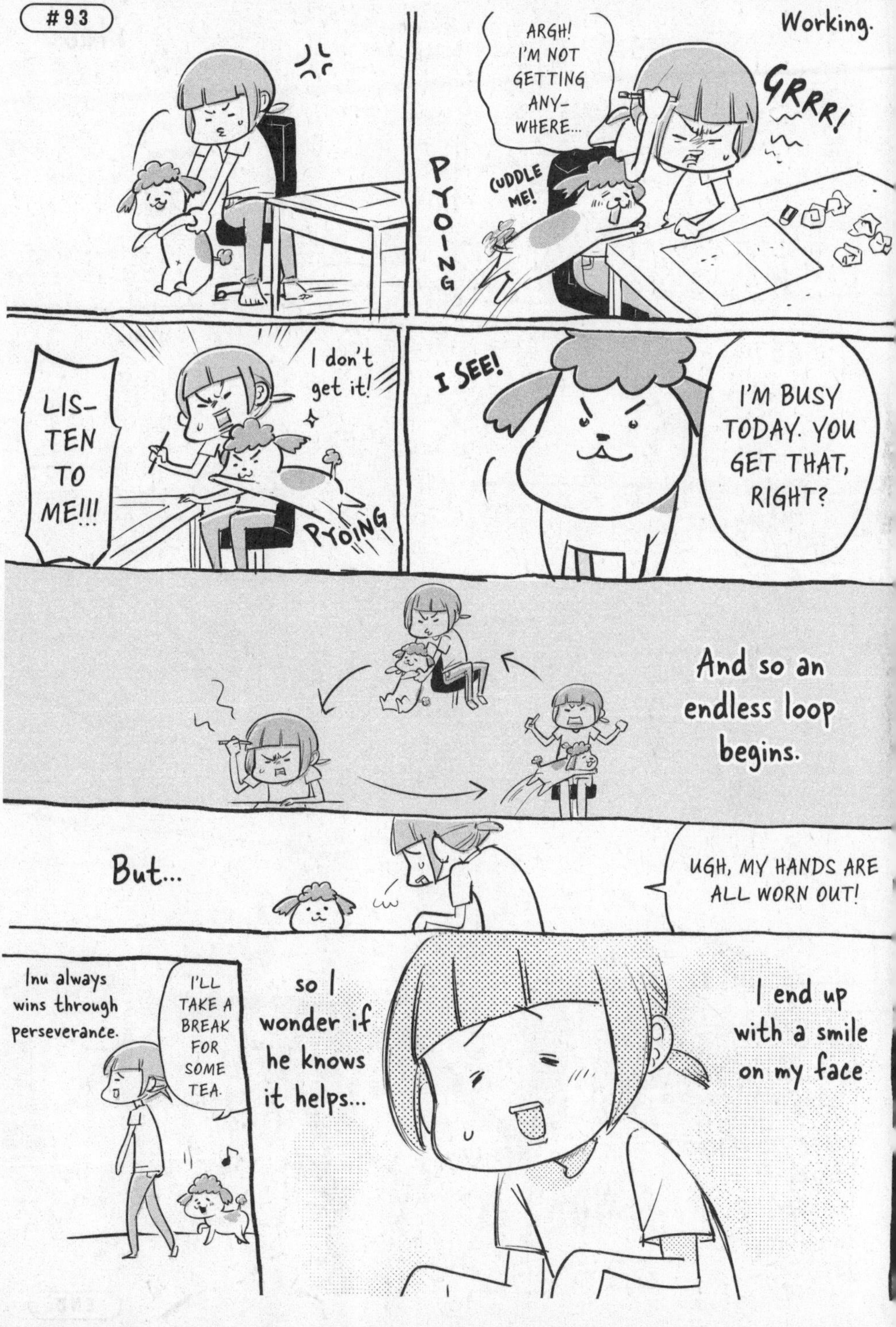
Working.
ARGH! I'M NOT GETTING ANY-WHERE...
GRRR!
CUDDLE ME!
PYOING
I'M BUSY TODAY. YOU GET THAT, RIGHT?
I SEE!
I don't get it!
LIS-TEN TO ME!!!
PYOING
And so an endless loop begins.
UGH, MY HANDS ARE ALL WORN OUT!
But...
I end up with a smile on my face
so I wonder if he knows it helps...
I'LL TAKE A BREAK FOR SOME TEA.
Inu always wins through perseverance.

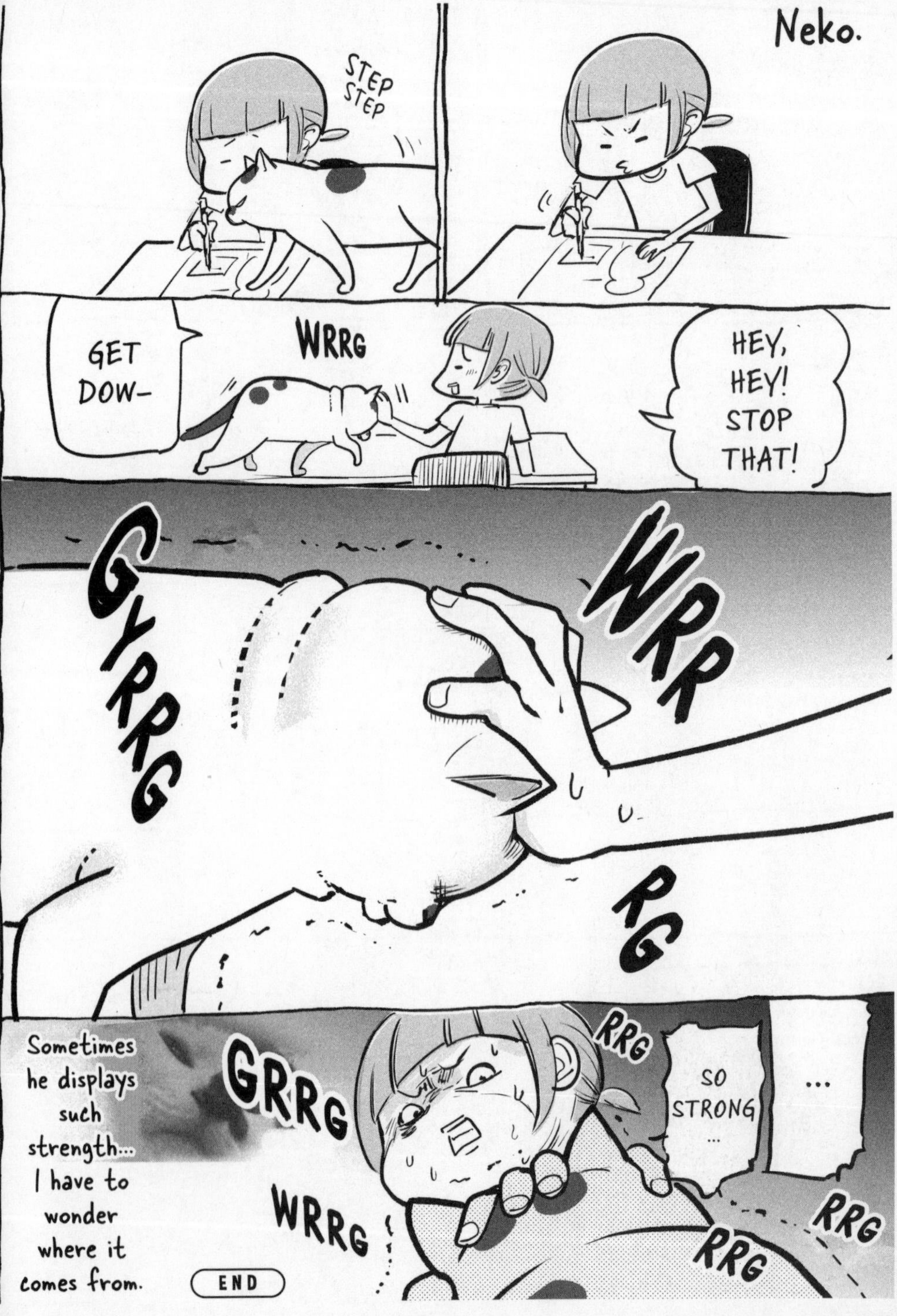

Neko.
STEP STEP
HEY, HEY! STOP THAT!
WRRG
GET DOW-
WRRR
GYRRG
RG
...
SO STRONG ...
RRG
GRRG
RRG
RRG
WRRG
Sometimes he displays such strength... I have to wonder where it comes from.
END

The fragrant paw pads of which he is so proud.

Newly-Drawn 4-Panel Strip

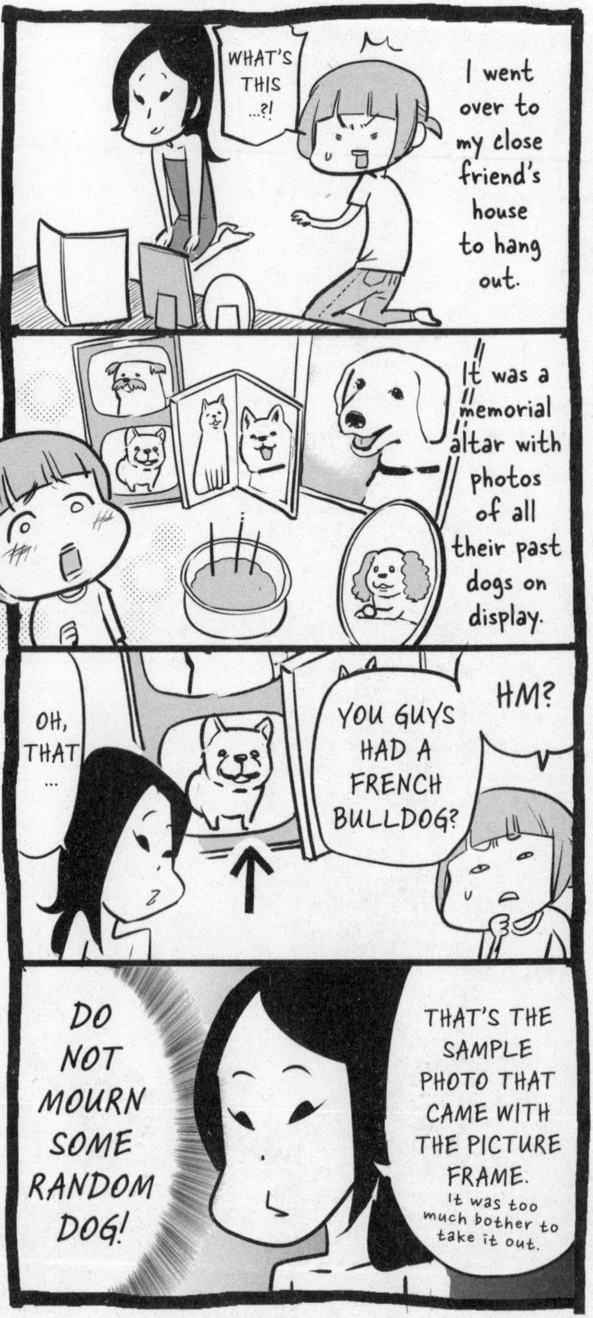
I went over to my close friend's house to hang out.
WHAT'S THIS ...?!
It was a memorial altar with photos of all their past dogs on display.
HM?
YOU GUYS HAD A FRENCH BULLDOG?
OH, THAT ...
THAT'S THE SAMPLE PHOTO THAT CAME WITH THE PICTURE FRAME.
It was too much bother to take it out.
DO NOT MOURN SOME RANDOM DOG!

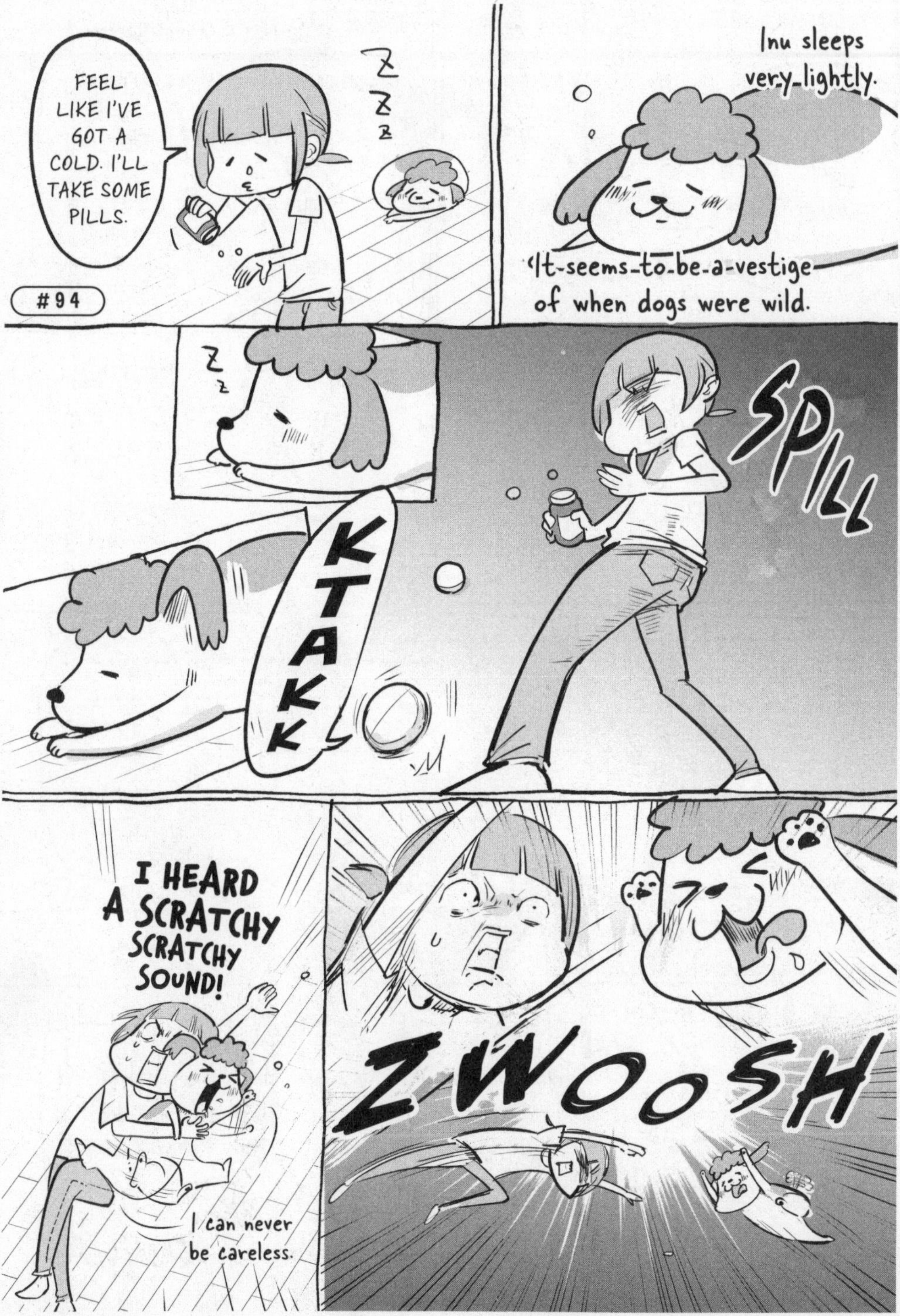
Inu sleeps very lightly.
It seems to be a vestige of when dogs were wild.
Z Z Z
FEEL LIKE I'VE GOT A COLD. I'LL TAKE SOME PILLS.
#94
SPILL
Z Z
KTAKK
ZWOOSH
I HEARD A SCRATCHY SCRATCHY SOUND!
I can never be careless.

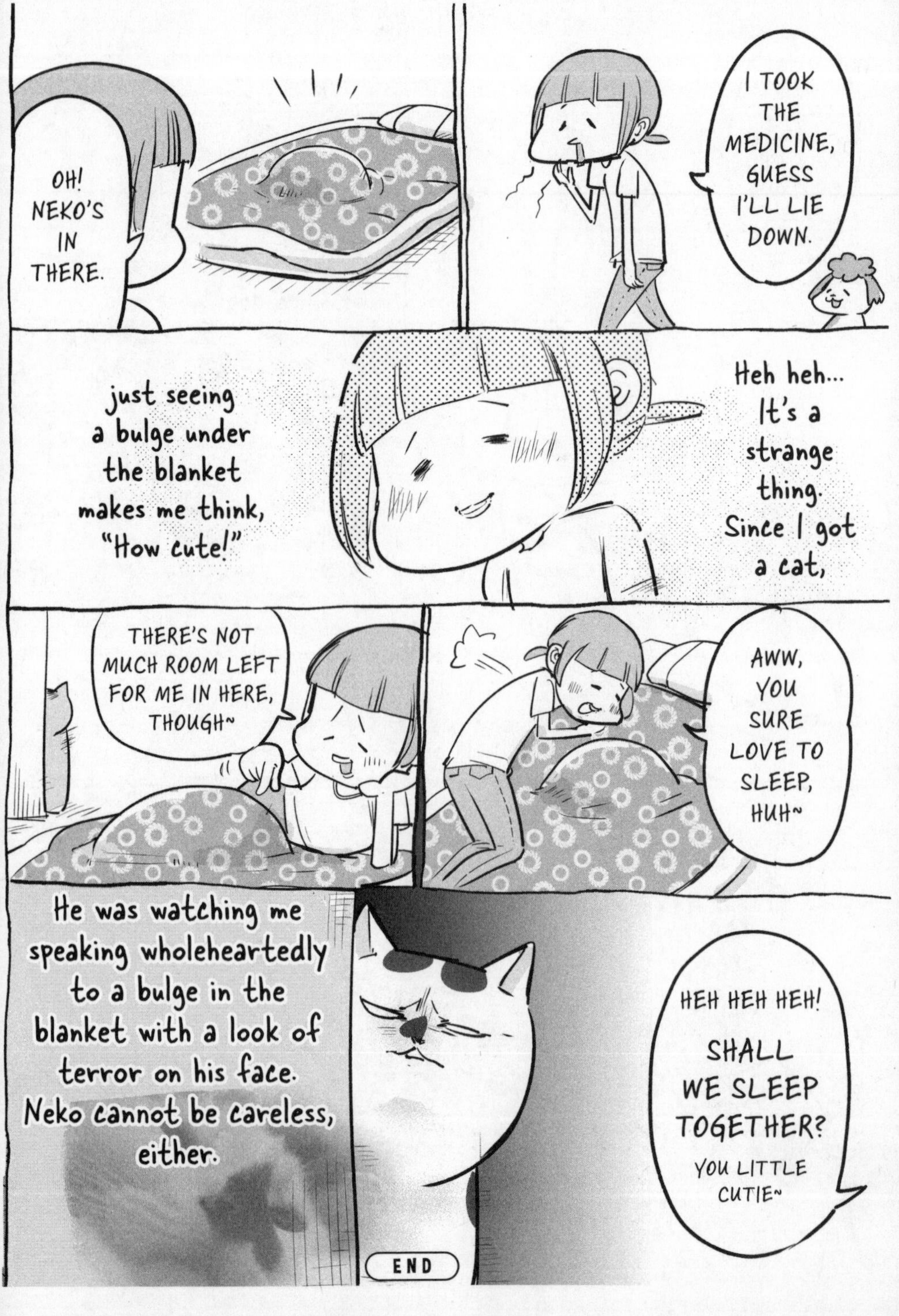
I TOOK THE MEDICINE, GUESS I'LL LIE DOWN.
OH! NEKO'S IN THERE.
Heh heh... It's a strange thing. Since I got a cat,
just seeing a bulge under the blanket makes me think, "How cute!"
AWW, YOU SURE LOVE TO SLEEP, HUH~
THERE'S NOT MUCH ROOM LEFT FOR ME IN HERE, THOUGH~
HEH HEH HEH! SHALL WE SLEEP TOGETHER? YOU LITTLE CUTIE~
He was watching me speaking wholeheartedly to a bulge in the blanket with a look of terror on his face. Neko cannot be careless, either.
END

More About #94

And underneath the bulge in the blanket was...

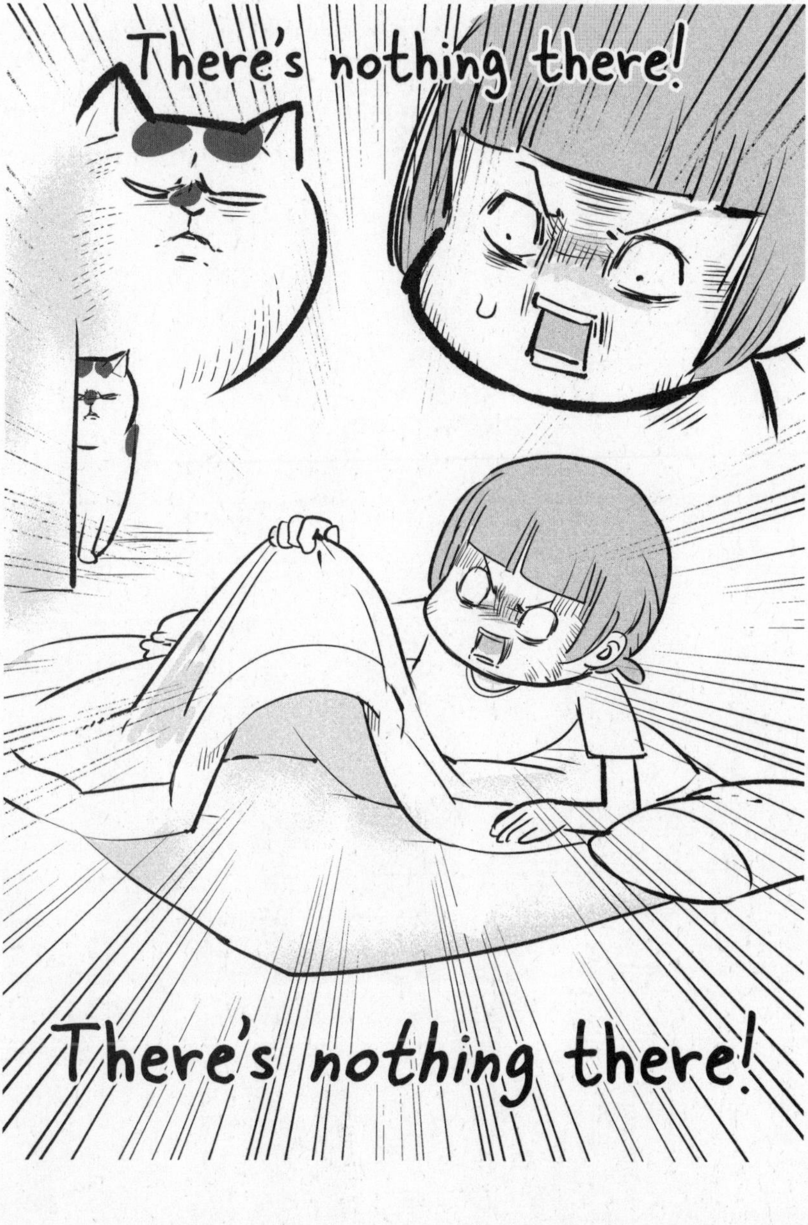
There's nothing there!
There's nothing there!

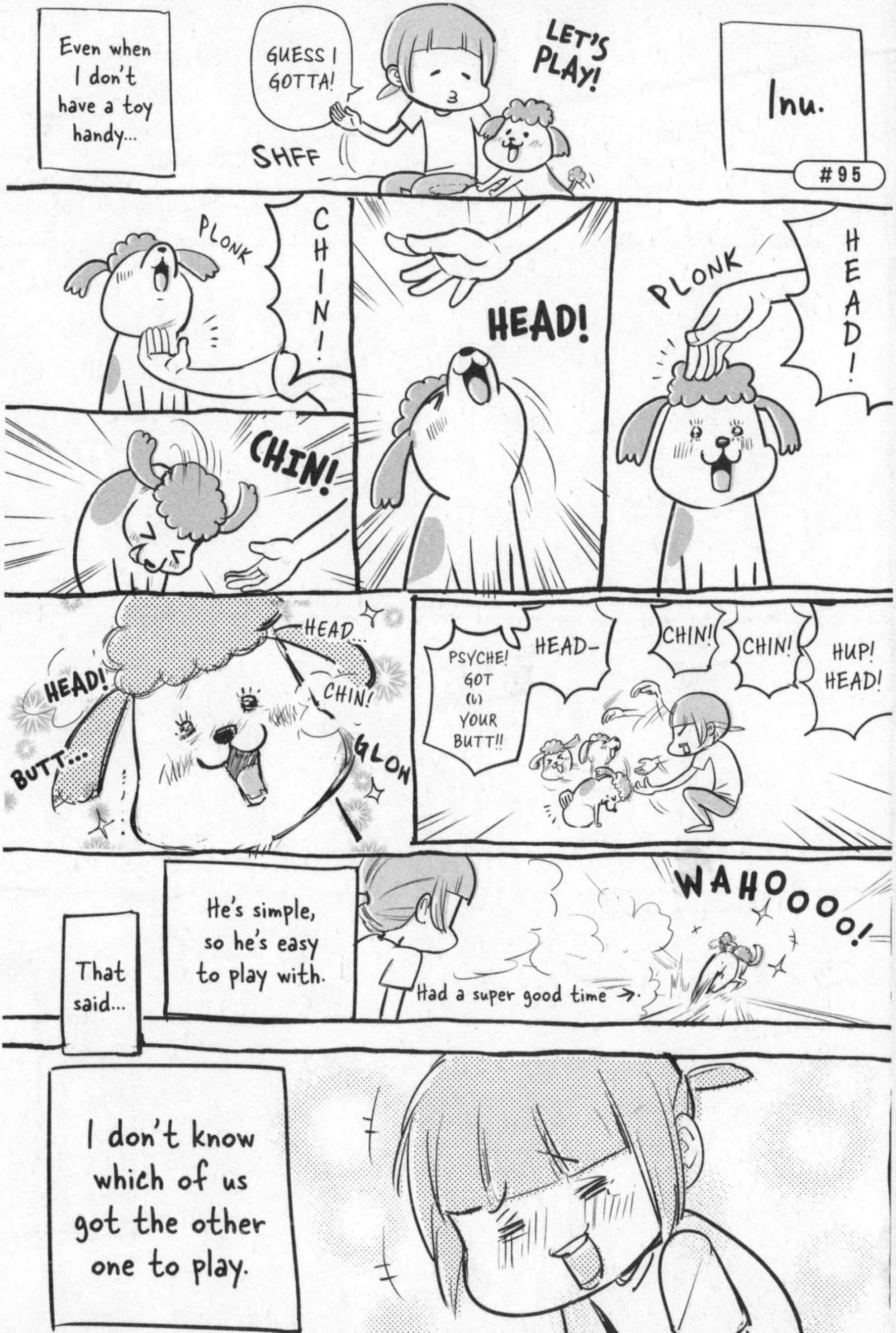

Inu.
#95
LET'S PLAY!
GUESS I GOTTA!
SHFF
Even when I don't have a toy handy...
PLONK
HEAD!
HEAD!
PLONK
CHIN!
CHIN!
HUP! HEAD!
CHIN!
CHIN!
HEAD-
PSYCHE! GOT (U) YOUR BUTT!!
HEAD
CHIN!
GLOW
HEAD!
BUTT...
WAHOOOO!
Had a super good time →
He's simple, so he's easy to play with.
That said...
I don't know which of us got the other one to play.

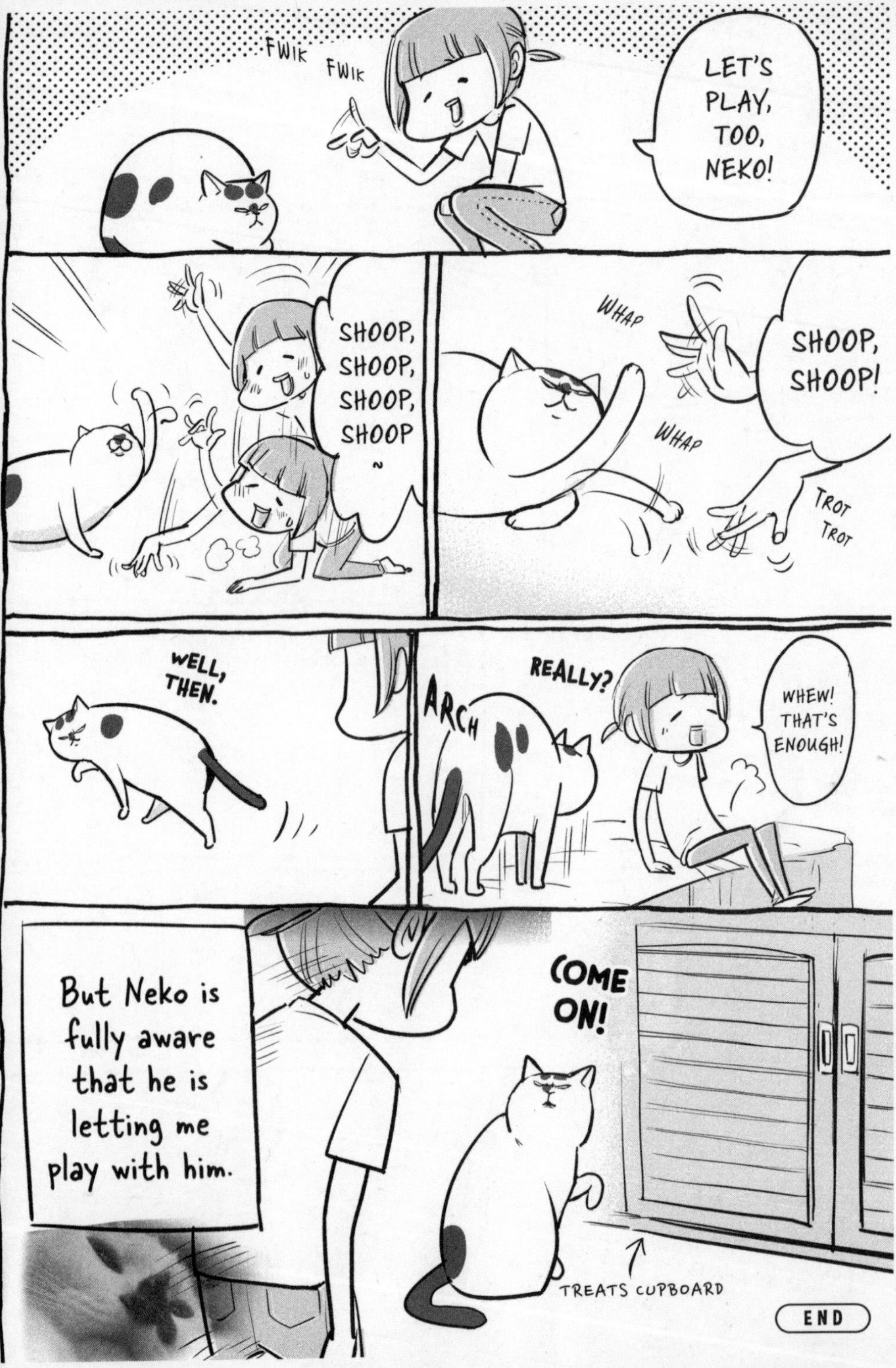
LET'S PLAY, TOO, NEKO!
FWIK
FWIK
SHOOP, SHOOP!
WHAP
WHAP
TROT TROT
SHOOP, SHOOP, SHOOP, SHOOP
WHEW! THAT'S ENOUGH!
REALLY?
ARCH
WELL, THEN.
COME ON!
But Neko is fully aware that he is letting me play with him.
TREATS CUPBOARD
END

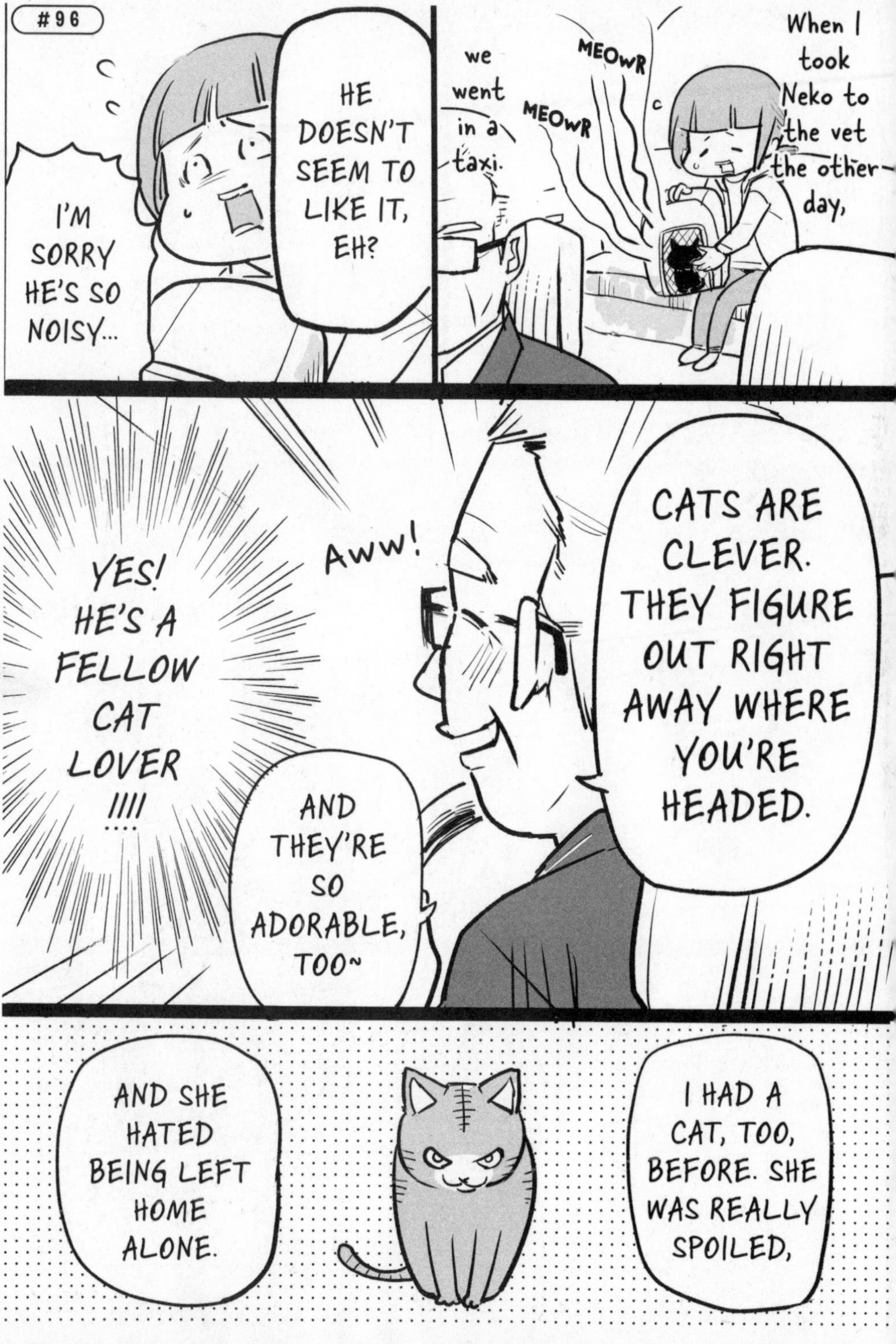
#96
When I took Neko to the vet the other day,
MEOWR
MEOWR
we went in a taxi.
HE DOESN'T SEEM TO LIKE IT, EH?
I'M SORRY HE'S SO NOISY...
CATS ARE CLEVER. THEY FIGURE OUT RIGHT AWAY WHERE YOU'RE HEADED.
AND THEY'RE SO ADORABLE, TOO~
AWW!
YES! HE'S A FELLOW CAT LOVER !!!!
I HAD A CAT, TOO, BEFORE. SHE WAS REALLY SPOILED,
AND SHE HATED BEING LEFT HOME ALONE.

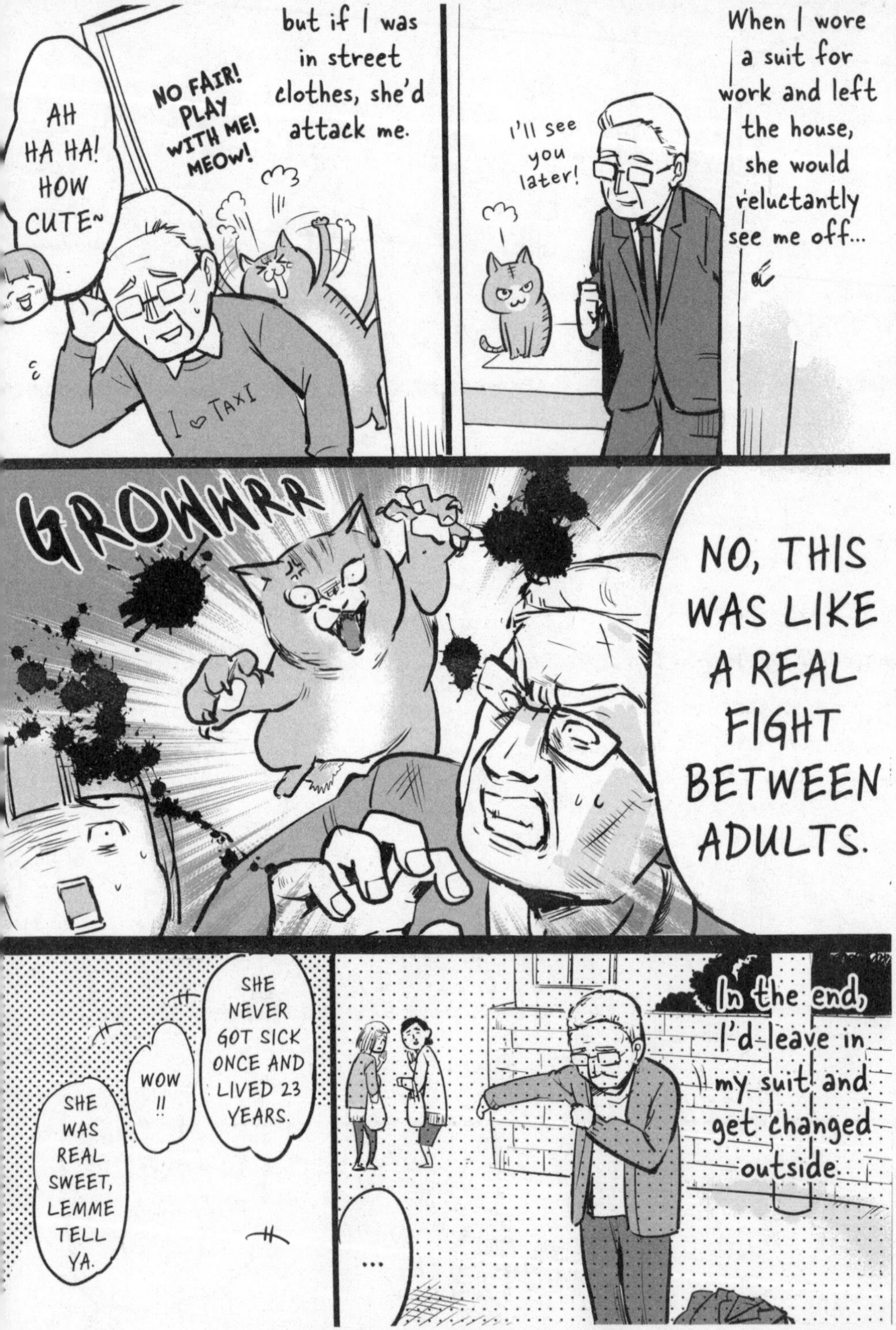

When I wore a suit for work and left the house, she would reluctantly see me off...
I'll see you later!
but if I was in street clothes, she'd attack me.
NO FAIR! PLAY WITH ME! MEOW!
AH HA HA! HOW CUTE~
I ♡ TAXI
NO, THIS WAS LIKE A REAL FIGHT BETWEEN ADULTS.
GROWWRR
In the end, I'd leave in my suit and get changed outside.
...
SHE NEVER GOT SICK ONCE AND LIVED 23 YEARS.
WOW !!
SHE WAS REAL SWEET, LEMME TELL YA.

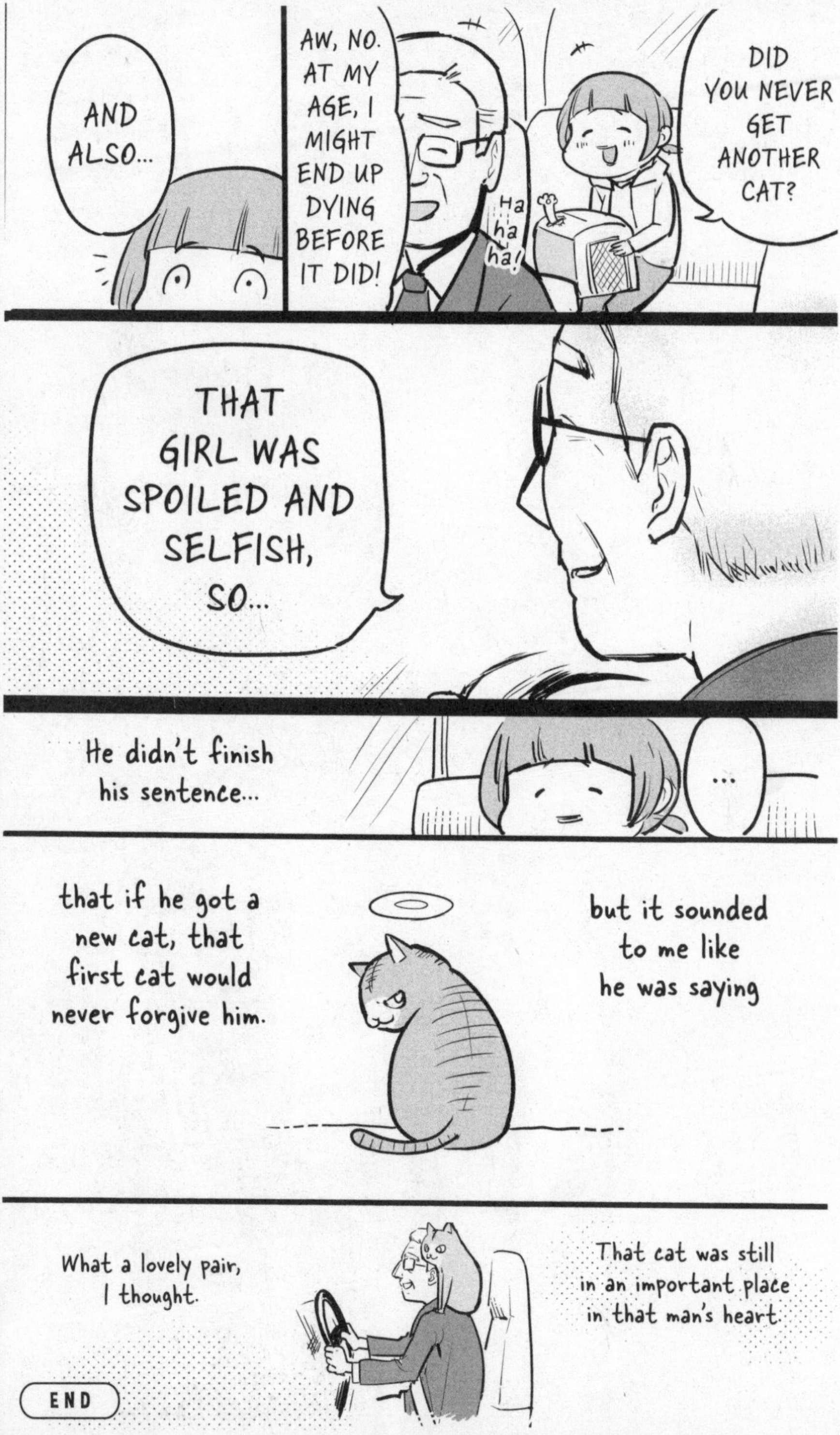
DID YOU NEVER GET ANOTHER CAT?
AW, NO. AT MY AGE, I MIGHT END UP DYING BEFORE IT DID!
Ha ha ha!
AND ALSO...
THAT GIRL WAS SPOILED AND SELFISH, SO...
...
He didn't finish his sentence...
but it sounded to me like he was saying
that if he got a new cat, that first cat would never forgive him.
That cat was still in an important place in that man's heart.
What a lovely pair, I thought.
END

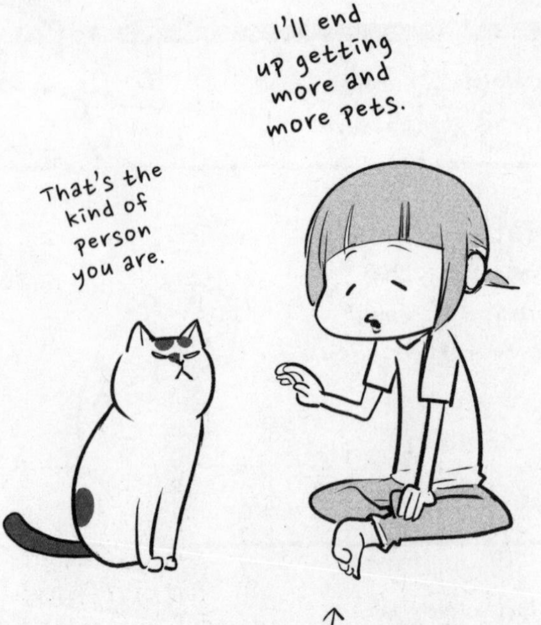
I'll end up getting more and more pets.
That's the kind of person you are.
THE BIG FAMILY TYPE

A morning treat.

Newly-Drawn 4-Panel Strip

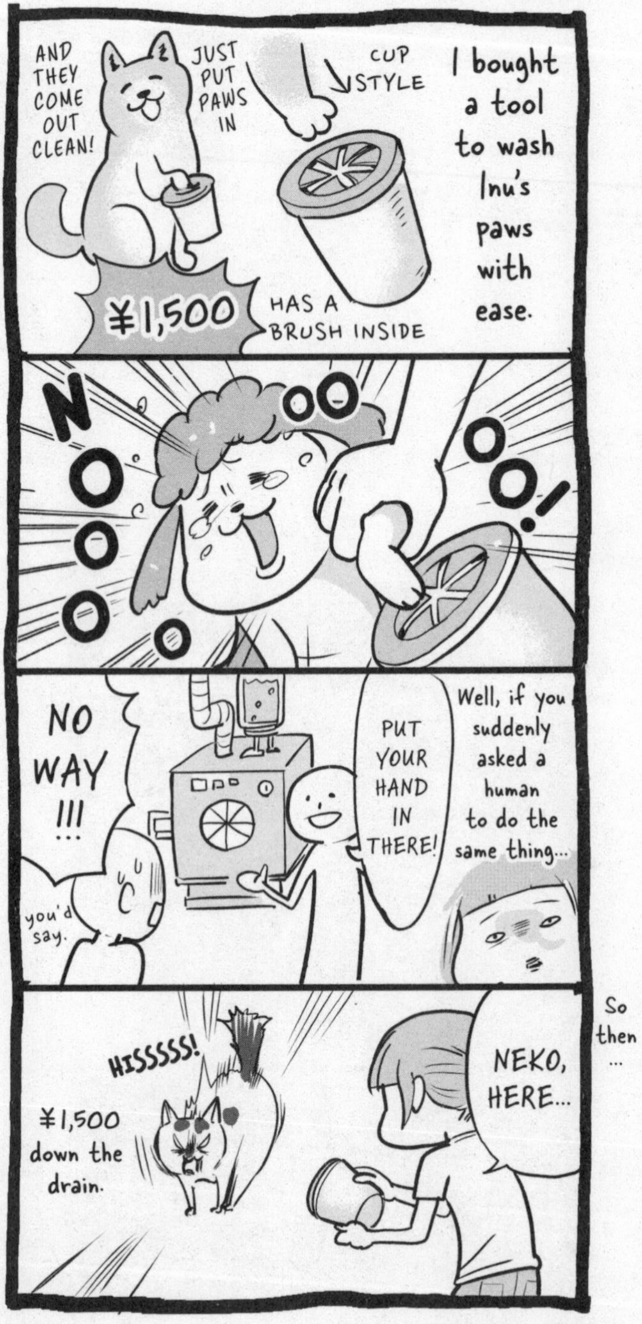
I bought a tool to wash Inu's paws with ease.
CUP STYLE
JUST PUT PAWS IN
AND THEY COME OUT CLEAN!
HAS A BRUSH INSIDE
¥1,500
NOOOOOOOOO!
Well, if you suddenly asked a human to do the same thing...
PUT YOUR HAND IN THERE!
NO WAY!!!...
you'd say.
So then...
NEKO, HERE...
HISSSSS!
¥1,500 down the drain.

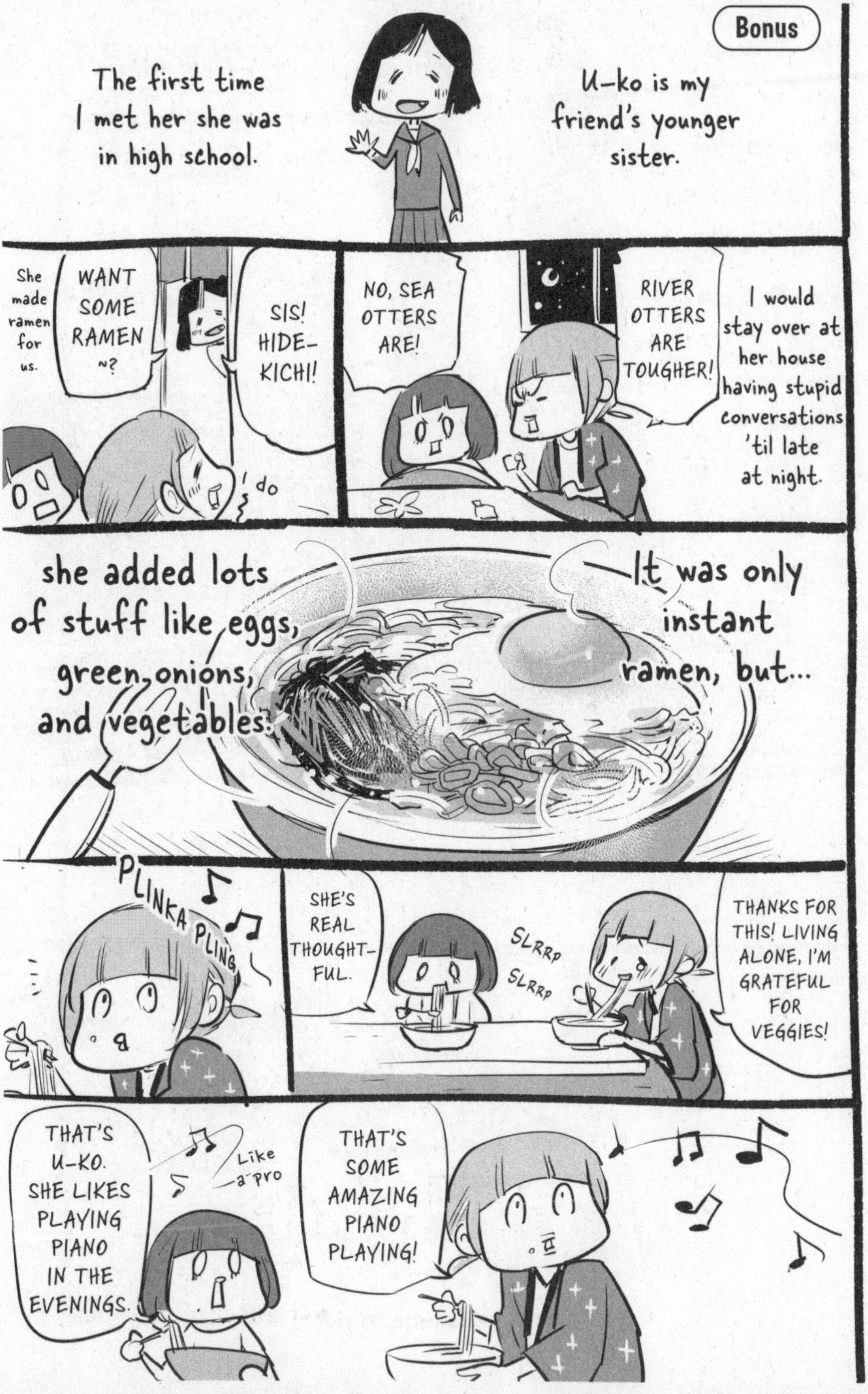
Bonus
U-ko is my friend's younger sister.
The first time I met her she was in high school.
I would stay over at her house having stupid conversations 'til late at night.
RIVER OTTERS ARE TOUGHER!
NO, SEA OTTERS ARE!
SIS! HIDE-KICHI!
WANT SOME RAMEN ~?
She made ramen for us.
I do
It was only instant ramen, but...
she added lots of stuff like eggs, green onions, and vegetables.
THANKS FOR THIS! LIVING ALONE, I'M GRATEFUL FOR VEGGIES!
SLRRP SLRRP
SHE'S REAL THOUGHT-FUL.
PLINKA PLING
THAT'S SOME AMAZING PIANO PLAYING!
Like a pro
THAT'S U-KO. SHE LIKES PLAYING PIANO IN THE EVENINGS.

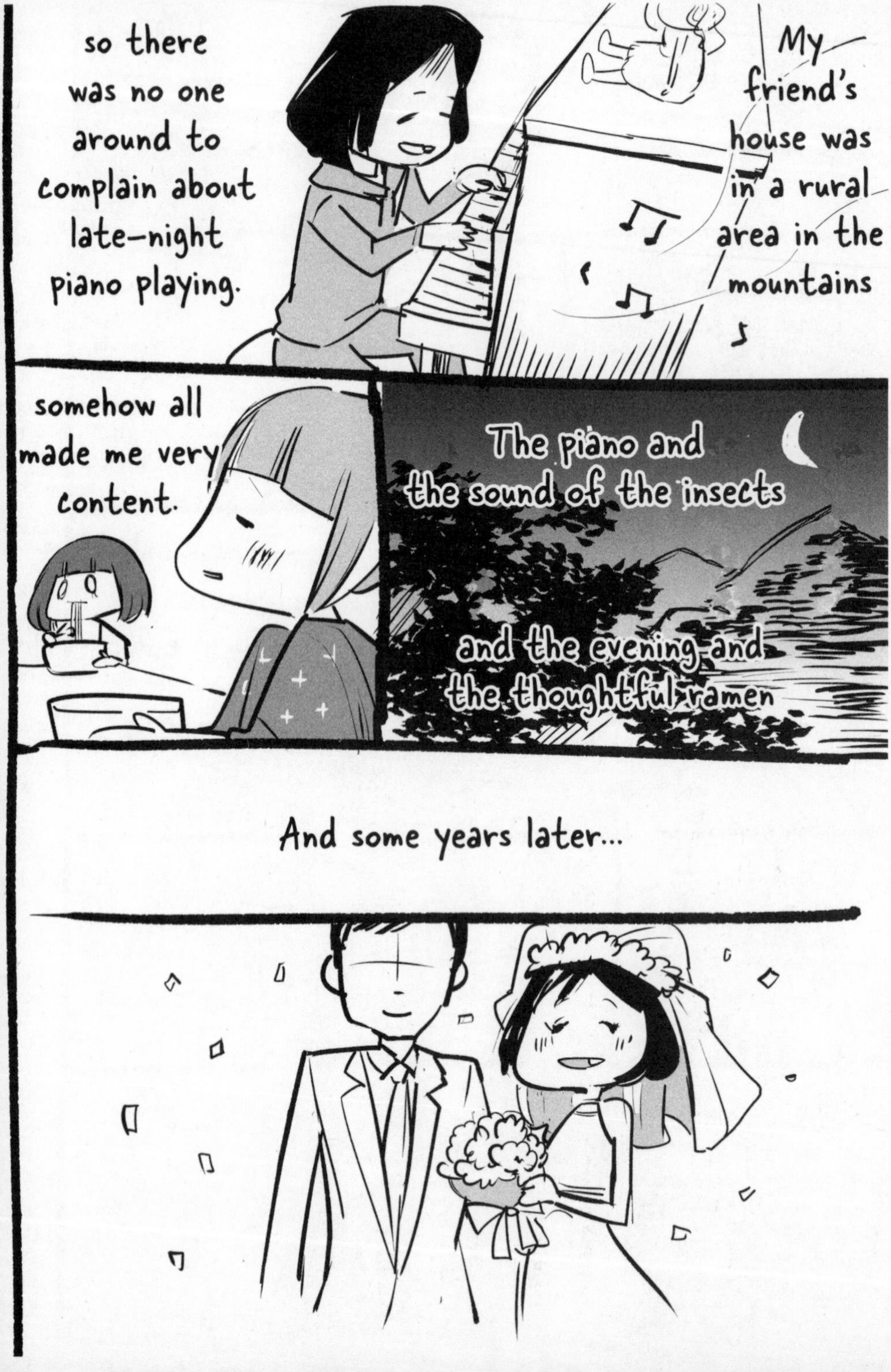
My friend's house was in a rural area in the mountains
so there was no one around to complain about late-night piano playing.
The piano and the sound of the insects
and the evening and the thoughtful ramen
somehow all made me very content.
And some years later...

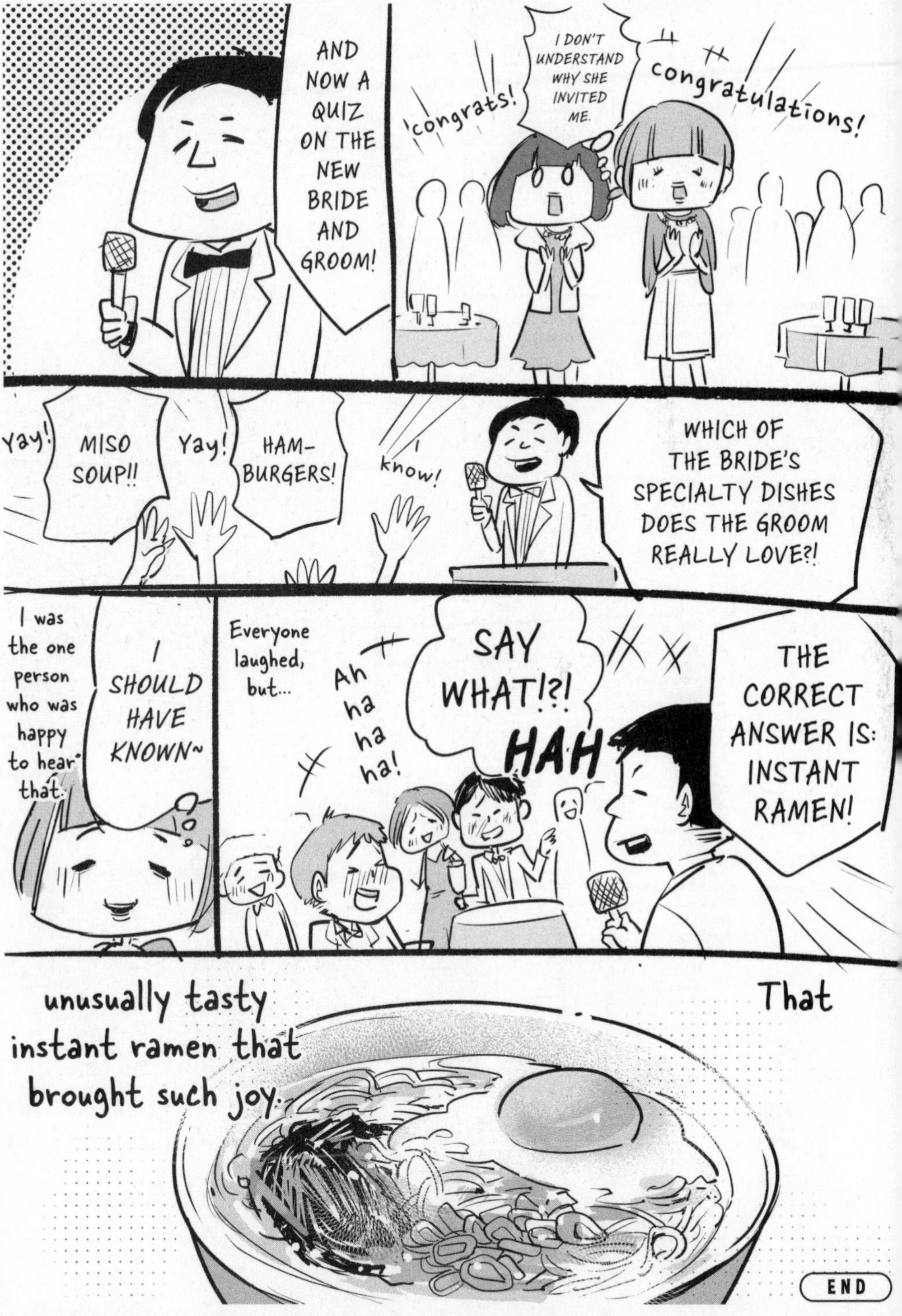
congratulations!
I DON'T UNDERSTAND WHY SHE INVITED ME.
congrats!
AND NOW A QUIZ ON THE NEW BRIDE AND GROOM!
WHICH OF THE BRIDE'S SPECIALTY DISHES DOES THE GROOM REALLY LOVE?!
I know!
HAM-BURGERS!
Yay!
MISO SOUP!!
Yay!
THE CORRECT ANSWER IS: INSTANT RAMEN!
SAY WHAT!?!
HAH
Ah ha ha ha!
Everyone laughed, but...
I SHOULD HAVE KNOWN~
I was the one person who was happy to hear that.
That
unusually tasty instant ramen that brought such joy.
END

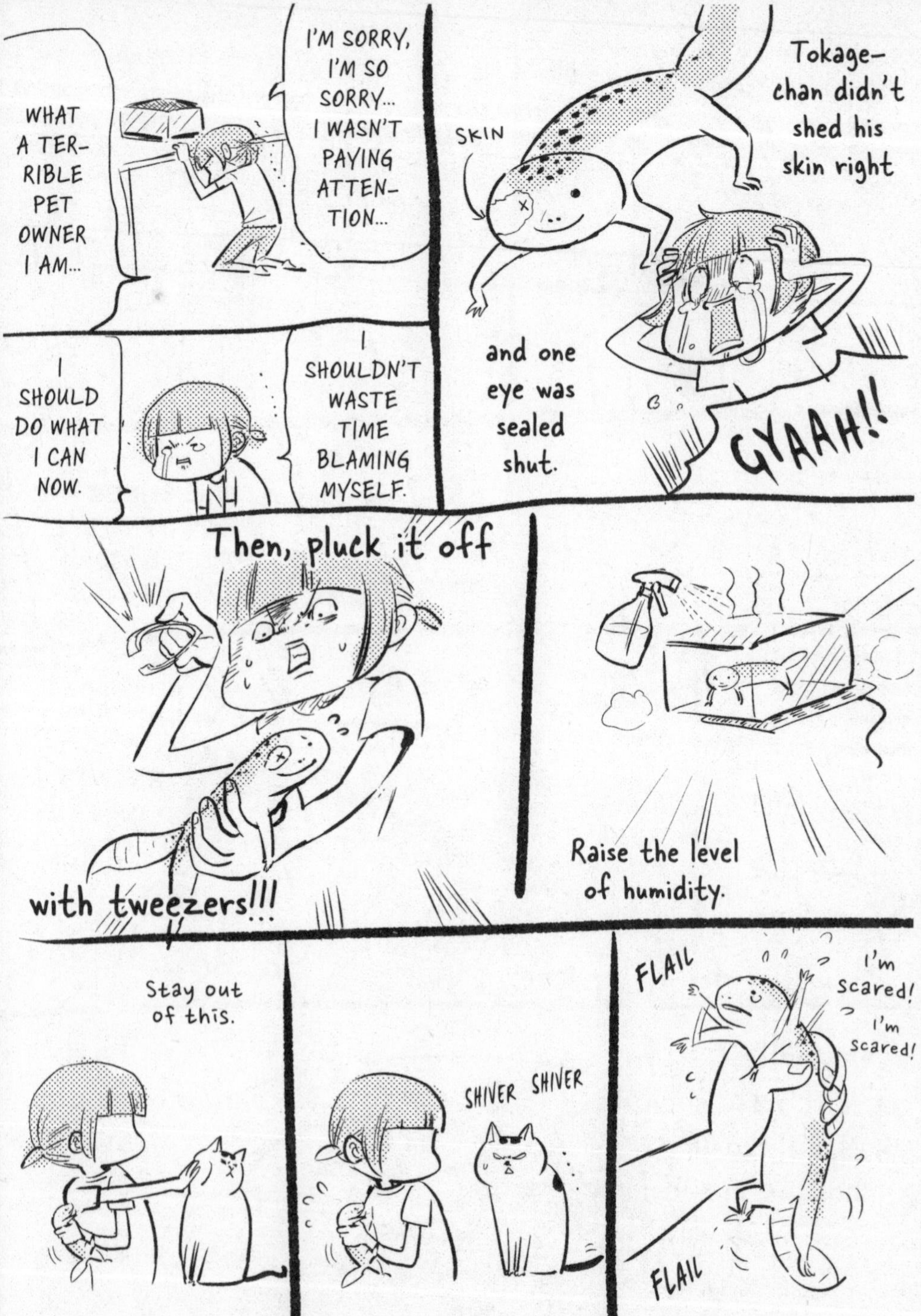
Tokage-chan didn't shed his skin right
SKIN
and one eye was sealed shut.
GYAAH!!
I'M SORRY, I'M SO SORRY... I WASN'T PAYING ATTENTION...
WHAT A TERRIBLE PET OWNER I AM...
I SHOULDN'T WASTE TIME BLAMING MYSELF.
I SHOULD DO WHAT I CAN NOW.
Raise the level of humidity.
Then, pluck it off
with tweezers!!!
FLAIL
I'm scared!
I'm scared!
FLAIL
SHIVER SHIVER
Stay out of this.

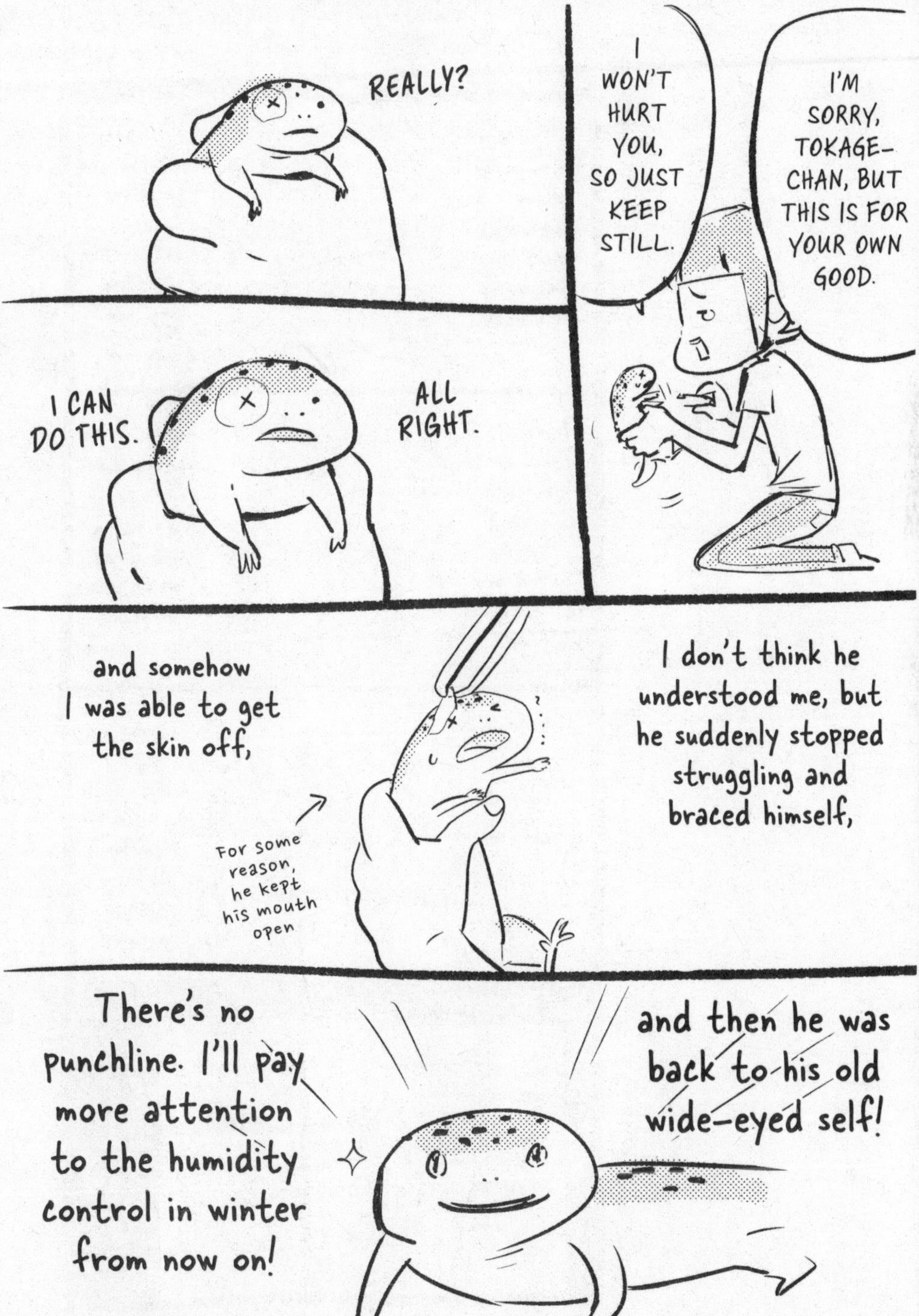

I'M SORRY, TOKAGE-CHAN, BUT THIS IS FOR YOUR OWN GOOD.
I WON'T HURT YOU, SO JUST KEEP STILL.
REALLY?
ALL RIGHT.
I CAN DO THIS.
I don't think he understood me, but he suddenly stopped struggling and braced himself,
and somehow I was able to get the skin off,
For some reason, he kept his mouth open
and then he was back to his old wide-eyed self!
There's no punchline. I'll pay more attention to the humidity control in winter from now on!
END

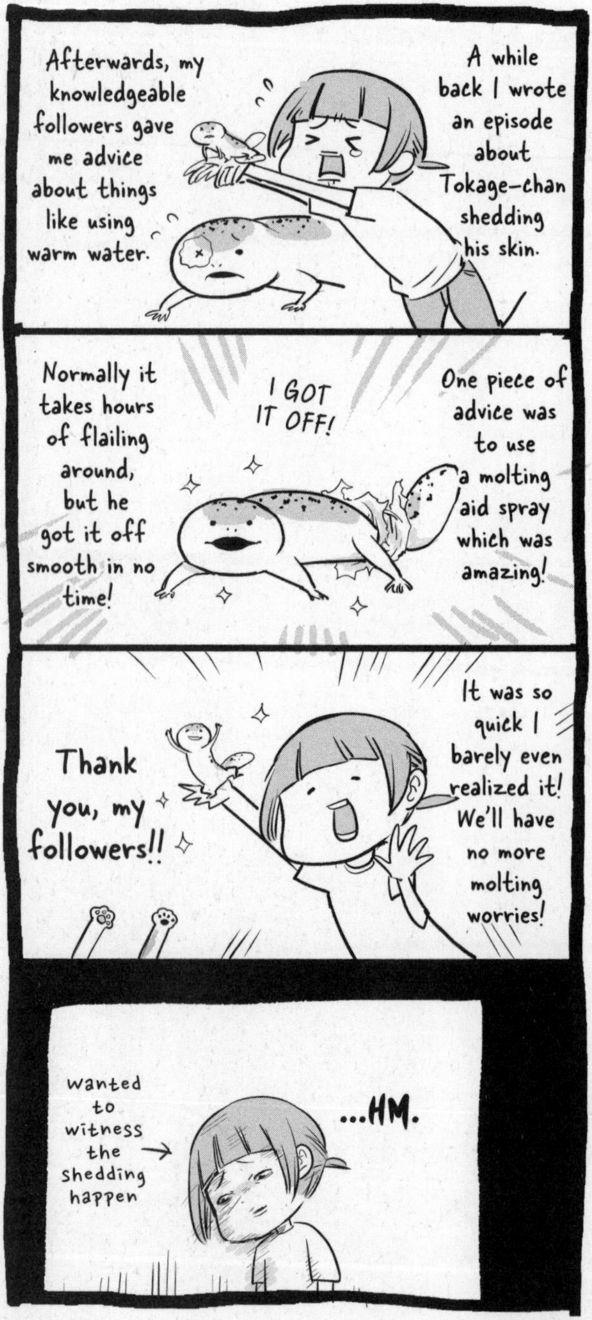
A while back I wrote an episode about Tokage-chan shedding his skin.
Afterwards, my knowledgeable followers gave me advice about things like using warm water.
One piece of advice was to use a molting aid spray which was amazing!
I GOT IT OFF!
Normally it takes hours of flailing around, but he got it off smooth in no time!
It was so quick I barely even realized it! We'll have no more molting worries!
Thank you, my followers!!
...HM.
wanted to witness the shedding happen

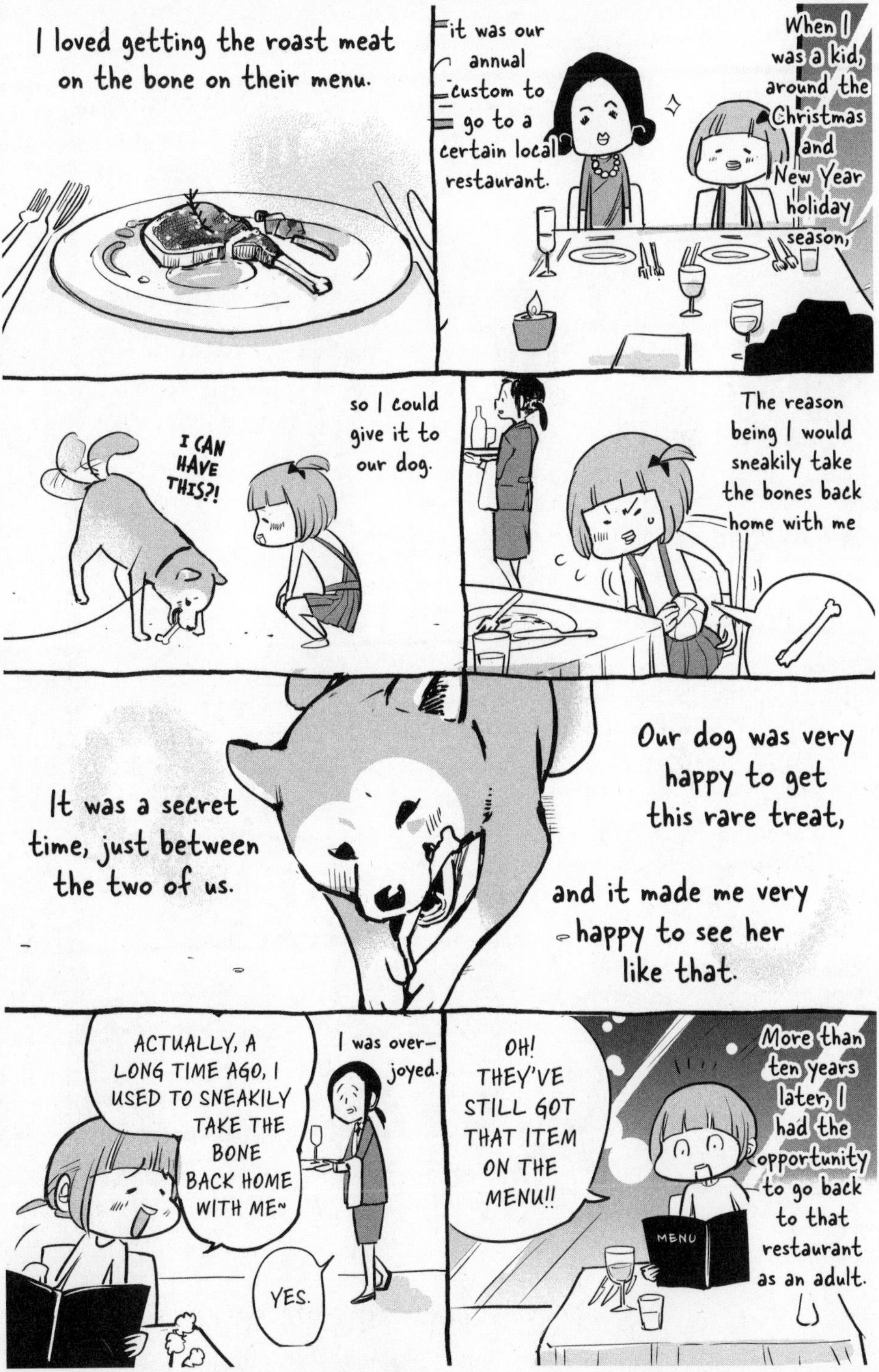
When I was a kid, around the Christmas and New Year holiday season,
it was our annual custom to go to a certain local restaurant.
I loved getting the roast meat on the bone on their menu.
The reason being I would sneakily take the bones back home with me
so I could give it to our dog.
I CAN HAVE THIS?!
Our dog was very happy to get this rare treat,
and it made me very happy to see her like that.
It was a secret time, just between the two of us.
More than ten years later, I had the opportunity to go back to that restaurant as an adult.
OH! THEY'VE STILL GOT THAT ITEM ON THE MENU!!
MENU
I was over-joyed.
ACTUALLY, A LONG TIME AGO, I USED TO SNEAKILY TAKE THE BONE BACK HOME WITH ME~
YES.

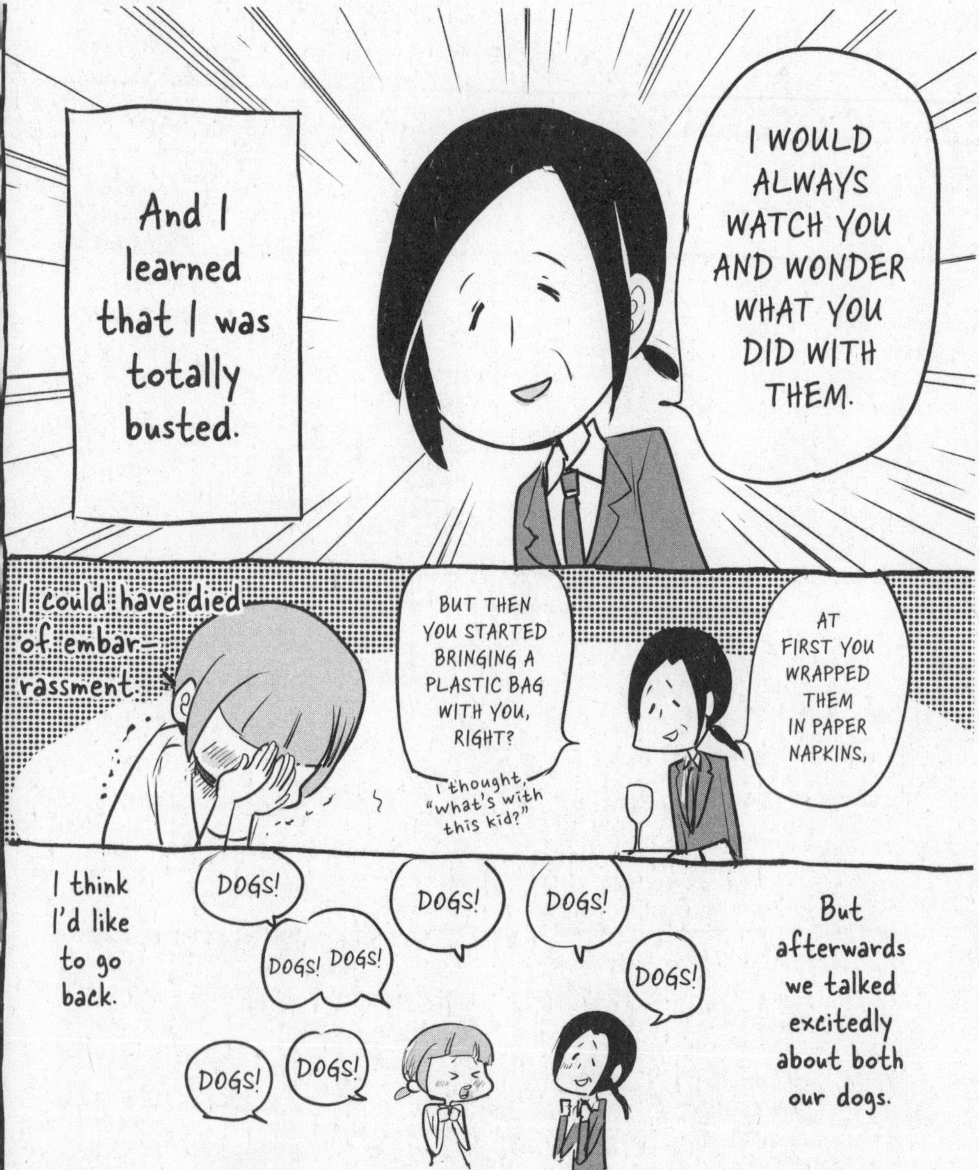
I WOULD ALWAYS WATCH YOU AND WONDER WHAT YOU DID WITH THEM.
And I learned that I was totally busted.
AT FIRST YOU WRAPPED THEM IN PAPER NAPKINS,
BUT THEN YOU STARTED BRINGING A PLASTIC BAG WITH YOU, RIGHT?
I thought, "what's with this kid?"
I could have died of embar-rassment.
But afterwards we talked excitedly about both our dogs.
DOGS!
DOGS!
DOGS!
DOGS!
DOGS! DOGS!
DOGS!
DOGS!
I think I'd like to go back.
END

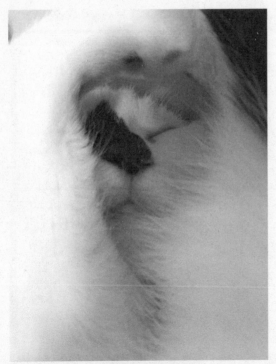

Uncommonly high levels of fluff.

Newly-Drawn 4-Panel Strip

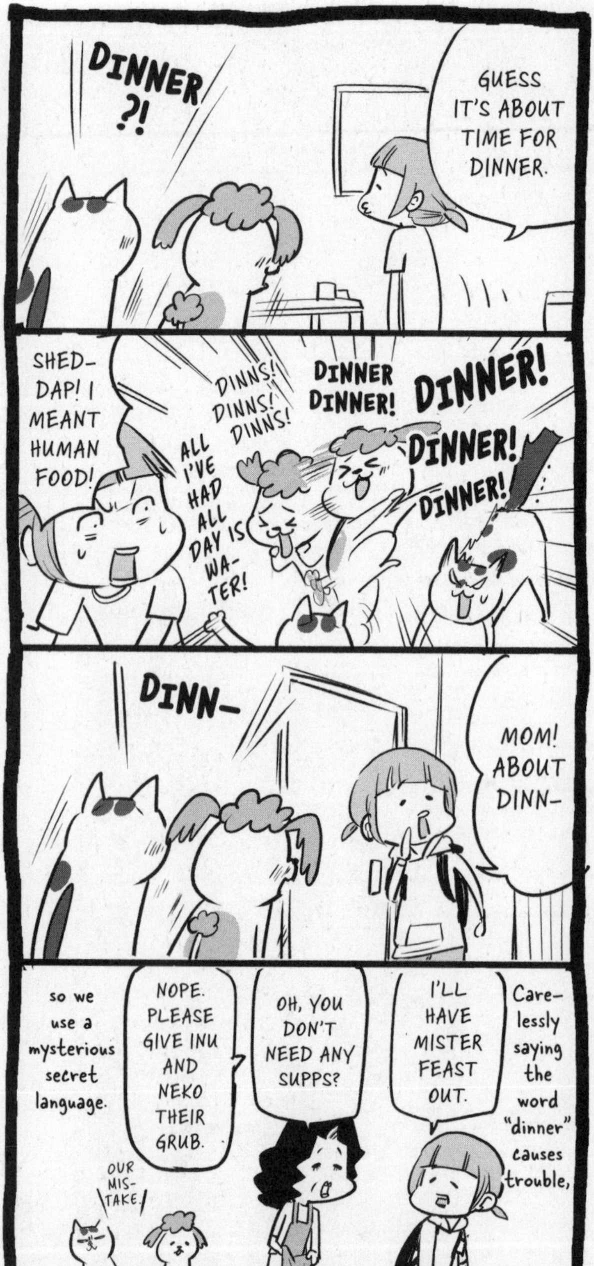
GUESS IT'S ABOUT TIME FOR DINNER.
DINNER ?!
DINNER!
DINNER!
DINNER!
DINNER DINNER!
DINNS! DINNS! DINNS!
ALL I'VE HAD ALL DAY IS WA-TER!
SHED-DAP! I MEANT HUMAN FOOD!
MOM! ABOUT DINN-
DINN-
Care-lessly saying the word "dinner" causes trouble,
I'LL HAVE MISTER FEAST OUT.
OH, YOU DON'T NEED ANY SUPPS?
NOPE. PLEASE GIVE INU AND NEKO THEIR GRUB.
OUR MIS-TAKE.
so we use a mysterious secret language.

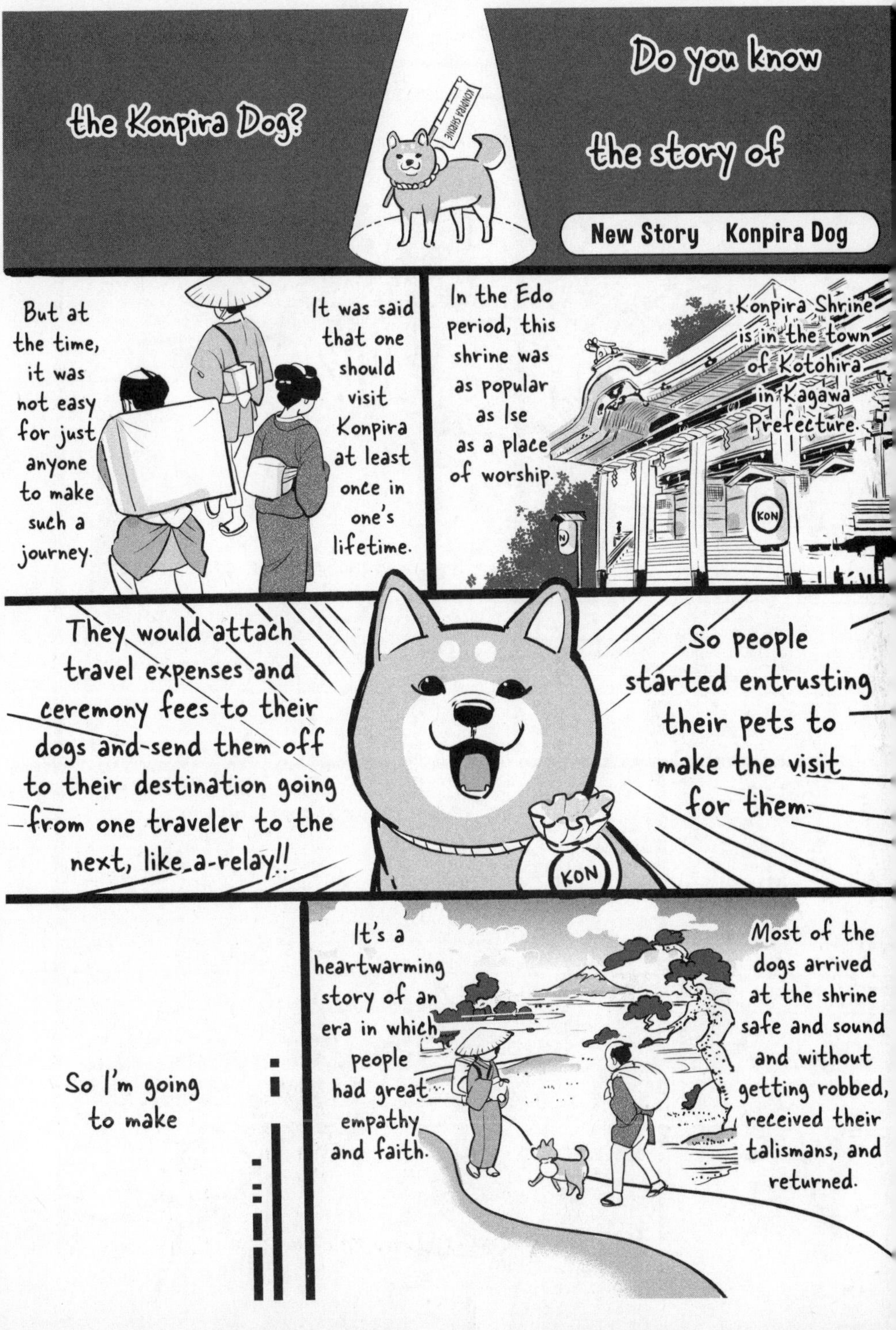
Do you know
the story of
the Konpira Dog?
KONPIRA SHRINE
New Story Konpira Dog
Konpira Shrine is in the town of Kotohira in Kagawa Prefecture.
KON
In the Edo period, this shrine was as popular as Ise as a place of worship.
It was said that one should visit Konpira at least once in one's lifetime.
But at the time, it was not easy for just anyone to make such a journey.
So people started entrusting their pets to make the visit for them.
They would attach travel expenses and ceremony fees to their dogs and send them off to their destination going from one traveler to the next, like a relay!!
KON
Most of the dogs arrived at the shrine safe and sound and without getting robbed, received their talismans, and returned.
It's a heartwarming story of an era in which people had great empathy and faith.
So I'm going to make

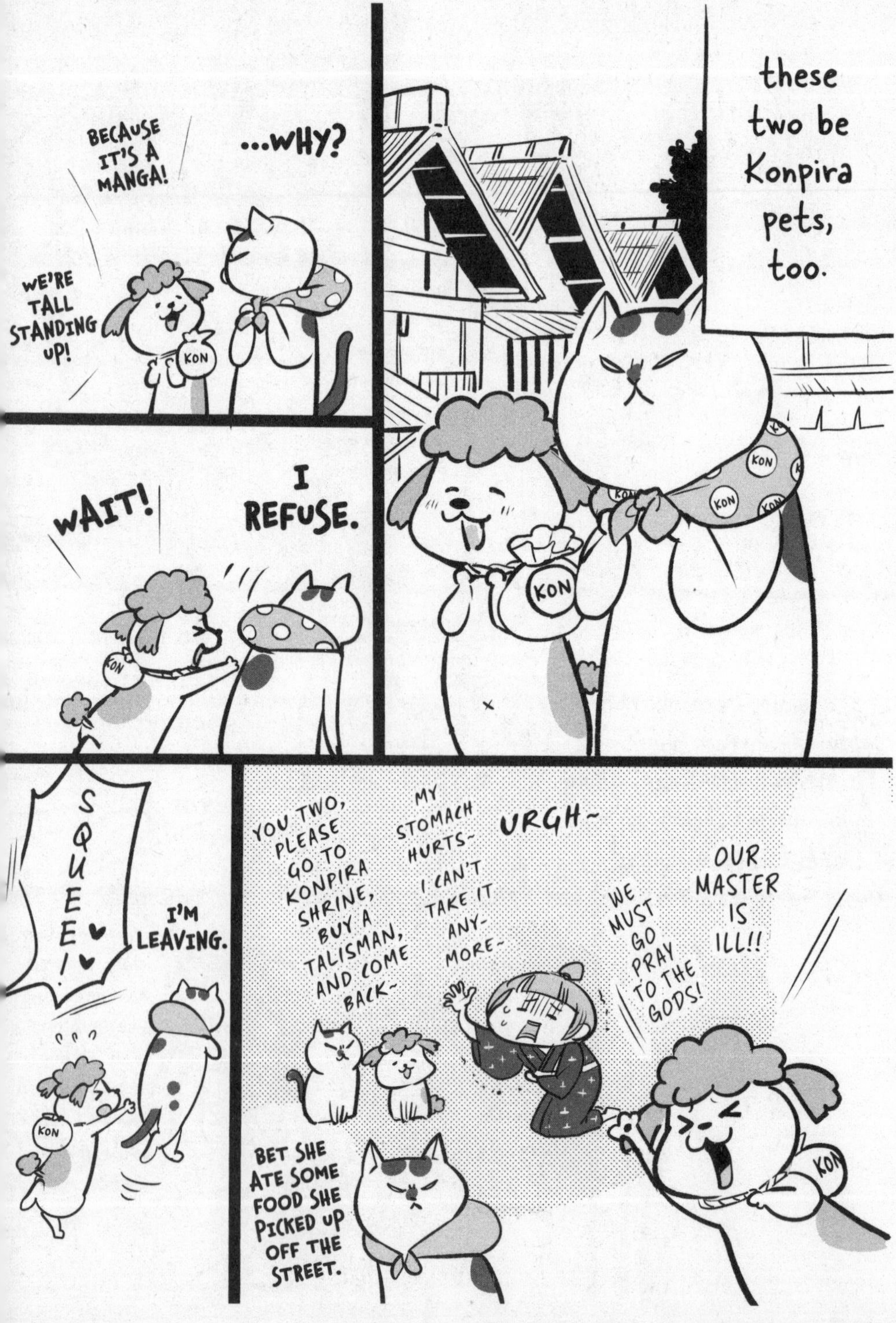
these two be Konpira pets, too.
...WHY?
BECAUSE IT'S A MANGA!
WE'RE TALL STANDING UP!
I REFUSE.
WAIT!
OUR MASTER IS ILL!!
WE MUST GO PRAY TO THE GODS!
URGH~
MY STOMACH HURTS~ I CAN'T TAKE IT ANY-MORE~
YOU TWO, PLEASE GO TO KONPIRA SHRINE, BUY A TALISMAN, AND COME BACK~
BET SHE ATE SOME FOOD SHE PICKED UP OFF THE STREET.
I'M LEAVING.
SQUEE!

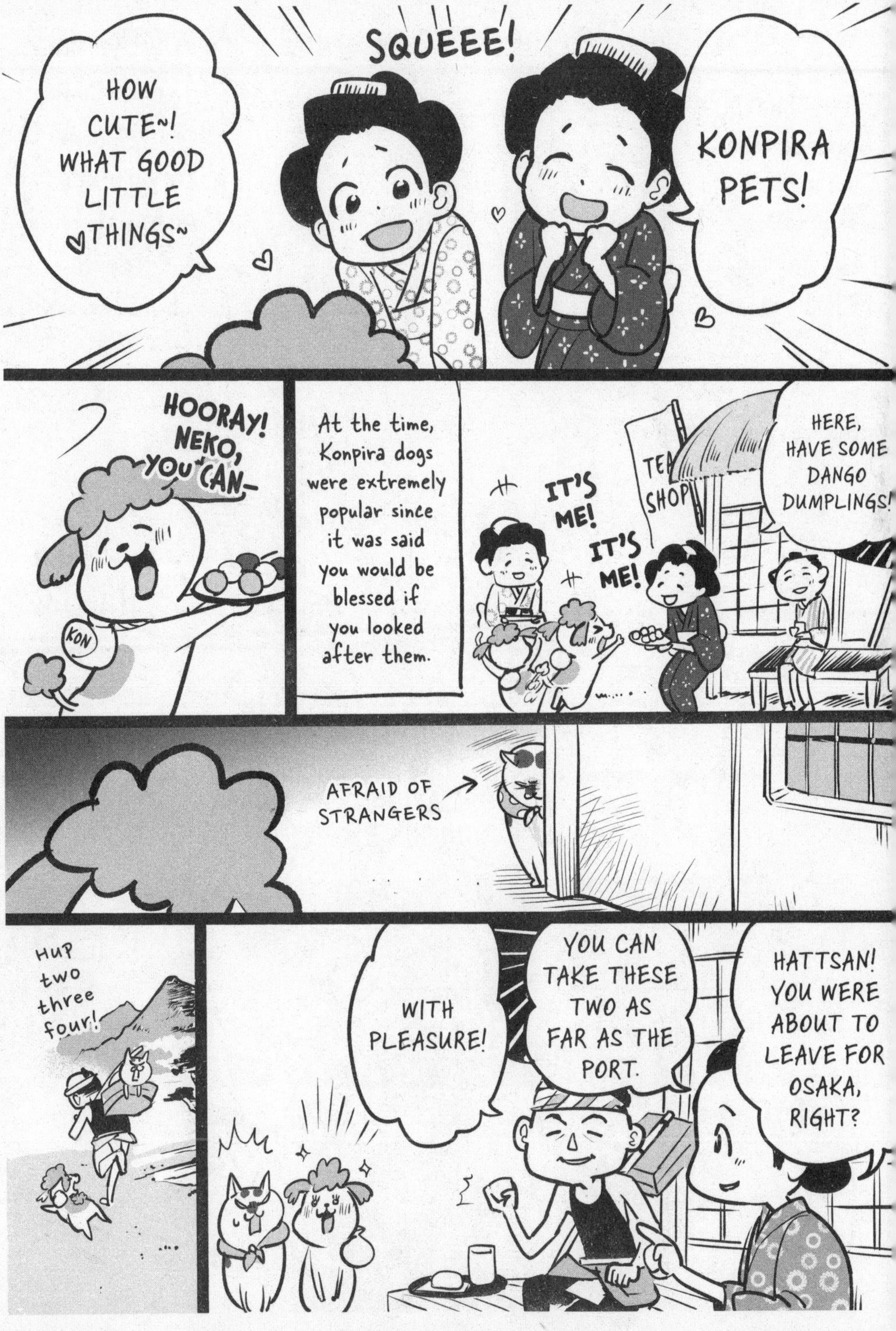

KONPIRA PETS!
SQUEEE!
HOW CUTE~! WHAT GOOD LITTLE THINGS~
HERE, HAVE SOME DANGO DUMPLINGS!
TEA SHOP
IT'S ME!
IT'S ME!
At the time, Konpira dogs were extremely popular since it was said you would be blessed if you looked after them.
HOORAY! NEKO, YOU CAN—
KON
AFRAID OF STRANGERS
HATTSAN! YOU WERE ABOUT TO LEAVE FOR OSAKA, RIGHT?
YOU CAN TAKE THESE TWO AS FAR AS THE PORT.
WITH PLEASURE!
Hup two three four!

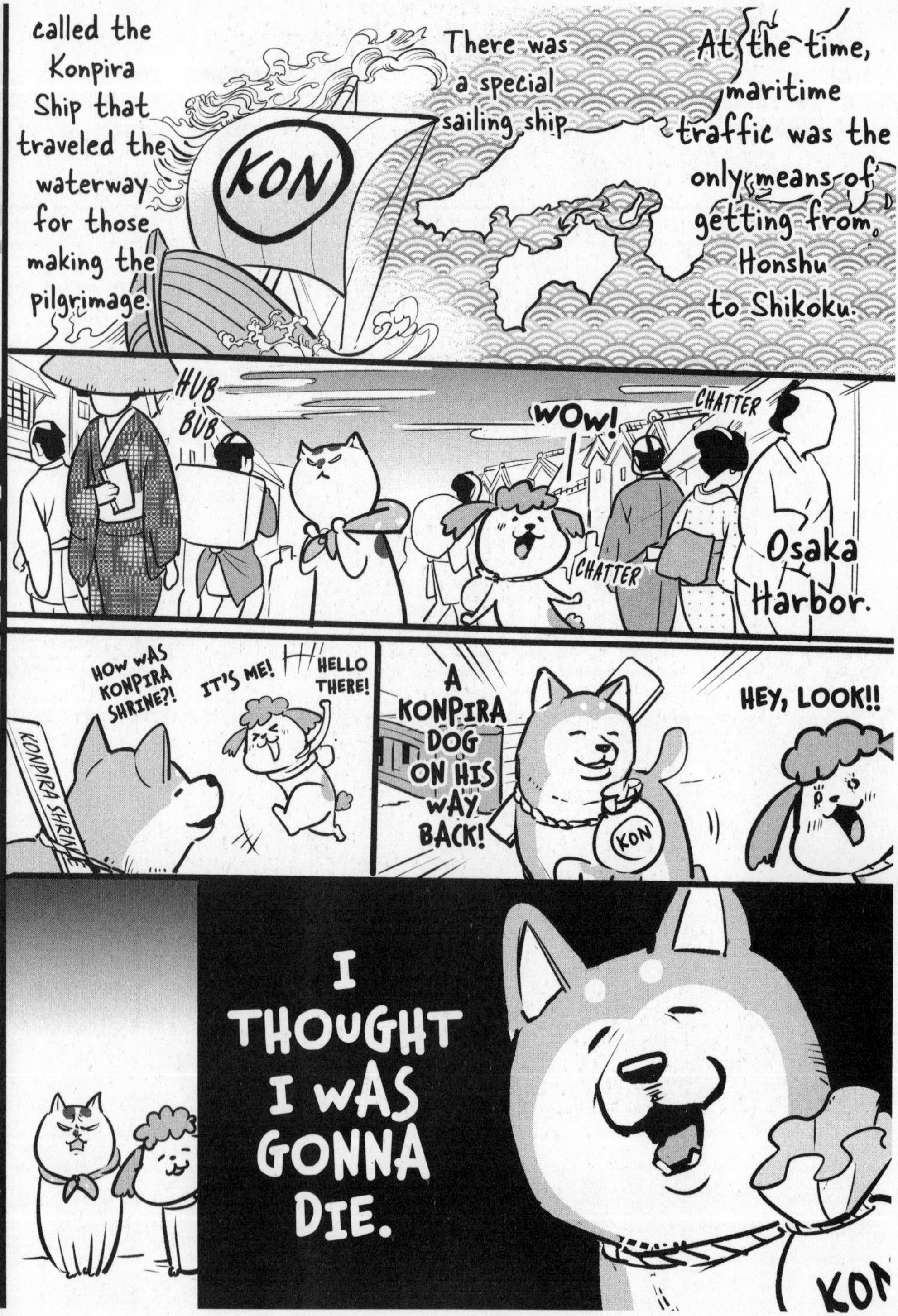
At the time, maritime traffic was the only means of getting from Honshu to Shikoku.
There was a special sailing ship
called the Konpira Ship that traveled the waterway for those making the pilgrimage.
KON
Osaka Harbor.
CHATTER
CHATTER
WOW!
HUB BUB
HEY, LOOK!!
A KONPIRA DOG ON HIS WAY BACK!
KON
HELLO THERE!
IT'S ME!
HOW WAS KONPIRA SHRINE?!
KONPIRA SHRINE
I THOUGHT I WAS GONNA DIE.

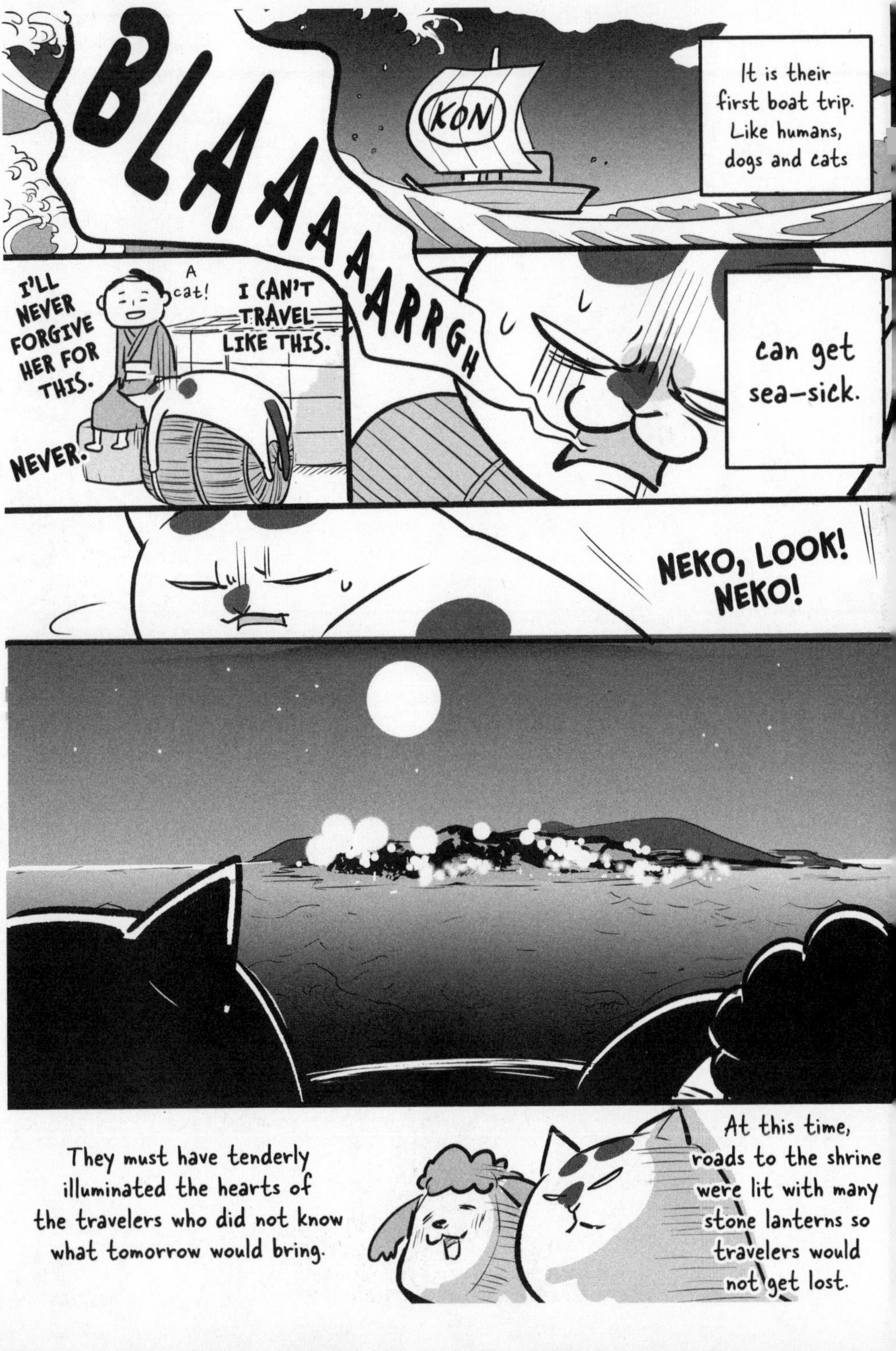

It is their first boat trip. Like humans, dogs and cats
KON
BLAAAAAARRGH
can get sea-sick.
I CAN'T TRAVEL LIKE THIS.
A cat!
I'LL NEVER FORGIVE HER FOR THIS.
NEVER.
NEKO, LOOK! NEKO!
At this time, roads to the shrine were lit with many stone lanterns so travelers would not get lost.
They must have tenderly illuminated the hearts of the travelers who did not know what tomorrow would bring.

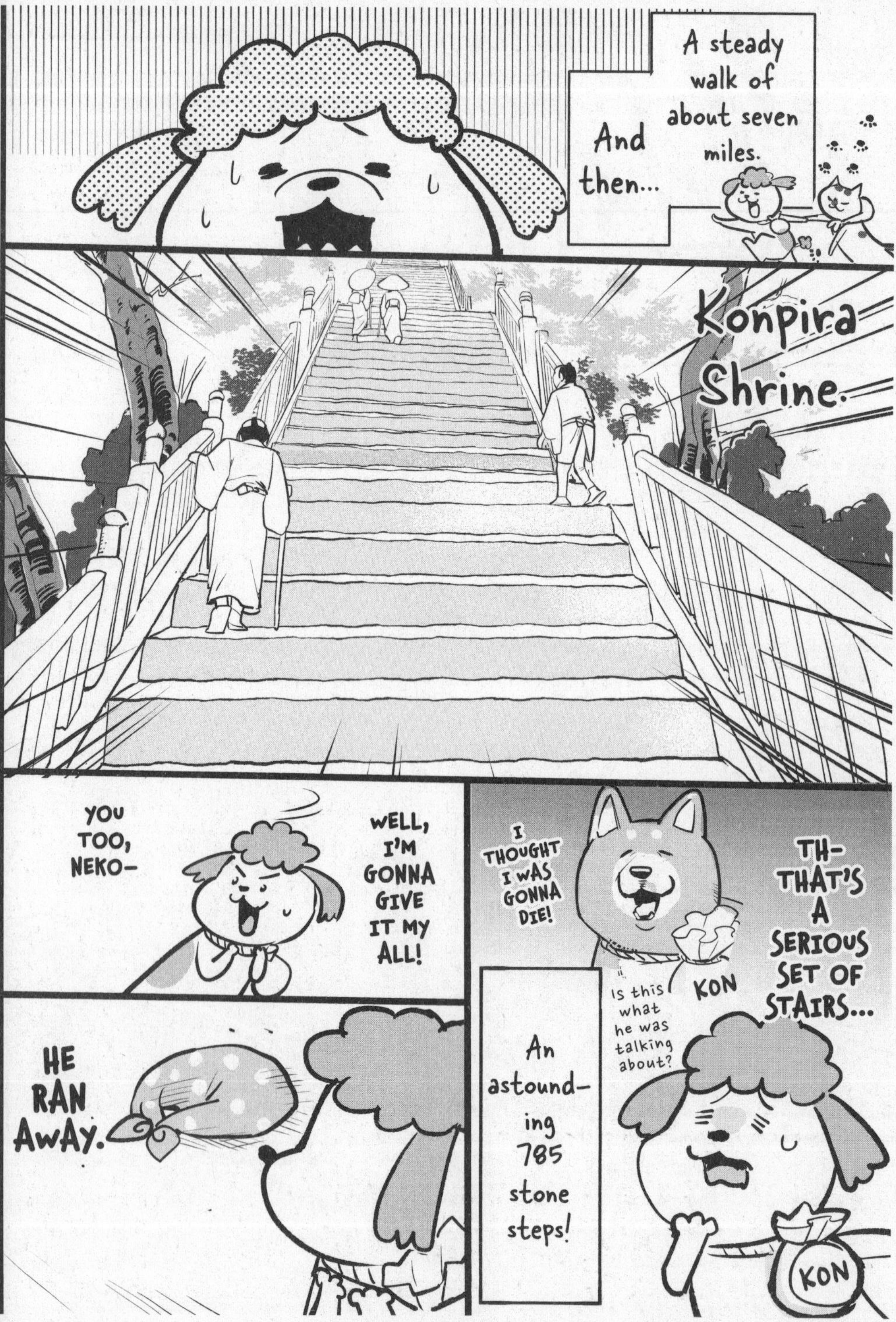
And then...
A steady walk of about seven miles.
Konpira Shrine.
TH-THAT'S A SERIOUS SET OF STAIRS...
I THOUGHT I WAS GONNA DIE!
KON
WELL, I'M GONNA GIVE IT MY ALL!
YOU TOO, NEKO-
Is this what he was talking about?
An astound-ing 785 stone steps!
KON
HE RAN AWAY.

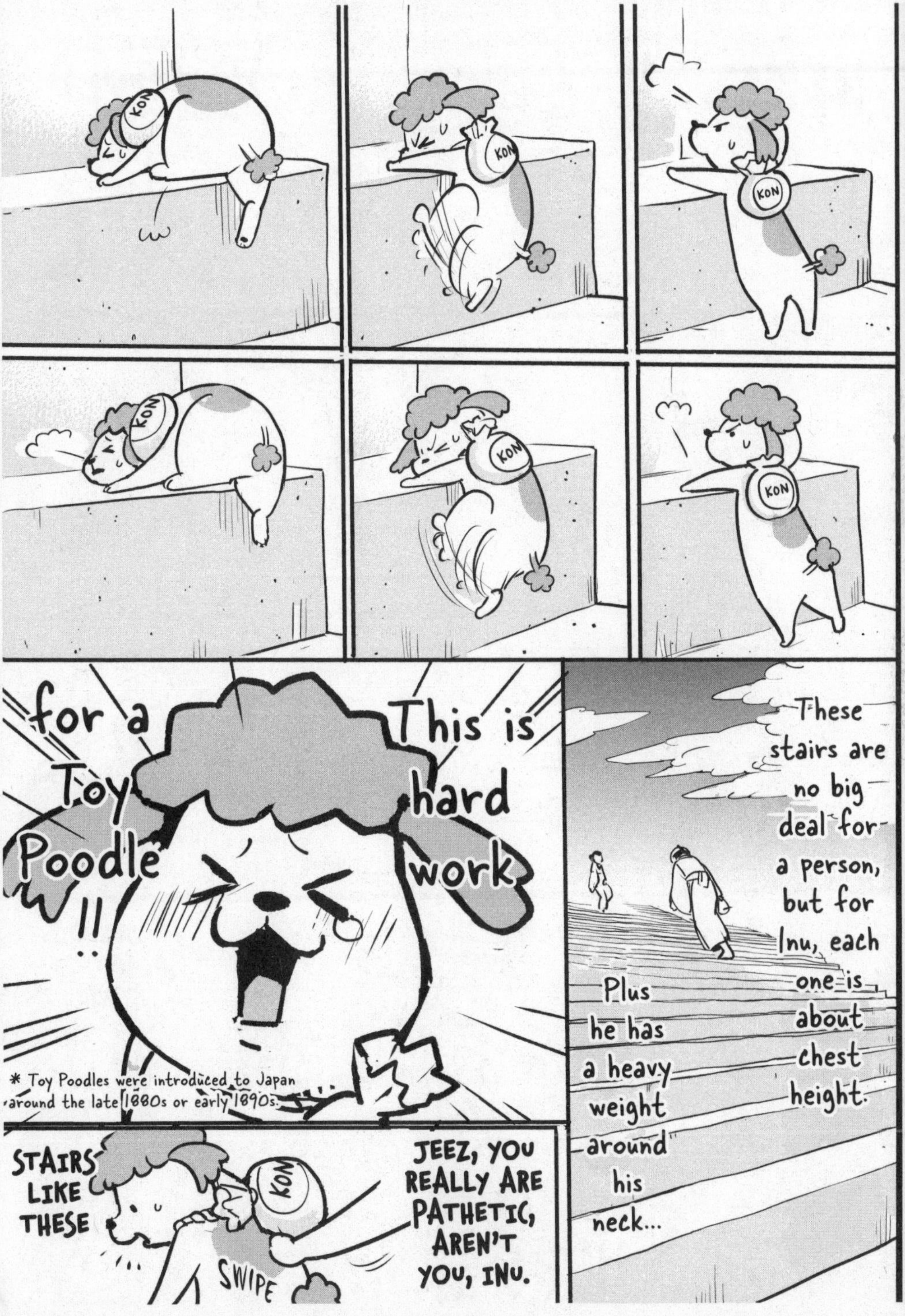

These stairs are no big deal for a person, but for Inu, each one is about chest height.
Plus he has a heavy weight around his neck...
This is hard work
for a Toy Poodle!!
* Toy Poodles were introduced to Japan around the late 1880s or early 1890s.
JEEZ, YOU REALLY ARE PATHETIC, AREN'T YOU, INU.
STAIRS LIKE THESE
SWIPE

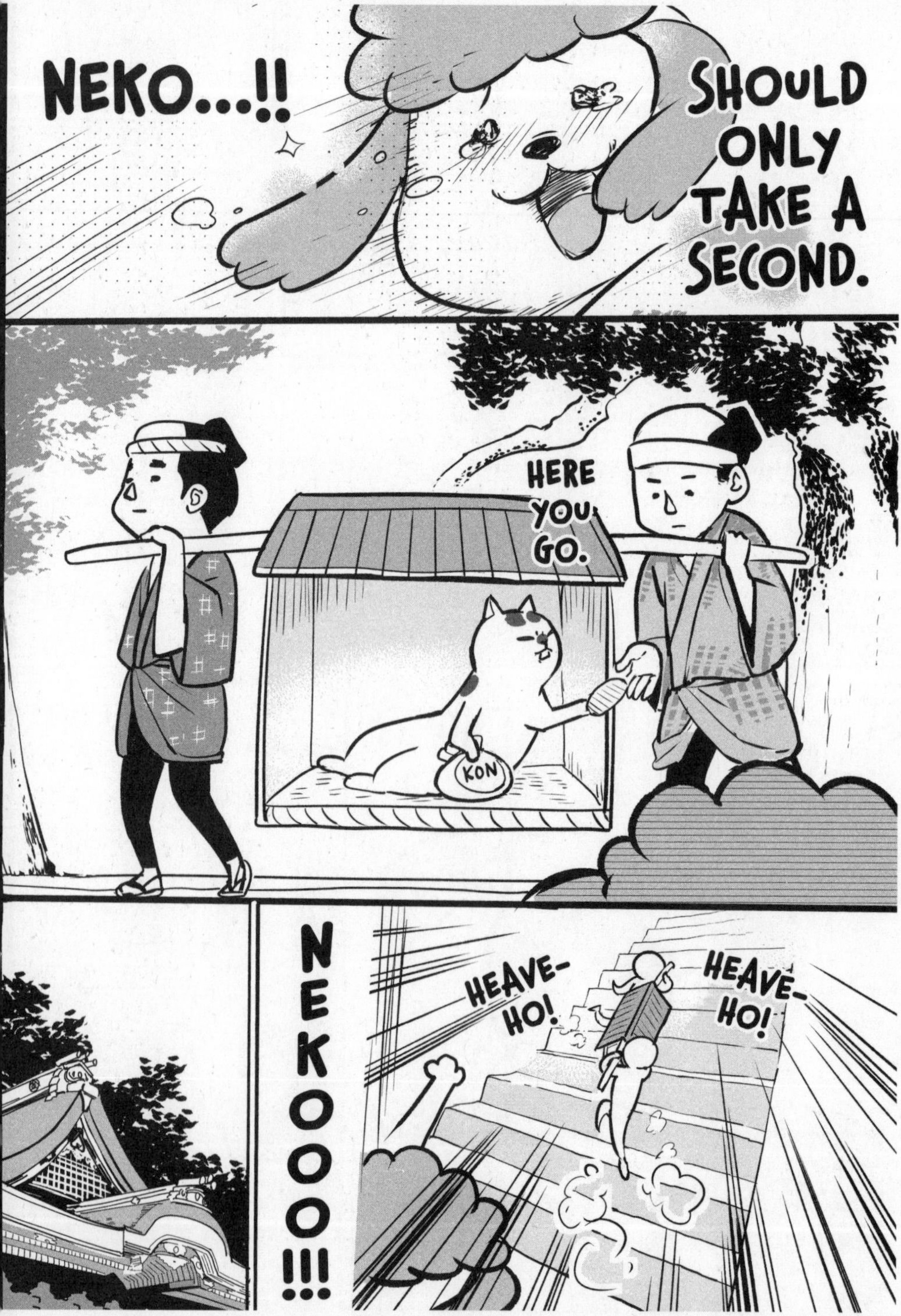
SHOULD ONLY TAKE A SECOND.
NEKO...!!
HERE YOU GO.
KON
HEAVE-HO!
HEAVE-HO!
NEKOOOO!!!

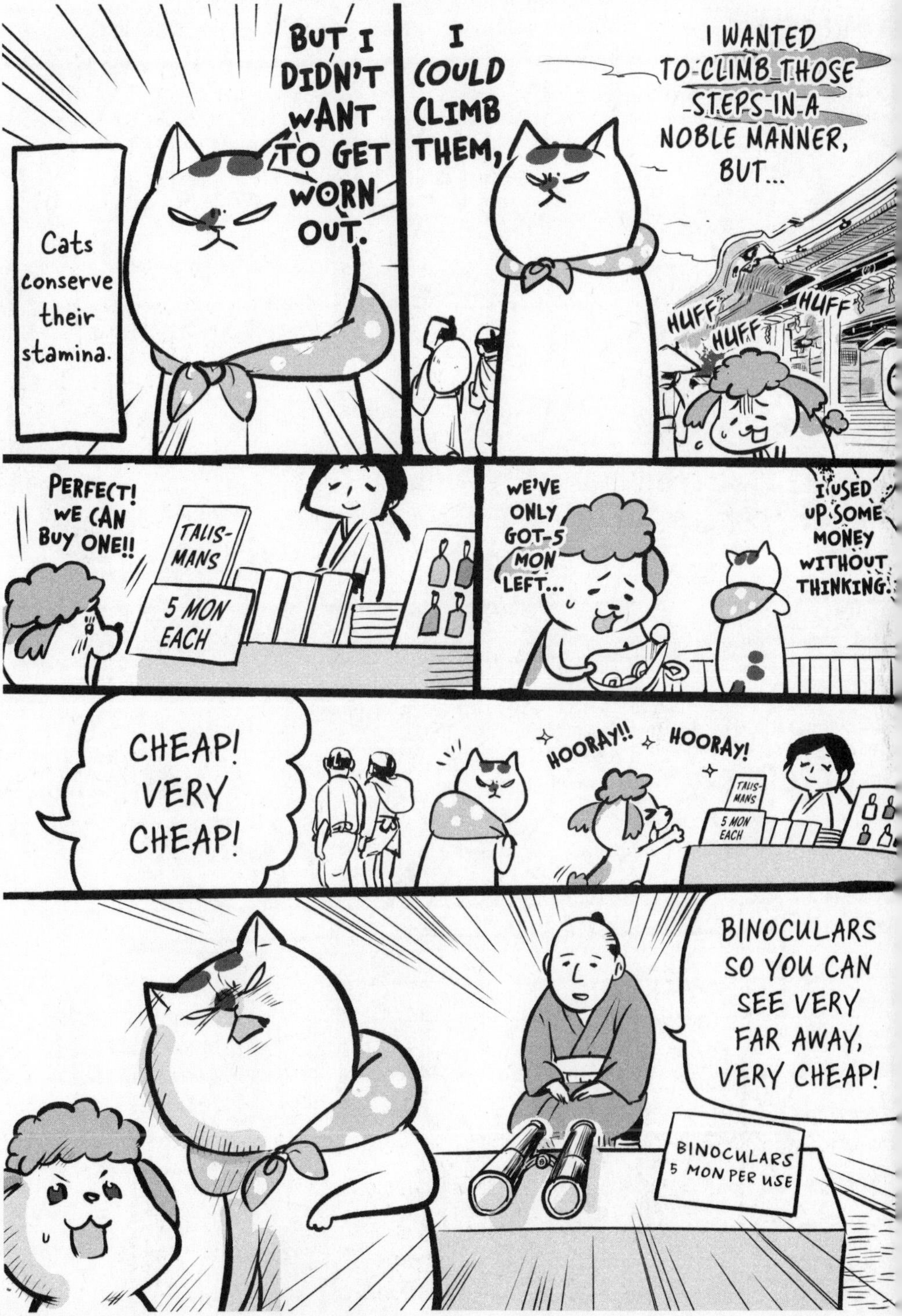
I WANTED TO CLIMB THOSE STEPS IN A NOBLE MANNER, BUT...
HUFF HUFF HUFF
I COULD CLIMB THEM,
BUT I DIDN'T WANT TO GET WORN OUT.
Cats conserve their stamina.
I USED UP SOME MONEY WITHOUT THINKING.
WE'VE ONLY GOT 5 MON LEFT...
TALIS-MANS
5 MON EACH
PERFECT! WE CAN BUY ONE!!
HOORAY!! HOORAY!
TALIS-MANS
5 MON EACH
CHEAP! VERY CHEAP!
BINOCULARS SO YOU CAN SEE VERY FAR AWAY, VERY CHEAP!
BINOCULARS 5 MON PER USE

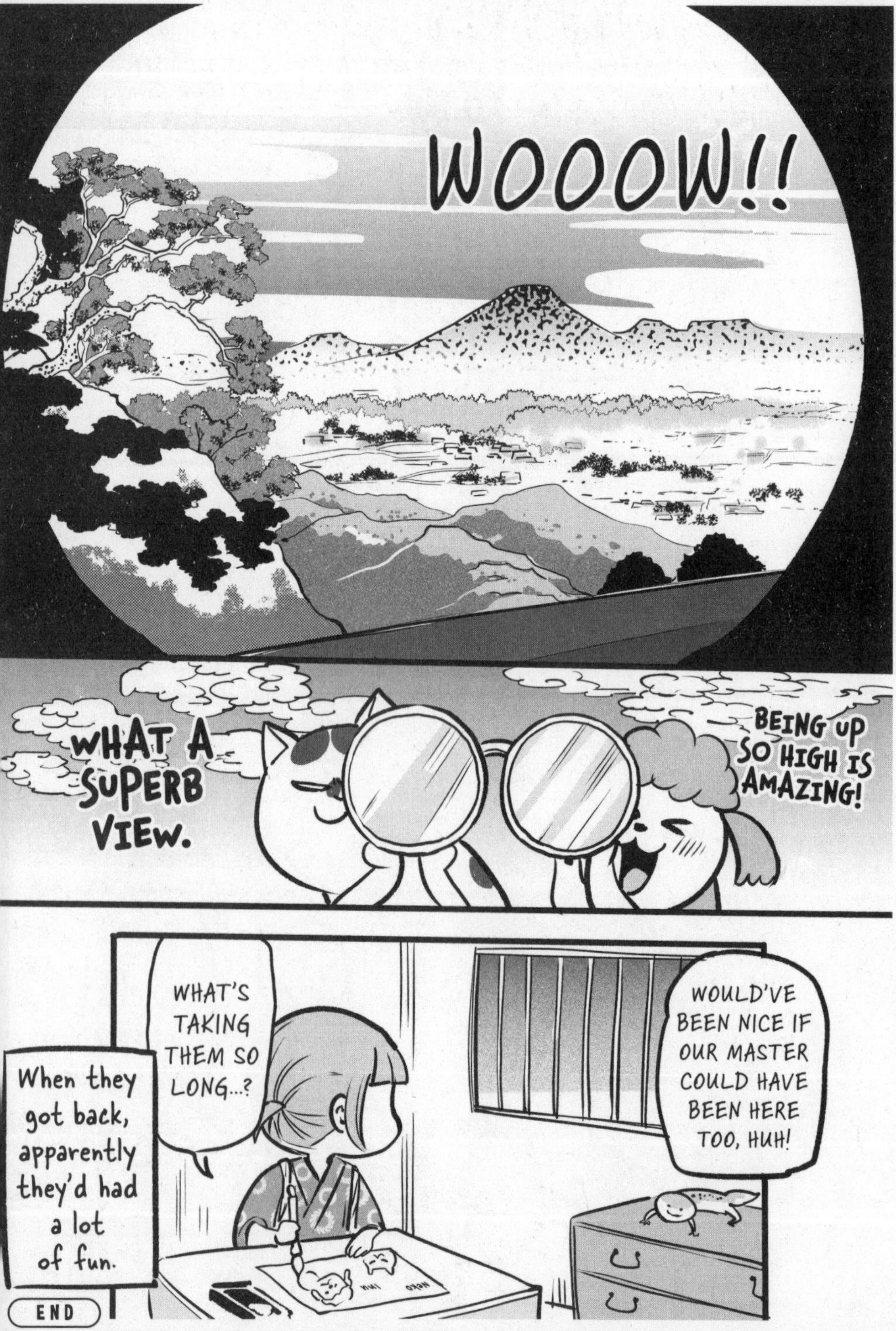
WOOOW!!
BEING UP SO HIGH IS AMAZING!
WHAT A SUPERB VIEW.
WOULD'VE BEEN NICE IF OUR MASTER COULD HAVE BEEN HERE TOO, HUH!
WHAT'S TAKING THEM SO LONG...?
When they got back, apparently they'd had a lot of fun.
END

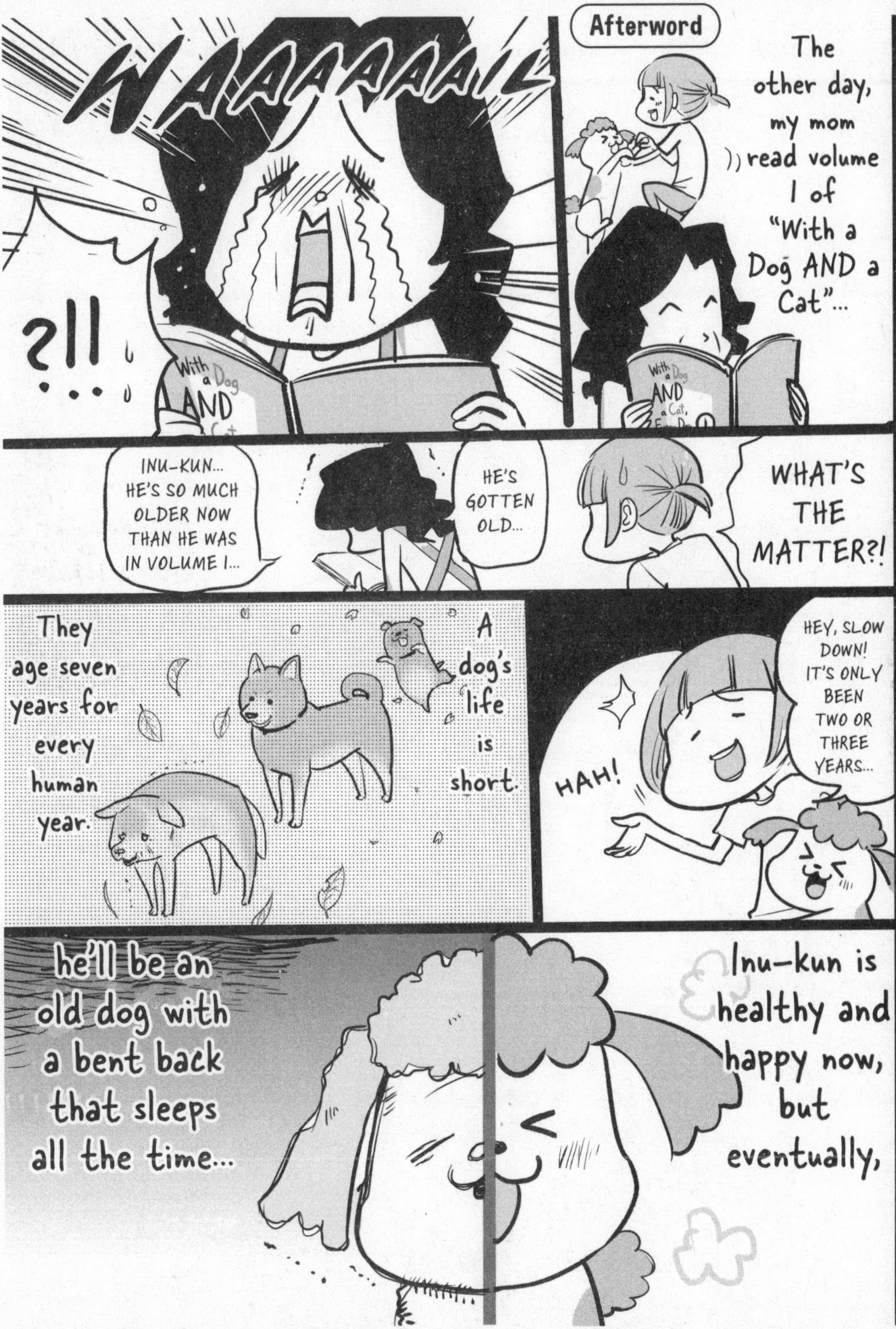
Afterword
The other day, my mom read volume 1 of "With a Dog AND a Cat"...
WAAAAAAA!
?!!
...
WHAT'S THE MATTER?!
HE'S GOTTEN OLD...
INU-KUN... HE'S SO MUCH OLDER NOW THAN HE WAS IN VOLUME 1...
HEY, SLOW DOWN! IT'S ONLY BEEN TWO OR THREE YEARS...
HAH!
A dog's life is short.
They age seven years for every human year.
Inu-kun is healthy and happy now, but eventually,
he'll be an old dog with a bent back that sleeps all the time...

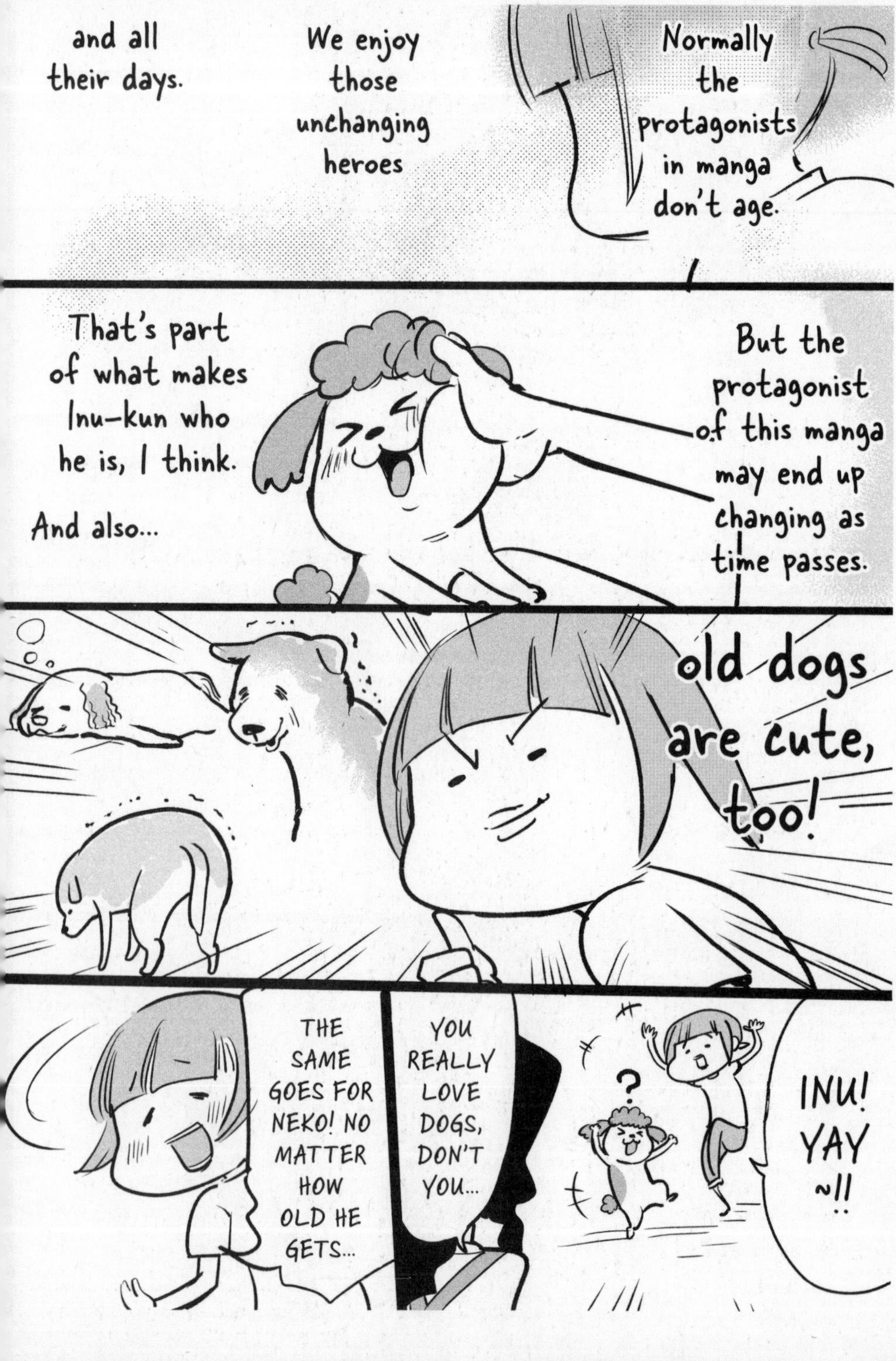
Normally the protagonists in manga don't age.
We enjoy those unchanging heroes
and all their days.
But the protagonist of this manga may end up changing as time passes.
That's part of what makes Inu-kun who he is, I think.
And also...
old dogs are cute, too!
INU! YAY ~!!
YOU REALLY LOVE DOGS, DON'T YOU...
THE SAME GOES FOR NEKO! NO MATTER HOW OLD HE GETS...

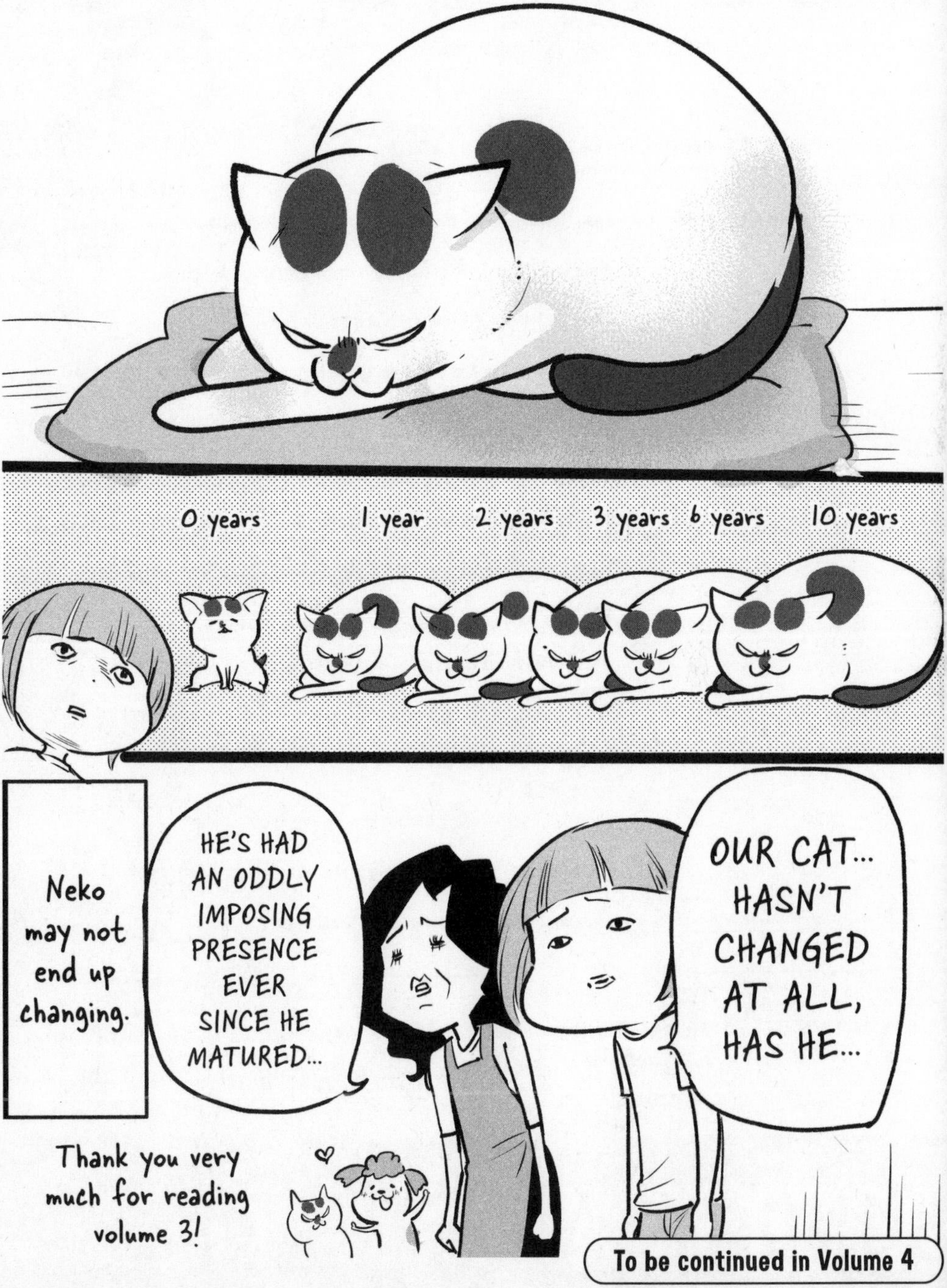
0 years 1 year 2 years 3 years 6 years 10 years
OUR CAT... HASN'T CHANGED AT ALL, HAS HE...
HE'S HAD AN ODDLY IMPOSING PRESENCE EVER SINCE HE MATURED...
Neko may not end up changing.
Thank you very much for reading volume 3!

To be continued in Volume 4

IS BEING SERIALIZED ON TWITTER! Information

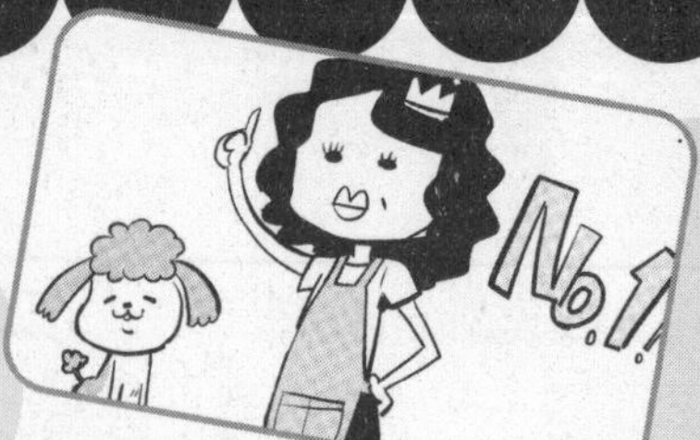
No.1!

VOLUME 3 EPISODE TITLES WHEN SERIALIZED ON TWITTER

#67 With a Dog AND a Cat, They Start the Day the Exact Opposite, So Every Day is Fun

#68 〃 They Can Read the Mood or Ruin It, So Every Day is Fun

#69 〃 They Look Down on You, So Every Day is Fun

#70 〃 Even if You're Sick in Bed, Every Day is Fun

#71 〃 It's a World Which Doesn't Need Words or Maybe Does, So Every Day is Fun

#72 〃 Incidents Happen at the Vet and it's Fun Every Time

#73 〃 They are Considerate of Their Master, and Every Day is Fun

#74 〃 They Trust Themselves to You So Differently That Every Day is Fun

#75 〃 Feeling Moved by Their Maturing Makes Every Day Fun

#76 〃 The Way They Fit into Places Makes Every Day Fun

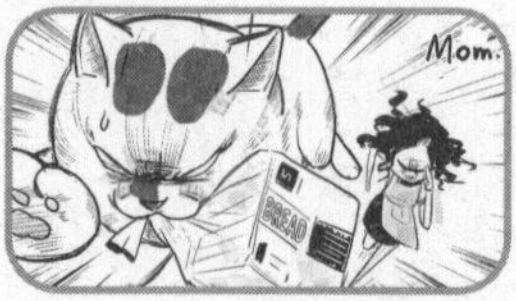
Mom.

#77 〃 They're Photogenic, and Every Day is Fun

#78 〃 Even When They Get Bored of Playing, Every Day is Fun

#79 〃 They Get Excited Over Strangers, So Every Day is Fun

#80 〃 Their Attitudes are Completely Different, So Every Day is Fun

#81 〃 They've Got Good Ears, So Every Day is Fun

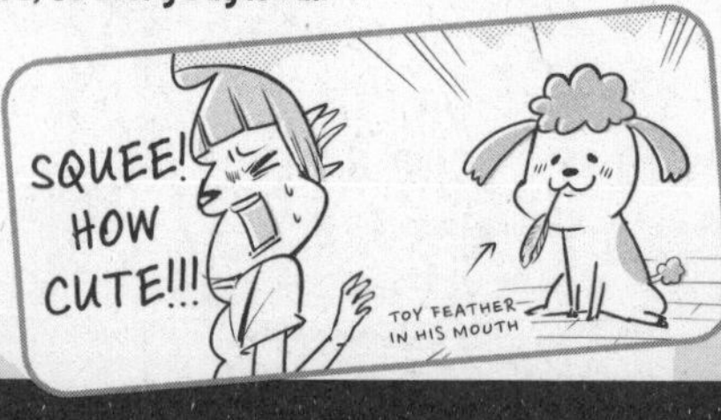
SQUEE! HOW CUTE!!!
TOY FEATHER IN HIS MOUTH

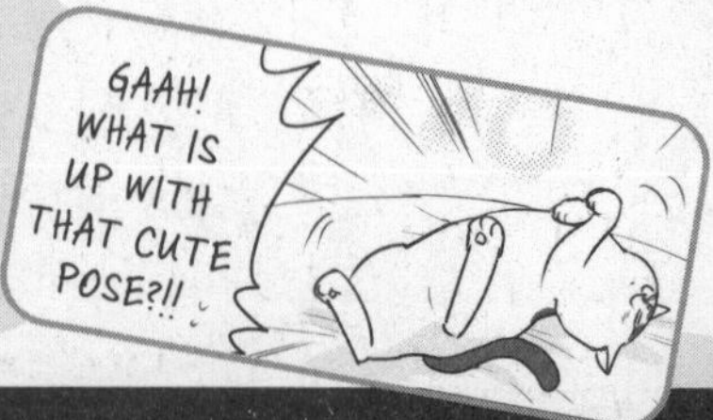
GAAH! WHAT IS UP WITH THAT CUTE POSE?!!

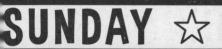

SUNDAY ☆

(AND TRYING NOT TO TAKE ANY WEEKS OFF!)

"WITH A DOG AND A CAT, EVERY DAY IS FUN"

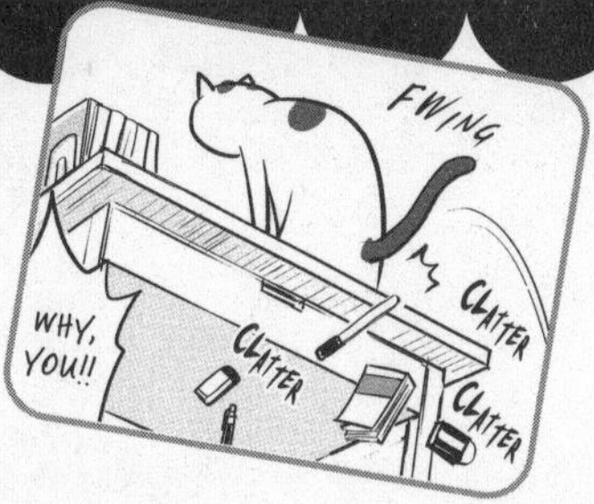
FWING
CLATTER
CLATTER
CLATTER
WHY, YOU!!

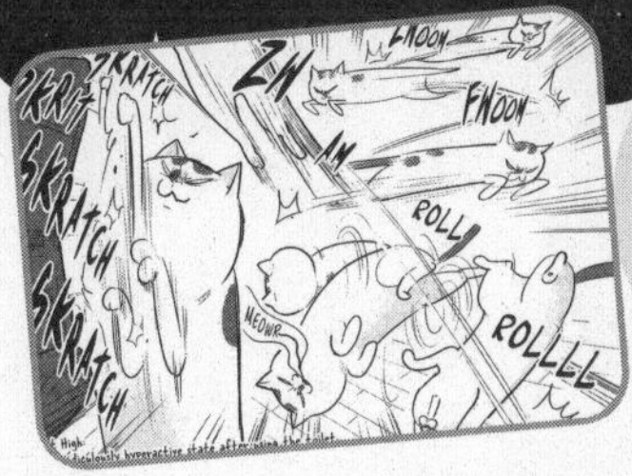
SKRATCH
SKRATCH
SKRATCH
SKRATCH
ZW
FWOOM
FWOOM
ROLL
ROLLLL
MEOWR

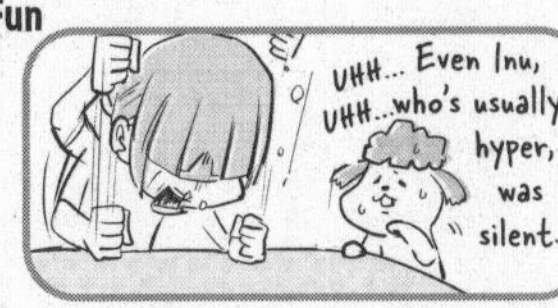
UHH... Even Inu, UHH...who's usually hyper, was silent.

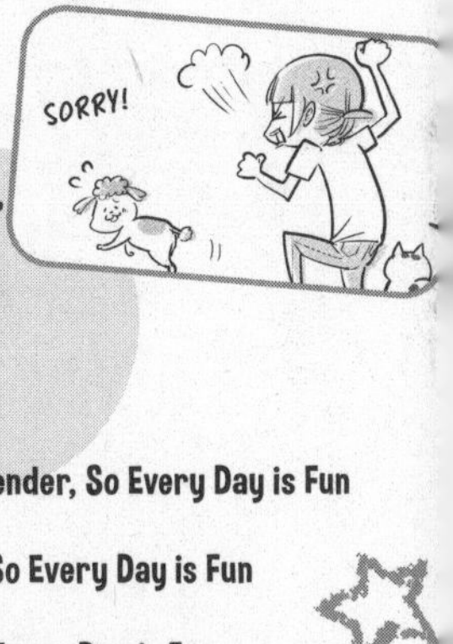
SORRY!

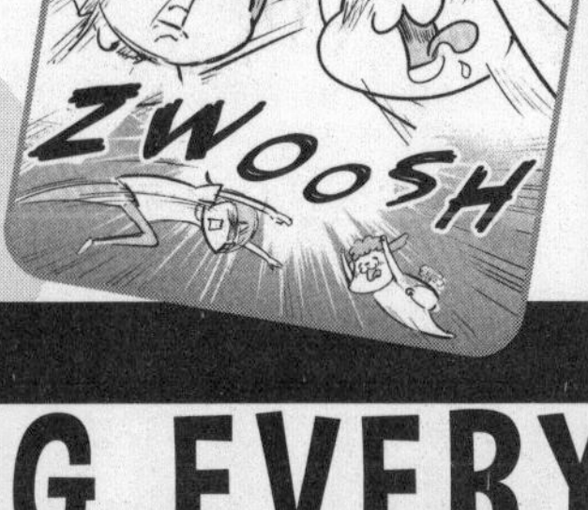
ZWOOSH

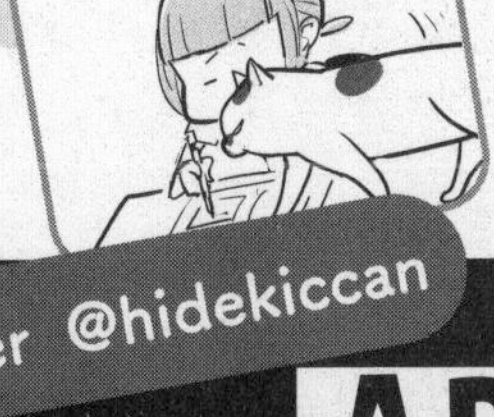
STEP STEP

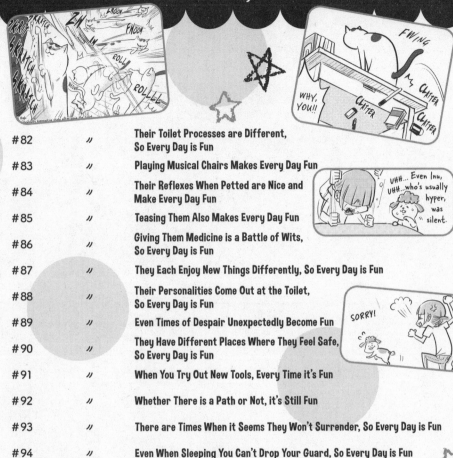

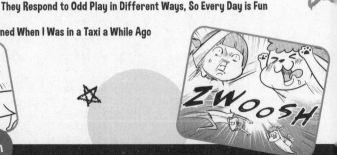

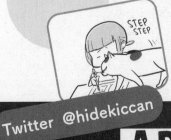

Twitter @hidekiccan

APPEARING EVERY

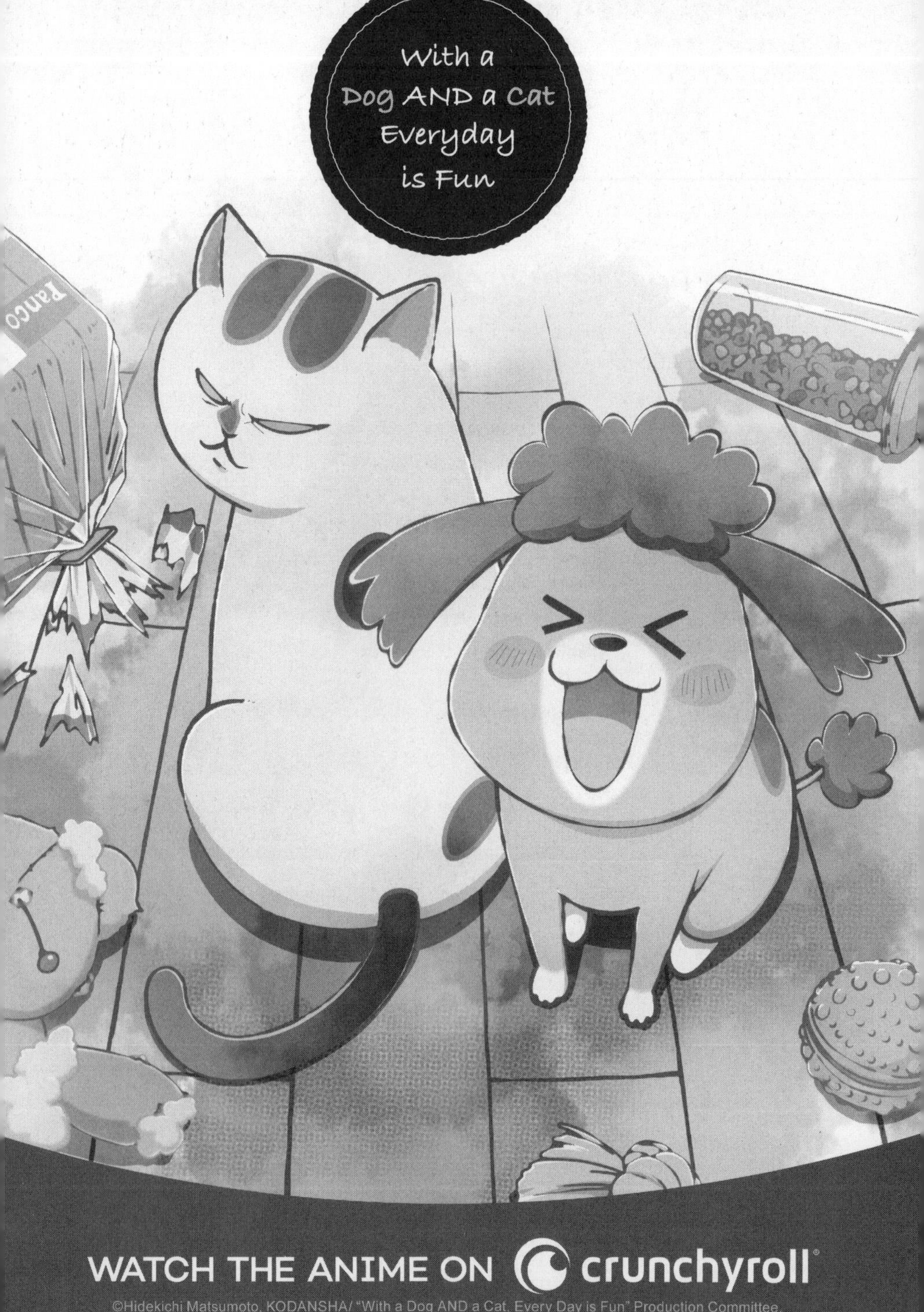
With a
Dog AND a Cat
Everyday
is Fun
WATCH THE ANIME ON crunchyroll

Own this Purr-fect Collection!

The Complete
Chi's Sweet Home
Box Set

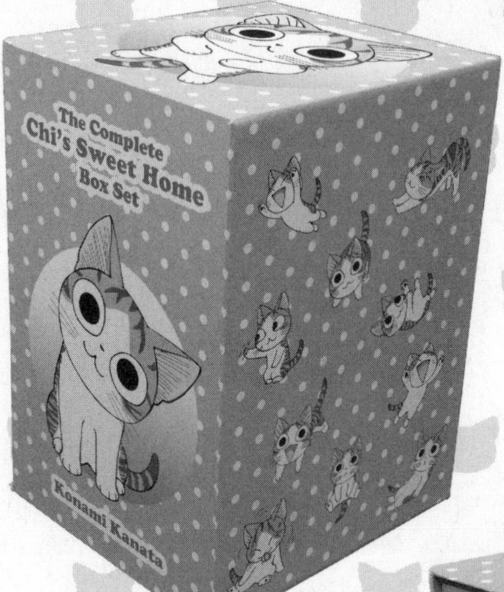
The Complete
Chi's Sweet Home
Box Set
Konami Kanata

The New York Times best-selling cat comic *Chi's Sweet Home* is now available in a complete box set!

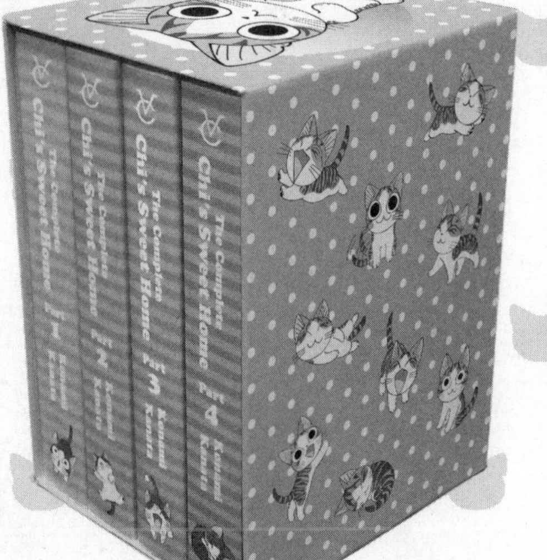
The Complete
Chi's Sweet Home
1
2
3
4

Contains all 4 volumes of the series in a cute collector's edition box.

60 cute stickers included!

Available Now!

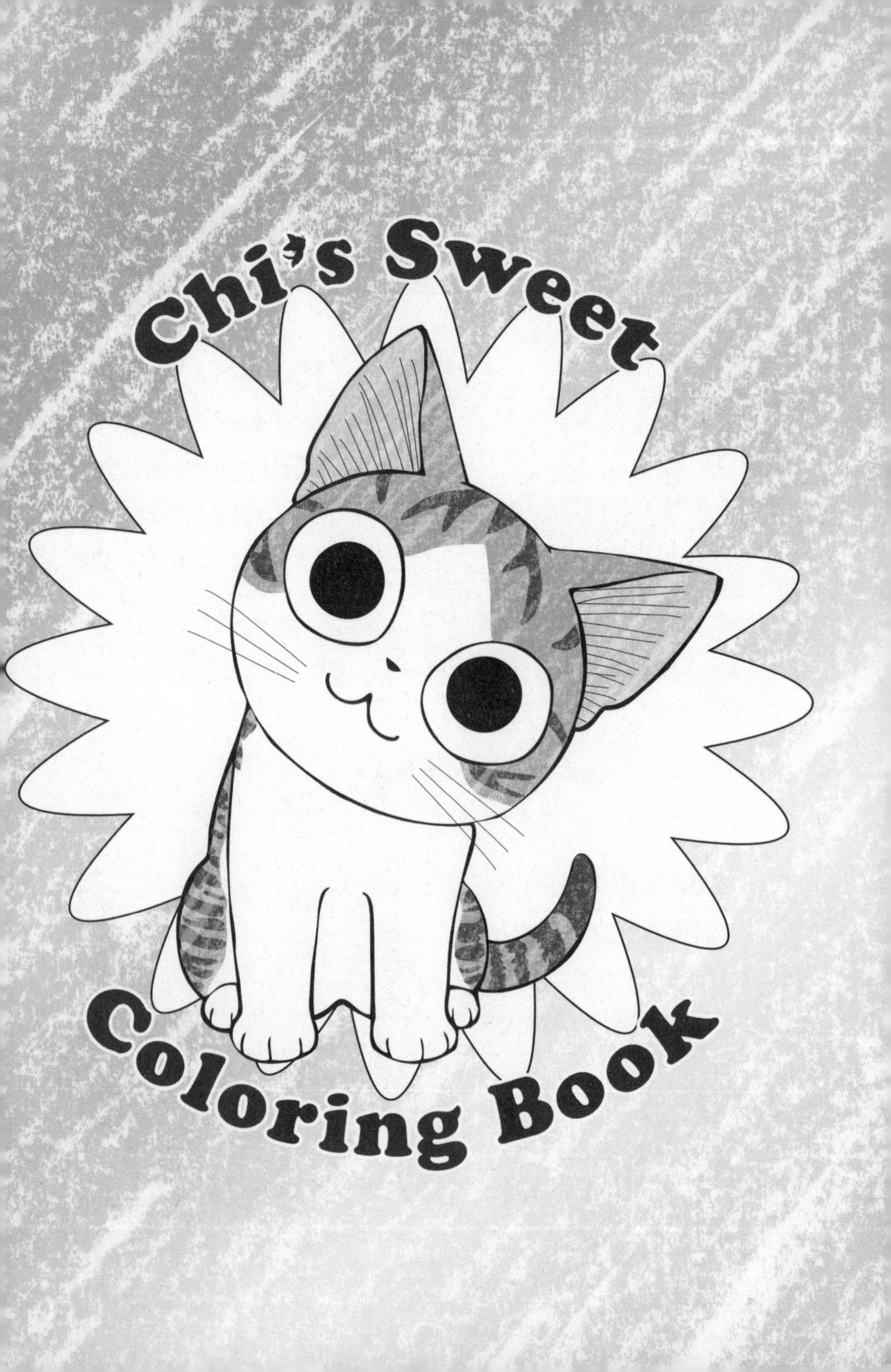
Chi's Sweet
Coloring Book

Chi returns to the US in a coloring book
featuring dozens of cute and furry illustrations from
award-winning cartoonist Konami Kanata.

Available Now!

Created by Konami Kanata
Adapted by Kinoko Natsume

Chi is back! Manga's most famous cat
returns with a brand new series!
Chi's Sweet Adventures collects dozens
of new full-color kitty tales made
for readers of all ages!

Volumes 1-4
On Sale Now!

Chi's

Sweet Adventures

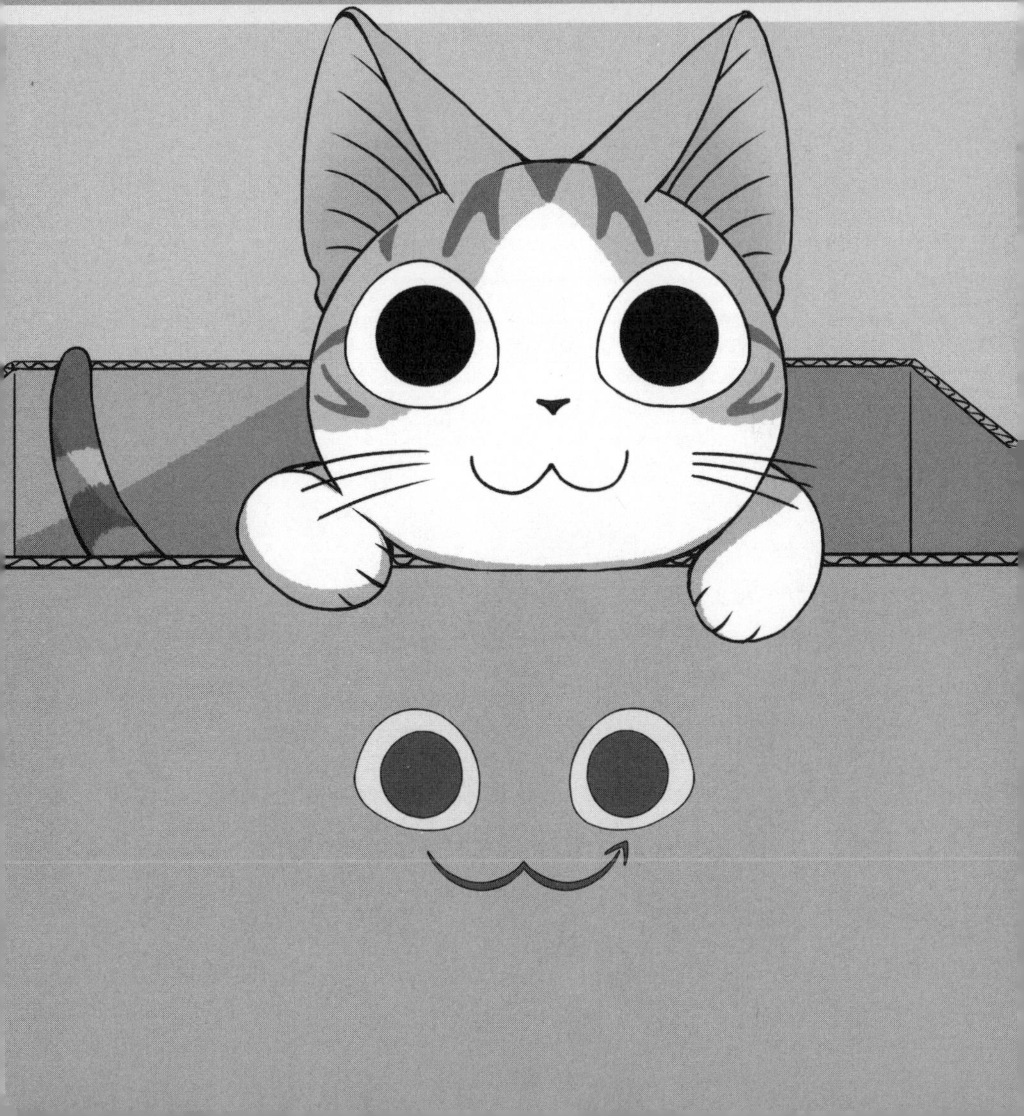

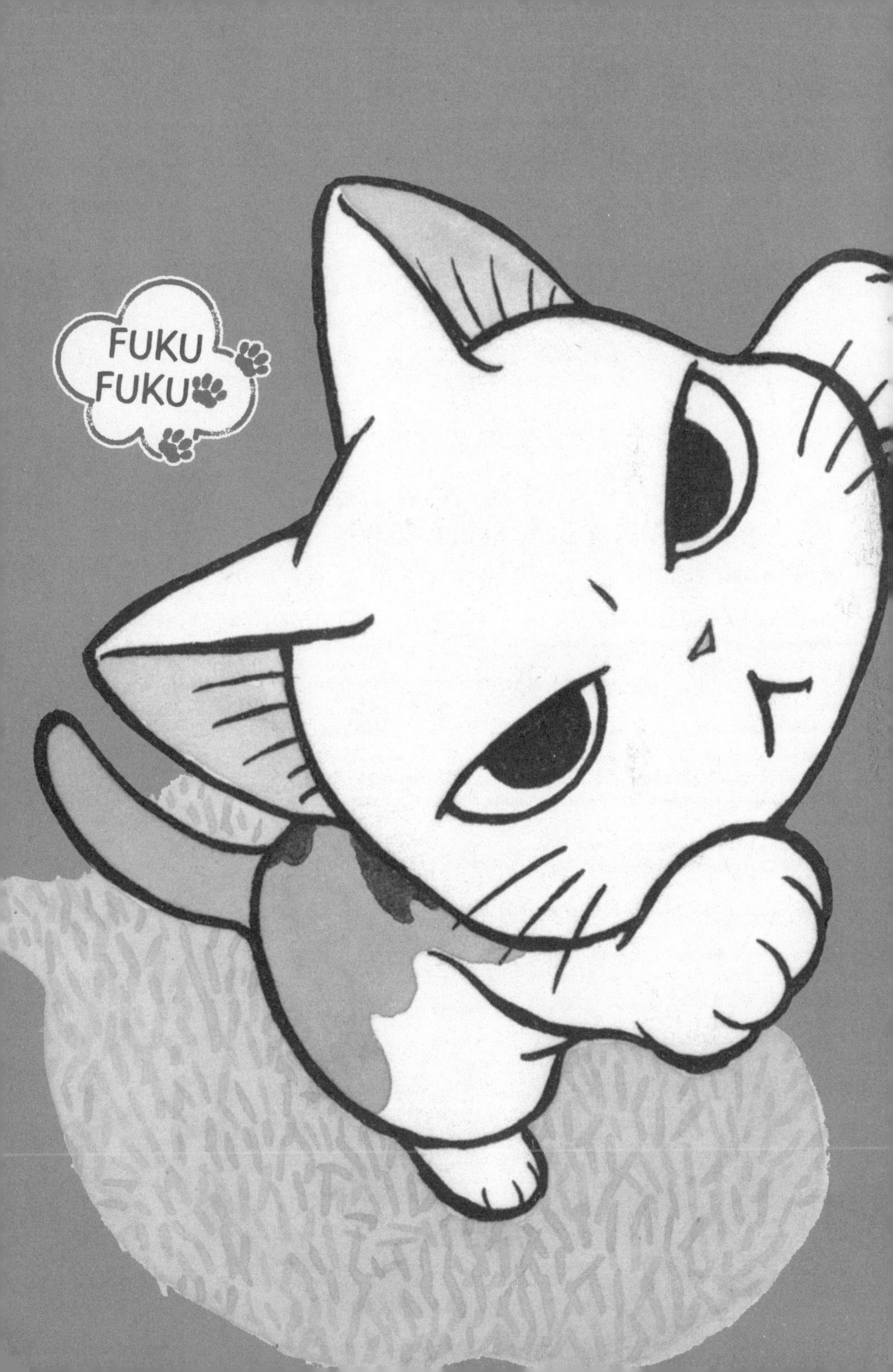
FUKU
FUKU

With a Dog AND a Cat, Every Day is Fun 3

A Vertical Comics Edition

Translation: Kumar Sivasubramanian
Production: Risa Cho
　　　　　　　Eve Grandt
　　　　　　　Alexandra Swanson (SKY Japan Inc.)

First published in Japan in 2019 by Kodansha, Ltd., Tokyo
Publication rights for this English edition arranged through Kodansha, Ltd., Tokyo
English language version produced by Vertical Comics, an imprint of Kodansha USA Publishing, LLC

Translation provided by Vertical Comics, 2021
Published by Kodansha USA Publishing, LLC, New York

Originally published in Japanese as *Inu to Neko Docchimo Katteru to Mainichi Tanoshii 3* by Kodansha, Ltd., 2019

This is a work of fiction.

ISBN: 978-1-64729-002-3

Manufactured in the United States of America

First Edition

Kodansha USA Publishing, LLC
451 Park Avenue South
7th Floor
New York, NY 10016
www.readvertical.com

Vertical books are distributed through Penguin-Random House Publisher Services.

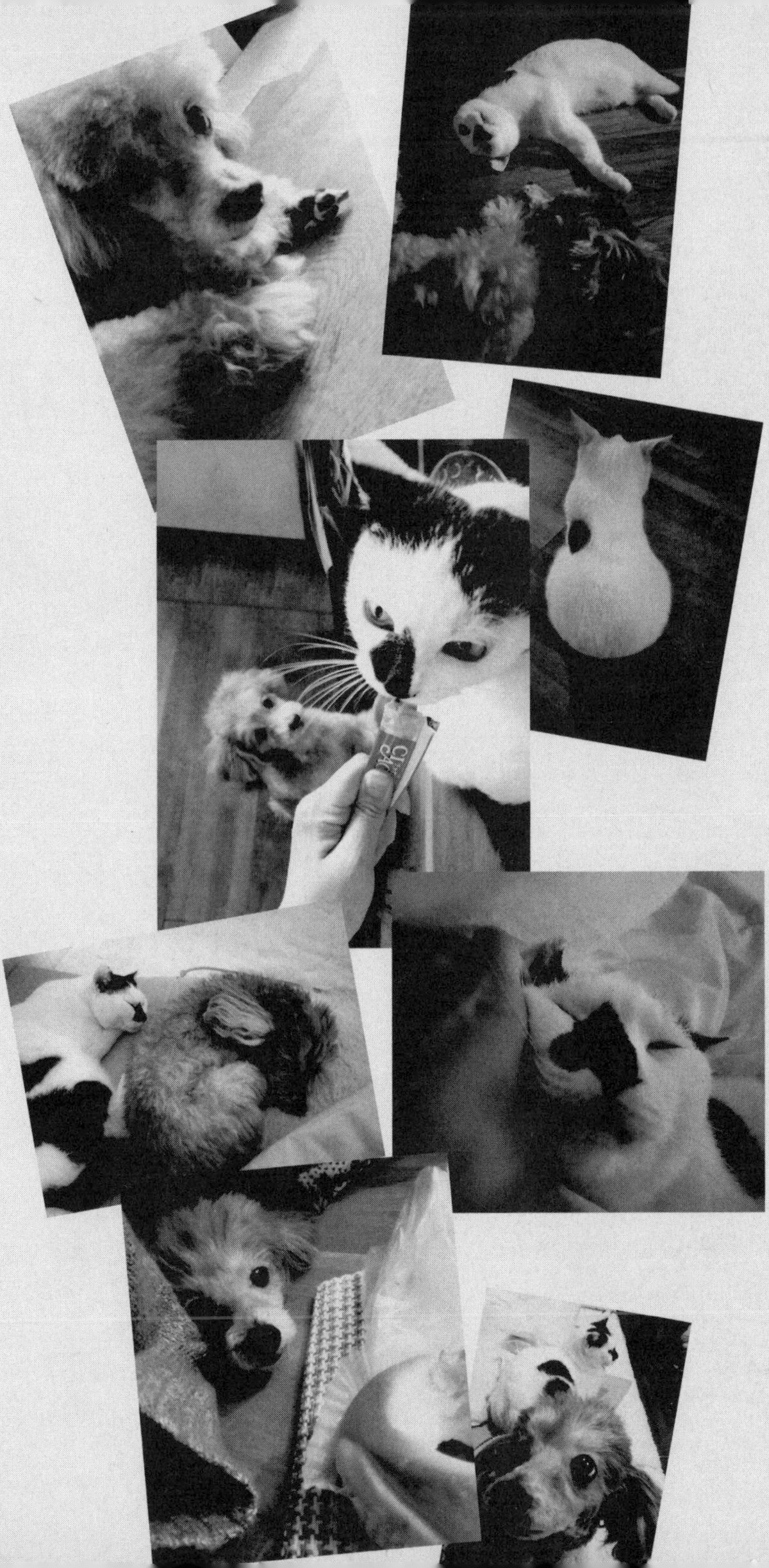

KASKAASH

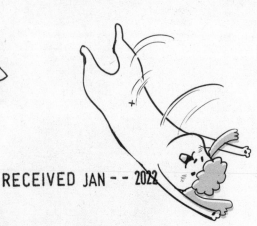

ZNOo

NEKOOO!

DASH